Insurgency and
Counterinsurgency
in Algeria

INDIANA UNIVERSITY
INTERNATIONAL STUDIES

Insurgency and Counterinsurgency in Algeria

ALF ANDREW HEGGOY

INDIANA UNIVERSITY PRESS
BLOOMINGTON | LONDON

Contents

v

Maps

Charts

Preface

Writing about the recent past, about questions such as insurgency and counterinsurgency in Algeria, presents the historian with obvious problems. The most important difficulty is that arguments about the Algerian Revolution have not yet become the province of academic disputations. Second, the sources are for the most part committed ideologically to one side or the other. Hence the nature of available documentation is a problem in itself. And yet it is possible to begin analyzing what happened in Algeria between 1954 and 1962, to go beyond what has been written by journalists, who, on the whole, did some excellent work.

The basic argument of this study is that the French adapted themselves well, on the technical and military level, to the revolutionary war forced on them by the National Liberation Front (FLN) and the National Liberation Army (ALN). By the middle of 1956 France had robbed the insurgents of the initiative they had seized in November 1954. The nationalists, however, responded effectively to the changing circumstances and obtained their own ends by shifting the emphasis from the military to the political aspects of the struggle. In the end, the FLN-ALN robbed the French of victory.

This study of insurgency and counterinsurgency in Algeria ends in 1958, although the war continued until 1962. By 1958 the rebels had lost the military struggle. But they had managed to sow doubt in the minds of many Frenchmen and political leaders in France about the desirability of imposing a French solution to the Algerian question. In other words, the essential problems after 1958 were not problems of insurgency and counterinsurgency. The all-important considerations were political and involved the necessity of keeping some Frenchmen, be they officers or *colon* leaders, from forcing their own solutions on the government of France. These difficulties were met by President de Gaulle after he came to power. Since numerous studies of the Fifth Republic have suggested answers to these problems, there is no need to continue the present study beyond 1958.

Several academic institutions thoroughly gathered information pertinent to the topic, thereby facilitating research on the period between 1954 and 1958. Three French centers of documention have particularly noteworthy collections: the Centre de Récherches sur l'Afrique Mediterranéenne (CRAM) in Aix-en-Provence; the Centre de Haute Etudes d'Administration Musulmane, which has become the Centre de Hautes Etudes Administratives sur l'Afrique et l'Asie Moderne (both share the same initials, CHEAM) in Paris; and the libraries of the Fondation Nationale des Sciences Politiques (FNSP), also in Paris.

The bibliography only suggests the reading done in preparation for this study. To list everything read would yield a list of articles and books longer than the book itself. The FNSP has card catalogues that give abstracts of practically all newspaper and review articles on important political questions including, of course, Algerian topics. Equally helpful, but not as thorough, is a similar card catalogue at the CRAM. The advantage of this second research tool is that it indicated unpublished studies in the CRAM collection and in the library of the CHEAM. The value of the CHEAM collection, composed of unpublished memoirs by administrators and officers with experience in Algeria, is obvious. The three depositories discussed above probably contain nearly all the information available at the present, although other resources will become available when official archives are opened in some fifty years.

Research was also done in North Africa in the national libraries of Algiers and Tunis, and in the departmental archives of Bougie, Constantine, and Fort National in Algeria. Other depositories might have been consulted, but these were poorly organized. In any case, the depositories consulted represent a fair sampling. Finally, some of the information was gathered from interviews with participants, most of whom are Algerians who served in the ALN.

Former ALN soldiers, unfortunately, were not very talkative. While there was an occasional failure to communicate because of language difficulties, a more imposing barrier was the rebel soldiers' reluctance to talk about military activities; even after the war, their training stuck. Former rebel officers, on the other hand, were willing informants. As a group, however, they gave little information not available in print. Another source of information was the Algerian refugee population in Tunis, around Aix-en-Provence, and elsewhere. Whenever oral sources were used, specific references are not made in notes; instead, the reader's attention is directed to published material and available manuscripts that touch on the problems revealed in interviews. While this device is not entirely satisfactory, it respects my informants' strongly expressed desire to remain anonymous.

The semantic problem faced in writing about recent events in Algeria reveals a great deal about the nature of most of the available written record. Most sources, even some prepared by nationalists and their allies, use colonialist terminology. For example, *Muslim* is widely used in a racial sense to refer to Algerians as opposed to Europeans. Logically, the latter should have been legally described as Christians, but the colonial administration, staffed by Frenchmen, was not logical on this point. Algerians themselves object to *native*, which tends, they feel, to be debasing. The colonial administration became aware of the political implications of these terms and, in 1956, began referring to Frenchmen of European Origin *(Français de Souche Européenne)* and to Frenchmen of North African Origin *(Français de Souche Nord Africaine)*. Use of these awkward descriptions is also avoided in the present study because the terms represent poor attempts to hide the prejudices evident in the earlier official distinctions. If terms such as *Muslim* or *native* remain in the text, these are meant to reflect the nature of the documentation and some of the flavor of the colonial situation. On the whole, however, these words are avoided and *Algerian* is used to refer to all but the European settlers and the armed personnel of France.

In writing this book it is the author's intent to present a specific study of the Algerian experience, which until now has not been analyzed in detail. Nevertheless, comparisons between this revolutionary and anticolonial situation and similar extreme social and political experiences in other parts of the colonial world naturally suggest themselves. Brief references in the text and in the notes reflect this, although the effort to focus on Algeria is maintained throughout. For those interested in the comparative approach to the subject, a parallel reading of similar studies might be profitable. There are, for example, several somewhat brief case studies in D. M. Condit, Bert H. Cooper, Jr., and others, *Challenge and Response in International Conflict*, vol. III: *The Experience* in *Africa and Latin America* (Washington: Center for Research in Social Systems, 1968). Other books on specific case studies are also easily available, as are more general approaches to guerrilla warfare as a whole. Several excellent journalists' accounts, all of them mentioned in the bibliography, deserve continued interest.

A. A. H.

Acknowledgments

I am indebted to so many that I dare not mention names. To do so would inevitably lead me to commit a cardinal offense, to fail to mention one or two names of persons without whose help I could not have completed this monograph. I hope those who helped me will accept this collective expression of debt and my warmest "thank you."

The staffs of CHEAM (Centre de Hautes Etudes d'Administration Musulmane), of FNSP (Fondation Nationale de Sciences Politiques) and of CRAM (Centre de Recherches sur l'Afrique Mediterranéenne) were particularly helpful. I also wish to thank the directors of the national libraries of Algiers and Tunis, and the archivists of the departmental depositories in Bougie, Constantine, and Fort National. Perhaps my warmest expression of gratitude should go to Algerians and

Europeans who knew much of what I wanted to know first hand and who agreed to talk to me.

On another plane, I would like to thank the institutions that enabled me to devote my full attention to North African and Algerian topics during a period of two years. Duke University gave me a travel grant which helped to meet the expense of getting to the Maghrib and to France. The Institute of International Education supported my efforts financially during the academic year 1963–1964, when I spent my time reading about the origins and development of Maghribi nationalism. The Army Research Office in Durham, North Carolina, gave me the grant that enabled me to turn my full attention to the problems of insurgency and counterinsurgency in Algeria. The basic research for this monograph was done with AROD support during the year 1964–1965.

Some of my colleagues at the University of Georgia, but especially Professors Joseph R. Berrigan, Roger Nichols, and Ronald R. Rader, members of my family, particularly my wife and my father, and staff members of the School of Insurgency Warfare at Fort Bragg have read various chapters of my study and have contributed valuable comments. I must, of course, take full responsibility for any mistakes of a factual or interpretive nature still to be found in the text of my study. A final expression of gratitude goes to typists and graduate students who helped prepare the final draft.

Athens, Georgia   A. A. H.

Abbreviations

ALN   *Armée de Libération Nationale* (National Liberation Army)

CCE   *Comité de Coordination et d'Exécution* (Executive and Co-ordinating Committee)

CCI   *Centre de Coordination Interservice* (Interservice Coordinating Center)

CHEAM *Centre de Hautes Etudes Administratives sur l'Afrique et l'Asie Moderne* (Center for Advanced Administrative Studies on Modern Africa and Asia)

CNRA   *Conseil National de la Révolution Algérienne* (National Council of the Algerian Revolution)

CRAM   *Centre de Recherches sur l'Afrique Mediterrannéene* (Research Center on Mediterranean Africa)

CRUA   *Comité Révolutionnaire d'Unité et d'Action* (Revolutionary Committee for Unity and Action)

DOP   *Dispositif Opérationnel de Protection* (Operational Security Organization)

DPU   *Dispositif de Protection Urbaine* (Urban Security Service)

ENA   *Etoile Nord-Africaine* (North African Star)

FEM   *Fédération des Elus Musulmans* (Federation of Elected Muslims)

FLN   *Front de Libération Nationale* (National Liberation Front)

FNSP   *Fondation Nationale des Sciences Politiques* (National Political Science Foundation)

GPRA   *Gouvernement Provisoire de la République Algérienne* (Provisional Government of the Algerian Republic)

MNA   *Mouvement National Algérien* (Algerian National Movement)

MTLD   *Mouvement pour le Triomphe des Libertés Démocratiques* (Movement for the Triumph of Democratic Liberties)

OPA   *Organisation Politique et Administrative* (Political and Administrative Organization)

OS   *Organisation Secrète,* also known as *Organisation Spéciale* (Secret Organization, or Special Organization)

OAS   *Organisation de l'Armée Secrète* (Secret Army Organization)

PCA   *Parti Communiste Algérien* (Algerian Communist Party)

PCF   *Parti Communiste Français* (French Communist Party)

PPA   *Parti du Peuple Algérien* (Algerian People's Party)

SAR   *Sections d'Amélioration Rurale* (Rural Improvement Sections)

SAS   *Sections Administratives Spécialisées* (Special Administrative Sections)

SAU   *Sections Administratives Urbaines* (Urban Administrative Sections)

UDMA   *Union Démocratique du Manifeste Algérien* (Democratic Union of the Algerian Manifesto)

Ulama   *Association des Ouléma Réformistes Algériens* (Association of Algerian Reformist Ulamas)

Insurgency and Counterinsurgency in Algeria

1 | The Origins and Early Development of Twentieth-Century Algerian Nationalism

ALGERIA'S HISTORY IN THE TWENTIETH CENTURY REFLECTS A synthesis of Muslim, African, and European characteristics. Algerian nationalism combines Islamic and pan-Arab ideologies taken from the Middle East with political, cultural, social, and revolutionary concepts borrowed from France, particularly from the French Communists, and native egalitarianism as well as other largely Berber attitudes and emotions. In a sense, Algerian nationalism is similar to that of most Arab countries; it was, at least in the earlier stages, a predominantly middle-class movement. But the bourgeoisie quickly yielded to the proletarian leaders of the North African Star (ENA), the political party most closely associated with the men who led the Revolution of 1954. This nationalism was a reaction to a colonial situation, and as an anticolonial movement it resembled in many respects anticolonial movements in other non-Western areas.[1]

The French imperium in Algeria, however, lasted longer and was more intensive than that over any other Maghribi country.[2] The officials who followed the conquering armies to Algeria in 1830 destroyed the central administrative institutions of the last Turkish Dey of Algiers. They expelled all the Turks, the only people who held positions of importance before 1830, the only leaders who knew how the system worked. The Turkish officials were replaced by Frenchmen, who imposed on Algeria a complex of ill-adapted French institutions. An entirely different policy was followed later in Tunisia and Morocco. When they conquered Tunisia in 1881, and Morocco in 1912, the French allowed native institutions and a skeleton of the established governments to survive. The result was that nationalism developed in these countries much more quickly than in Algeria. By 1907, for example, the Tunisians had created a viable nationalist movement, after a colonial period of only twenty-seven years.[3] In Morocco the eighteenth year of French control saw the development of a strong sense of nationalism and opposition to foreign rule.[4] Over a century passed, however, before the Algerians, deprived of their institutions and symbols around which they might have united, were able to spawn their own brand of anticolonial and revolutionary nationalism. There were, then, two modes of French colonial rule in the Maghrib. That used in Algeria made it more difficult to resist the imposition of foreign control.

Opposition to the French rule in Algeria, often characterized by a reluctance openly to attack the colonial power, made a false start around 1910. The Young Algerians, a disorganized group of *élites,* men who had been educated in French schools or who had served France in the administration or in the army, began to criticize the system which granted Muslims no voice in the affairs of their own country. These *élites* can hardly be classed with the modern nationalists, however, since what they demanded was merely the rights of French citizens.[5] Their protest, cut short by the advent of World War I, was nevertheless the genesis of Algerian nationalism.

During the First World War thousands of Algerians were drafted by the French army and saw action in metropolitan France. Countless other Berbers and Arabs went to Europe in search of work, to replace Frenchmen who left the factories to serve in the trenches.[6] While in France these Algerians were exposed to the propaganda of the Allies and the Central Powers alike. They listened to discussions of Wilsonian principles, absorbing the notion that nations ought to determine their own destinies. These soldiers and workers saw the glaring contrast between their right to vote while in France and their disenfranchisement at home.[7] The most thoughtful of these expatriates realized that reforms were urgently needed, and the leading politicians of France were quick to recognize this fact. In 1915 Georges Clemenceau and Georges Leygues proposed a bill designed to correct some of the inequities of the Algerian system.

At that time the French held absolute control in Algeria, and all important decisions were made by French officials. The European settlers *(colons)* received virtually automatic preference with respect to political rights and economic opportunities.[8] While the Europeans elected their own representatives in Algeria's central consultative assemblies, the Muslims were represented by officials appointed by French administrators. This political imbalance was reinforced by economic realities. While the vast majority of Algerians were wretchedly poor and eked out a meager existence in the traditional sector of the economy, the *colons* tended to work in the modern sector or in the administration and were relatively rich. These political and economic inequities were clearly illustrated by the peculiar organization of the administrative institutions of the country.

Although theoretically composed of three overseas departments of France, Algeria had special institutions. An appointed governor-general headed the government. Elsewhere, the position of governor-general was an exclusively colonial office. Equally unique were the two local assemblies constituted to advise the governor, the Financial Delegation *(Délégation Financière)* and the High Council *(Conseil Supérieur)*. The latter, a type of provincial senate, had fifty-eight members, of whom the governor or his staff appointed a majority of twenty-four Europeans, mainly officers and prefects, and nine carefully screened Algerian notables. The remaining twenty-five seats were elective, ten representing the Financial Delegation and fifteen the departmental General Councils *(Conseils Généraux)*. In the Financial Delegation, only twenty-one of the sixty-nine delegates were Algerian. Until 1919 these twenty-one natives were appointed, although their European counterparts were elected. Of the Algerians, fifteen represented the Arabs and six the Kabyles and other Berbers.[9]

The Europeans dominated the three departmental assemblies as well, and also the communal administrations. In native communes, that is in areas where very few or no Europeans had settled, French military chiefs controlled all local administrations. *Caïds,* native administrative officials who were usually chosen from among the local leaders, assisted the chiefs. But there were no elected positions. Wherever even a small number of Europeans had settled, the French created so-called mixed communes. In such areas local power was exercised by Municipal Commissions composed of government-appointed settlers while *caïds* controlled native affairs. Finally, full-fledged communes on the metropolitan models were organized where there were important concentrations of Europeans. Although the settlers rarely constituted a majority of the population in any commune, the law stipulated that three-fourths of the seats of the Municipal Council of the full communes be reserved for European representatives.

Algerians in both France and North Africa were inevitably

angered by this discrimination. By 1910 the Young Algerians were demanding justice. During the First World War M. Clemenceau and M. Leygues, moved by the bravery of the North African conscripts during the war, also proposed broadening the rights of the Algerians. Most of the *élites,* those few Algerians who had profited from the French presence in their country, wanted to become citizens equal in every respect to other Frenchmen. Under law they could do this only by renouncing certain special rights which the French had guaranteed to Muslims in their 1830 treaty with the last Turkish Dey of Algiers. Among the most important of these was the right to be tried in their own courts and according to Qur'anic law. In effect, Algerian Muslims were required to isolate themselves from their culture in order to participate in the government of their own nation. In 1919 this injustice was partially remedied by the passage of the bill originally proposed by Clemenceau and Leygues in 1915. Under the new statute the Muslims were given a second electoral college and the right to elect half the members of the consultative assemblies. The Europeans, who constituted roughly ten per cent of the country's population, voted as the first electoral college, electing the other half of the representatives. This fact, together with some procedural rules, assured the settlers of a decided advantage over the Algerians. Among the rules that served the settlers well, for example, was the possibility of demanding a majority of two-thirds of the votes to decide on most important issues debated in the Financial Delegation or in the High Council.

Although the proposed bill of 1915 was moderate, and although it was further weakened by numerous compromises, it was bitterly opposed by the *colons* and their representatives.[10] By 1919, when a modified version of the bill was passed, Clemenceau had become Premier of France. He then used his considerable personal prestige and the power of his office to force the Chamber of Deputies to accept his proposed reforms.[11] His opponents, however, did not change their minds and they warned of the perils to come, of the dangers unleashed by the new law. The Algerians were also unhappy because they felt the reforms were granted as a reward for services rendered, while they considered them to be intrinsic rights. They were, no doubt, also angered and discouraged by the disparity of power revealed during the struggle to pass the bill. While the *colons* had been well represented by their own deputies and senators, and by an effective lobby in Paris, the Muslims had been forced to rely on the sympathies of a few leftist deputies. This imbalance of power was not subsequently remedied, nor were the injustices of the basic premises corrected.

Thus Clemenceau's reform bill can hardly be regarded as a giant step toward freedom and equality for all. The law had the limited objective of extending certain rights of citizenship to a restricted number of Muslims. Benefiting most were World War I veterans of the French army and native administrative officials who had been decorated by the government. For these special categories the law of 1919 simplified the naturalization process, but to enjoy all the privileges of French citizenship, and hence to vote in the first electoral college, the applicants were still required to accept French laws, thus relinquishing their protected personal status under Qur'anic law. Separation of church and state was a concept completely alien to Muslims, and few Algerians dared to abandon their Islamic law and religion, thus cutting themselves off from their friends and families. Between 1919 and 1935 only 1,631 Muslims were naturalized.[12]

Other provisions of the Clemenceau law guaranteed a few political rights to the vast majority of Muslims who were not French citizens. The franchise was given to men over twenty-five who had served in the French Army, those who owned property or commercial establishments, government employees, and those who held university degrees. These men, who numbered some 421,000, voted separately as the second electoral college. The first college, until 1919 the only body to send representatives to the Algerian deliberative assemblies, was still reserved for settlers and the minute number of naturalized Algerians. The newly created second electoral college could send its own representatives to the assemblies, although not to the Chamber of Deputies or to the Senate in Paris. Still other provisions established fiscal equality by abolishing some pre-1919 "Arab taxes." Finally, those Muslims who had not chosen naturalization were henceforth to be admitted to public employment on the same basis as Frenchmen but with one important exception: positions of authority remained the preserve of Europeans. To this legal reservation might be added a factual limitation: because many government positions were filled through competitive examinations based on the French educational system, the Algerian applicants were at a considerable disadvantage.

Despite these disadvantages the Algerians made some meager political and economic advances in 1919. The creation of an electorate of some 421,000 people was especially important. This was a necessary precondition for the development of a body of native politicians who would be responsive to the needs of the second electoral college and the Muslim population as a whole. Though they could elect only half of the members of the Algerian consultative assemblies, the Muslims now had their own delegates who might stand up to the settlers. During the 1930's all the elected members of the second college, with the exception of the Communists, coalesced into three departmental Federations of Elected Muslims, an embryonic but truly Algerian political party.

In the early 1930's, before the organization of the first Federation of Elected Muslims in the department of Constantine, only one political party in Algeria expressed policies that represented Algerian interests as opposed to those of the settlers. This was the Algerian branch of PCF (French Com-

munist Party). Since 1919 party members had sought assiduously the votes of the second electoral college. Still, while
the Communists called for the eventual independence of
Algeria, most of the party's members and leaders were Europeans in origin and culture. Then in 1935 the connection with
the PCF was severed and the independent PCA (Algerian
Communist Party) came into being. A concerted effort was
made to recruit Arab and Berber members and to give as many
party positions as possible to Algerians.[13] This "native" policy
was sufficiently successful to enable the PCA to participate in
the organization of the first Algerian Muslim Congress in
1936.[14] In spite of their best efforts, however, the Communists
did not become the spokesmen of the Algerian interests. Of
those Berbers and Arabs who were politically active, most preferred to support organizations created by their fellow Muslims rather than the Communist Party with its taint of
European connections.

The first Algerian institution of this kind was not a political
party but a religious group whose cultural and educational
program proved to be fertile soil for the growth of a national
spirit. This gathering of religious scholars called itself the Association of Reformist Ulama. The Association was founded
in 1931 by Cheikh Abd-el-Hamid Ben Badis, a learned Muslim
theologian and a resident of Constantine, where he taught
Arabic. The Cheikh came from a conservative bourgeois
family; he shunned personal involvement in the political
currents of the time and he exhorted the organization to do
likewise. He and his disciples, however, were unable to adhere
to his original high-minded principles. As faithful and conscientious Muslims, the Ulama could not maintain the distinction between "church" and "state" which Ben Badis had
pronounced but which was so alien to the culture of the entire
Muslim world.[15]

While they did not seek political power, the Ulama developed their own brand of nationalism and Ben Badis was probably the first nationalist of twentieth-century Algeria. Except for the ENA (North African Star, a proletarian party which was gaining the allegiance of most of the Algerian workers in France during the early 1930's under the leadership of Messali Hadj) the Association of Reformist Ulama did more than any other movement to turn the Algerian people against their French overlords.* Unlike the ENA, however, the Ulama were active in Algeria itself, not in France, and theirs was essentially a religious and cultural struggle. Their avowed purpose was to protest and try to correct all the social ills that afflicted Algeria by proclaiming Islamic principles. While they were sincere in wishing to avoid a direct confrontation with the French administration, the Ulama called on their people to return to a purer and more primitive form of Islam. The implication was clear that a truly Muslim state and society, such as that which God had revealed to His Prophet, Muhammad, could never exist in a nation administered by infidels.

French bureaucrats were aware of the potential danger of the Ulama's program, but found it difficult to oppose them without seeming to infringe on protected religious rights. This fear, however, did not keep the government from closing the pulpits of official mosques to the Ulama, who it feared might deliver subversive sermons to the masses. These grounds were naturally unacceptable to the Muslims, since the ruling went against the sense of Islamic tradition and practice. The French simply argued that only the official agents of the Muslim cult could speak from official pulpits.[16] A xenophobic religious reaction, which might have been expected, was avoided because the government's appointed religious leaders supported the administration in the mosques. In so doing they were protecting their own position from a

---

* For a full discussion of the origin, development, and significant role of the ENA in the events leading up to the Revolution of 1954, see chapter 2.

seemingly dangerous challenge by progressive Ulama, who
were often better educated than those appointed by the colonial regime. These appointees, however, were by no means
alone in their opposition to the reformists. In their teachings
the Ulama of the Association had challenged a variety of re-
religious or pseudo-religious leaders including the marabouts,
leaders of cults of local saints, and the chiefs of the Muslim
brotherhoods that had strayed from the Ulama's strict con-
ception of Islam. While the Ulama protested their expulsion
from the official mosques, they turned to more practical solutions. They created, for example, a system of private discussion clubs, within which they were assured of a receptive
audience. While the administration watched the Association
with a wary eye, it grew apace.

Ben Badis and his followers found their greatest success in
their publications and their system of private schools. They
published *Ech Chihab* and *El Basaïr* in Arabic, and *La Défense*
in French. Their educational program, however, was by far
their more important task. In their schools the Ulama taught
Arabic and a number of other subjects whose nature permitted
a strong Islamic emphasis. By 1936 the Ulama had 130 schools
in the department of Constantine alone. While less aggressive
in the other departments, they spread their influence there as
well. French officials have estimated that some 10,000 pupils
attended Ulama schools each year in the early 1940's. Even in
the mid-1930's their nationalism was outspoken; Ben Badis'
original prohibition of political involvement was discarded.
The pupils absorbed a telling slogan: "Islam is my religion;
Arabic is my language; Algeria is my fatherland."[17] This for-
mula, apparently devised by Ahmed Tawfiq el-Madani, did
not square with the Association's official principles. There
was no mention of Algeria's position vis-à-vis France, but the
Ulama were clearly preparing a generation of Algerians to
think in terms of Arabic and Islamic culture.

The French administrators could have closed the educational facilities run by the Asociation of Reformist Ulama. Most of these schools did not meet established standards and were located in inadequate, crowded, and unhealthy quarters. On the whole, the staffs did not meet French certification requirements. But government officials did not insist on the law. They wished to avoid challenging the Algerian people on such an emotional issue as Arabic language education, a question which was sure to lead to political agitation. In addition the closing of the Ulama schools would not further the French ideal of *mission civilisatrice.* The government's own schools, despite consistent efforts, could not meet Algerian needs. According to government figures, for example, there were 53,000 Muslim pupils in school in 1914, and some 104,000 by 1938.[18] This expansion, however, hardly kept pace with the high Algerian birthrate. As a result, tens of thousands of school-age children were condemned to illiteracy. Most students in the Ulama's schools were drawn from this group. In any case numerous Muslim youth continued their studies in these schools that existed on official sufferance. At the same time the Association of Reformist Ulama left active participation in Algeria's political affairs to others.

In 1934 a second middle-class organization, the Federation of Elected Muslims, appeared in the department of Constantine.[19] Two additional Federations, one each for the departments of Algiers and Oran, were created shortly thereafter. The Elected Muslims were politicians who sought changes in the French system in Algeria. But unlike the Ulama, they were not nationalists. Most members of the new organizations came from a new middle class whose rise was a result of the French presence. Dr. Ben Djelloul, the founder of the first Federation, and Ferhat Abbas, another well-known Elected Muslim, were both educated in French schools. Their families had risen within the colonial administration. These and other Elected Muslims were part of a new group of professional politicians who came, as a result of the application of the reform bill of 1919, to represent the second or Algerian electoral college.

While admiring and benefiting from the culture and civilization of France, the Elected Muslims were also aware of the situation of those fellow Algerians who had not been directly affected by French domination and who continued to cling to their traditional society. The new politicians wished to bridge the chasm between France and Islam by securing for all Algerians an escape from their position as semi-subjects, a condition that had remained unaffected by the reforms of 1919. To this end they hoped to see the rights of full citizenship extended to all Algerians without the requirement that they abandon their special protection under Qur'anic law. These *évolués* or *élites* of the Federations of Elected Muslims did not seek to divorce Algeria from France but rather to make their country a part of France in fact as well as in theory.

The position of the Federations of Elected Muslims can easily be defined by quoting from Ferhat Abbas' now famous description of the Algerian problem in 1936:

If I had discovered the Algerian nation, I would have become a nationalist . . . I did not discover it. I looked to history, I questioned the living and the dead. I could not find it. I visited cemeteries: no one mentioned it to me. I did, of course, find the Arab Empire, the Muslim Empire which did honor to Islam and to our race. But these empires are dead. They were the equivalents of the Latin Empire and of the Germanic Holy Roman Empire of the medieval period. They were born for an epoch and a humanity that are no longer ours . . . we have therefore pushed aside all the clouds and [nationalist] dreams to definitely tie our future to the French achievement in this country. We have written as much. The safeguarding of this achievement is the pivot of our political activity.[20]

Although loyal to the French system, politically influential Algerian *élites* were also critical. Abbas would certainly have approved the spirit of a sentence written by one of his peers, R. Zenati:

It is, in short, inadmissible that it [the Algerian administration] should pretend to continue treating today's native, especially when he has been educated in the great French schools, like his grandfather of one hundred years ago.[21]

These statements by the loyal opposition to the colonial system were almost immediately challenged. Although they were prudent bourgeois who shunned public affairs, the Ulama could not let Abbas' explanation stand. Quite the contrary, as Ben Badis explained in *Ech Chihab*, was true:

We too have searched in history and in the present situation and we have observed that the Muslim Algerian nation has come into being and exists. . . . This nation has its own history . . . , it has its own religious and linguistic unity, its culture and its tradition. We then say that this Muslim Algerian nation is not France, cannot be France and does not want to be France.[22]

Ben Badis went on to explain that even assimilation could not make this rediscovered nation French. Two months later this leader of the Reformist Ulama further explained that independence is a natural right for all nations of the earth. He also expressed the hope that France would one day treat Algeria as England treated Canada, Australia, and the Cape Colony.

The Ulama obviously did not advocate a violent seizure of power, but they were just as clearly outspoken nationalists. Yet they usually did not seek to work closely with other nationalists. In terms of political goals, the Ulama and the Communists might have been expected to form an alliance. But cooperation between them was the exception rather than the rule. On the whole, the Ulama found it much simpler to cooperate with fellow middle-class leaders in the Federations of Elected Muslims. In this case, class interests and prejudices, complicated by religious and racial attitudes, apparently overrode other considerations. The Communists were predominantly proletarian and European while the members of the

Federations were bourgeois Algerians. When they did join with proletarian organizations from time to time, however, the middle-class groups found it easier to work with the Communists than with their fellow Muslims in the ENA. The leaders of the Ulama and the Federations probably felt that the ENA might challenge their leadership of the Muslim masses. With their suspect foreign connections, the Communists seemed less likely to mount such a challenge.

The Ulama, the PCA, and the Federations together formed the Algerian Muslim Congress, which met twice in 1936. The preparations for these meetings, and the proceedings themselves, clearly delineate the contrasting interests and attitudes of these groups. The ENA, whose claim to speak for the Algerian proletariat was probably more valid than that of the PCA, was not invited to participate.[23] Their exclusion was certainly due to a bourgeois fear of association with an organization that had been outlawed in Algeria as soon as it had appeared in France. Also, it could be argued that the ENA had not played a significant role in Algerian affairs before 1936 and had few roots inside Algeria itself. It was, however, the party of thousands of Algerians in France. In any case, the three groups within the Congress were strange bedfellows; the nationalist Ulama worked with the assimilationists of the Elected Muslims and the suspect Communists. Nevertheless, the Ulama shrank from any hint of cooperation with the ENA whose leader, Messali Hadj, was probably a nationalist even before Ben Badis organized the Ulama.

In 1936 the leaders of the second electoral college who were active inside Algeria believed in the possibility of achieving acceptable conditions for their constituents within the French system. The chances for meaningful reform appeared particularly bright because Léon Blum and his Popular Front came to power in June. The Left, and particularly the Socialists, had often helped Algerians and other colonial peoples improve their position within the French imperial system. Between

1915 and 1919, for example, the Socialists had served as spokesmen for the Algerians, who were not represented in Paris. In this capacity they opposed the *colon* representatives, deputies and senators, who tried to stop passage of Clemenceau's Algerian reform bill. Now with the Socialists in power, new and better reforms appeared to be within reach. With this in mind, the first Algerian Muslim Congress met. The delegates mildly criticized the French colonial government, then sent a delegation to Premier Blum with a list of demands.

The tone of the document was not in the least nationalistic; while recognizing the distinctive features of Algeria, it tended to move the country more deeply into the French orbit. The Charter of Muslim Demands, as it became known, asked that Algeria become truly a part of France. The only reservation was that the personal status of Muslims should remain protected. Toward this dual end all laws of exception that applied only to Algeria and all special institutions, such as the office of governor-general, the Financial Delegation, and the mixed communes, should be suppressed. The Muslims as well as the *colons* should be represented in the French parliament; universal suffrage and the abolition of the two-college system should determine the choice of representatives. The two educational systems, the purely French and the modified, unequal native system, should be fused together. Unemployment and social security payments, and other social and economic services of the state of Algeria, should be the same for non-Europeans as for the settlers. Finally, Arabic should be taught freely and the Arabic press should be free.[24]

Although many approved of the Charter only with reservations and misgivings, the mild demands represented a consensus that was acceptable to most delegates at the Algerian Muslim Congress. The Ulama, for example, liked the demands concerning the language question and the insistence that the legal status of Muslims should not be changed as a condition of citizenship. By using a free press and Arabic education they could work more openly than ever. Time might take care of the rest. The PCA could not be too critical of the French since the Communists in the mother country were cooperating with the Popular Front. Finally, the Elected Muslims were, in 1936, not yet nationalists; the Charter thus suited their aspirations for Algeria. The first session of the Congress came to an end as a delegation of the participants left for Paris, there to meet with Blum and to present their demands.

Just as the law of 1919 had been revolutionary in allowing the rise of native Algerian politicians who spoke out against the representatives of the *colons,* the first meeting of the Algerian Muslim Congress also represented an important breakthrough. It was the first public gathering at which thousands of Algerians met to discuss their political problems. It indicated the progress made since the end of World War I, and it gave voice to the Muslim's increasing awareness of their nation's problems and their willingness to criticize the colonial regime. The delegation having arrived in Paris with their Charter of Muslim Demands, the leader of the Popular Front was now in center stage.

Premier Blum was convinced of the need to satisfy at least some part of the Muslim Demands. He received the delegation of the Congress warmly, and the group returned to Algiers with an enthusiastic report. Unfortunately, the Popular Front was chiefly concerned with more pressing problems in Europe itself, although Blum genuinely wished to improve the lot of the Algerian people. He believed, for example, that Muslims should be granted political equality. At the same time, however, he and other leaders were of the opinion that the French public was not ready to concede this all at once. Nor were the Algerian masses believed to be ready for such rights. As a result, and after seeking the advice of Maurice Viollette, a former governor-general with a liberal reputation, Blum prepared a moderate project. The planned reform called for the extension of full French citizenship to the Algerian *élites* without prejudice to their personal status as Muslims. This citizenship would not be hereditary. *Élites* were further defined as ex-officers and noncommissioned officers, Muslims decorated for military valor, holders of certain degrees, official representatives of commerce and agriculture, elected officials and functionaries with decision-making powers, workers who had earned industrial medals, and labor union secretaries with ten years' experience. These Algerians, who were presumed to favor the French system, were to elect one deputy to the Chamber of Deputies for each 20,000 voters or fraction thereof. According to the best estimates, between 20,000 and 25,000 Algerians could have benefited. Although all social classes might be represented, social, economic, and educational conditions in Algeria limited the number of potential beneficiaries.[25]

The immediate effects of the proposed reforms would have been limited at best, although the plan had a truly revolutionary potential. As education spread, more and more Algerians would become eligible to participate fully in political affairs. The Ulama, for example, accepted the proposed reform, with reservations, because they could point to its future possibilities. But unfortunately for those Algerians who believed in the value of the French connection, the Blum-Viollette project was never discussed on the floor of the Chamber of Deputies. The Popular Front was too concerned with the international situation to aggressively promote reform for Algeria. War loomed and the French government would not endanger its North African position, and hence its Mediterranean strategy, in case of armed conflict with Germany. Finally, the two extreme groups in Algeria, the most outspoken representatives of the *colons* and the ENA, Messali Hadj's uncompromisingly anticolonial party, combined to help destroy the proposed reform. These strange allies helped to stamp out the early expectations of many Algerians which arose at the prospect of reform. In the end a potential well of Francophile sentiment was subverted because of the attacks against the plan and because the government failed to improve the lot of the Muslims after it had promised to do so.

Most hurt by Léon Blum's failure to make his reform bill into law were those organizations that participated in the preparation for the first Algerian Muslim Congress.[26] They had hoped to influence the French government to grant these reforms. But those *colons* who usually resisted concessions to the Muslims carried the day. Ultimately, however, the leaders of the radical ENA, particularly Messali Hadj, gained the most. During the second session of the Muslim Congress of 1936, as the delegates met once more to hear the report of those who had presented the Charter of Muslim Demands to the national government in Paris, Messali Hadj appeared on the rostrum. As an uninvited speaker, he harshly criticized the French administration and called on his fellow Algerians to become nationalists.[27] In a typically revolutionary maneuver, Messali Hadj had outflanked all the other politicians and public figures. He offered the Muslims a clear choice whose appeal could only be enhanced by the death of the Blum-Viollette project. Shocked and surprised, the delegates rose to cheer him. Messali Hadj, active among Algerians in France since 1926, had made his debut in the political life of Algeria itself.

2 | *From Political Participation to Revolutionary Nationalism*

AFTER MESSALI HADJ'S GRAND ENTRANCE INTO THE MAIN-
stream of Algeria's politics, Muslim demands became notice-
ably more radical. In Algeria, as in Tunisia, the failure to
achieve promised reforms in 1936 made it difficult for moderate North African politicians to maintain their posture. In
Tunisia Bourguiba had quickly recovered, preserving his control over the Tunisian anticolonial forces and becoming more
determined than ever to reach his ends by whatever means
necessary.[1] In Algeria, however, the leaders of the Federations
of Elected Muslims, who had sought concessions from the
French in an atmosphere of understanding, found themselves
in a difficult position. Although they clearly represented Muslim interests, they could not bring themselves to call for
independence. Now they had to compete for votes and popular support with an unquestionably nationalist party, the

ENA, and Messali Hadj shared the limelight with Dr. Ben Djelloul and Ferhat Abbas. The new pressure from the proletarian left forced the bourgeois political leaders to move, though ever so slowly, toward more radical demands and, in the end, toward nationalist positions.

The drift from moderation to uncompromising anticolonial agitation did not, however, cancel all French influence among Algerians. Even the proletarian leaders of the ENA had learned a great deal while in direct contact with Frenchmen. When Messali's party burst full-grown on the Algerian political scene in 1936, it had been active outside North Africa for a decade, first under direct French Communist tutelage, then as a close associate of the French Communist Party (PCF).

The ENA, which under a variety of acronyms was to be the party most closely associated with the outbreak of revolution in 1954, was not born in Algeria. It was born among Algerians in France, and its members were not bourgeois but proletarians who had migrated to Europe in search of work. It came to life in Paris with Communist assistance, then it was carried back to Algeria by returning workers. It was, then, a foreign import adopted and adapted by Algerians. The North African Star (ENA for *Étoile Nord Africaine*), as this proletarian party was originally named, was the first nationalist Algerian party. It was founded in Paris in 1926 by Hadj Ali Abd el Qader, a naturalized Frenchman and a member of the Central Committee of the French Communist Party. Leadership of the Star, however, quickly passed to Messali Hadj, an Arab from western Algeria with some Turkish blood. He remained its undisputed master until 1954, that is, until shortly before the outbreak of revolutionary warfare in November of that year.[2]

Messali Hadj was born to a poor family in the holy city of Tlemcen in 1898. He was educated along traditional lines mainly in Qur'anic schools, where the curriculum consisted largely of memorization of verses of the Qur'an, and was a member of the Derkawa Brotherhood. He moved to France while in his early twenties when he was drafted into the French army. Demobilized, he stayed in France, where he joined the Communist Party, from which he apparently learned a great deal. It is difficult to determine when he first became a nationalist. It is apparent, however, that he always advocated programs that combined the Islamic concepts he learned in the traditional Algerian schools with egalitarian social theories that he developed through his contacts with the Communists.[3]

In spite of Messali Hadj's close contact with the Communists, there was also a close connection between the ENA and the most important political currents of the Arab world. An accident in an eventful political career led Messali Hadj to Geneva in 1936. He was fleeing judicial proceedings initiated in Paris in connection with his political activities. Chekib Arslan, the father of pan-Arabism, happened to be in Switzerland. He met Messali Hadj, quickly converted him to pan-Arab ideas, and revived the flame of Islam in his heart. Messali Hadj was, of course, predisposed to such a conversion because of his family background and as a member of a Muslim brotherhood, the Derkawa.[4] With his conversion to pan-Arabism, Messali Hadj brought into Algerian nationalism the last important characteristic of that movement.

As leader of the ENA, Messali directed the fate of an institution created to defend the material, moral, and social interests of North African Muslims. In fact, Algerian Berbers, who were the most numerous North African migrant workers in France during the 1920's, made up practically the whole membership. Immediately after World War I, there were over 100,000 Algerian workers in France. This number grew until the time of the Great Depression. So the ENA had a wide potential clientele with which to work. To the party's official aims was quickly added a political program that included a call for the independence of all North Africa, the withdrawal of occupation troops, and the formation of one national revolutionary government. But Messali Hadj had no influence in Algeria itself until around 1936.

Because of the proletarian character of the ENA, and because of Messali's connection with the Communist Party of France, it is easy to see in his early program an application of the Communist doctrine of the time. That doctrine was aimed at liberating colonized peoples. But because the leadership of the ENA was all Algerian, the objectives of this organization quickly became solely Algerian. Finally, Messali Hadj's leadership quickly led to a break with the Communist sponsors as the Star became more and more closely asociated with various Arab movements.[5]

Outlawed in Algeria from the start, the ENA ran into legal trouble in France as well and was outlawed there in 1929. Very soon after its dissolution, however, it reappeared under another name and lived on clandestinely. Meanwhile, Messali Hadj had attended the anti-imperialist Congress of February 25, 1927, in Brussels, where he met, among others, Nehru. In 1930 he attended the Fifth Congress of the Profintern (the Red International of Labor Unions).[6] At these meetings, Messali Hadj met nationalist leaders from other colonized countries and these contacts led him to develop further his anticolonialism. On returning to France he created the newspaper, *El Oummah,* in which he continued to advocate the program of the ENA. As colonialists celebrated the hundredth anniversary in 1930 of the taking of Algiers, Messali saw to it that revolutionary and nationalist Muslim ideas entered his native land. Copies of *El Oummah,* or of other ENA publications that replaced it, were regularly smuggled into Algeria. In 1937 Messali's ENA, then known as the Glorious North African Star, was again outlawed. In the same year, however, the Algerian Peoples Party (PPA for *Parti du Peuple Algérien*) was created. Basically, only the name had changed.

During World War II political objections to French rule in North Africa were muted. Late in 1939 the PPA was outlawed;

Messali Hadj and most of his lieutenants were arrested and condemned to prison and exile terms ranging from life to several years. Native nationalists tried to cooperate in a waiting action. The PPA was to all appearances decapitated, but members of this proletarian party continued to work with middle-class nationalists of Ferhat Abbas' AML (Friends of the Manifest and of Liberty, a new party which united practically all the opponents of the colonial regime and replaced the pre-war Algerian Muslim Congress) and of the Ulama Association. Unlike some of their bourgeois colleagues, who were members of the Westernized *élite,* the followers of Messali Hadj did not feel hurt when France suffered defeat in 1940. They certainly did not volunteer for army service in Europe as did Ferhat Abbas and some of his friends. Nor did members of the Ulama, who were much too pro-Arab and Francophobe. Impatiently, members of the PPA infiltrated and subverted the other two organizations, especially the AML, during the war years. After the Allied landing in North Africa in 1942, and especially after 1943, the PPA was again in the news after a brief eclipse. But their most important work was done in secrecy.[7] Clandestinely, they prepared the Algerian population, particularly in eastern Algeria, for the violent Francophobe and anticolonial outbreak of May 1945.

The uprising of 1945 was characterized by the indiscriminate killing of Europeans by Algerian mobs that eventually cost 97 French lives. The repression that followed was even more cruel. Several thousand Algerians were killed or summarily executed while 4,500 Muslims, 3,700 of them in the department of Constantine, were arrested. Nearly 2,000 stood trial and were convicted, and 151 were sentenced to death. While only 28 were actually executed, the magnitude of the judicial proceedings and the total number of victims clearly indicates the seriousness of this upheaval.[8]

Politically, the uprising originated in the deep-seated dissatisfaction among Algerians at large, a generalized feeling of frustration that was exploited by the propagandists of the illegal PPA, many of whom had infiltrated into the middle-class groups led by Ben Badis, Ferhat Abbas, and others. The events themselves were triggered by nationalists who mingled with crowds of workers gathered to celebrate May Day. These nationalists waved white and green Algerian flags, chanted demands for the release of Messali Hadj from his French prison, and shouted slogans calling for independence. The attempts of the police to seize the leaders of the illegal disturbances led to scuffles, then to shooting, which resulted in two deaths and a dozen wounded in Algiers, one dead and several wounded in Oran. A week later, on May 8, PPA activists began a similar agitation while marching with crowds gathered to celebrate the signing of the armistice between the Allies and the Germans. When officials reacted again, the Algerians broke up into groups that roamed the streets, killing any European they happened upon.

The timing of the May 1945 uprising was somewhat surprising. The Free French had seemed to be in a conciliatory mood, as evidenced by an ordinance published on March 7, 1944. This official paper called for discussion of the principle of equality between Frenchmen and Muslims without prejudice to the latter's personal status. The document decreed that *élites*, a class still defined in much the same manner as in the ill-fated Blum-Viollette project, should immediately enjoy all the political rights of French citizenship. A more limited right of citizenship, to be defined in detail by a future Constituent Assembly, would be granted to other Muslims. For the moment, the latter would all be allowed to vote for representatives in local assemblies, while the proportion of Muslims in these bodies was set at two-fifths of the membership.[9]

This ordinance made enough concessions to meet the prewar demands of the Elected Muslims. But many of Dr. Ben Djelloul's followers had since become autonomists and were now in Ferhat Abbas' AML. Elected Muslims, Ulama leaders, members of the PPA and even of the PCA were represented in the AML ranks. PCA members, however, were reluctant participants because their relations with the PPA had deteriorated. The avowed nationalists who followed Messali Hadj found friends and protection in the AML, and they used this organization for their own purposes. Members of the illegal PPA and their Ulama colleagues in the AML were particularly dedicated in their efforts to subvert whatever gains the French administration might have made if the ordinance of March 1944 proved acceptable to the Muslims; they saw the law as an assimilationist tool that might encourage *élites* to resume their prewar role of loyal opposition. As already noted, Ferhat Abbas and many of his bourgeois peers had become autonomists or even mild nationalists. This had been one effect of the pressure from the left unleashed by Messali Hadj in 1936 and also of continued French failure to improve the political position of the Algerians. The agitation of PPA agents eventually led to the outbreak of May 1945, an event that made less likely than ever before a peaceful French solution to the problem of Algeria. The uprising and consequent repression left a bitter legacy of hatred. More immediately, the events forced the government to abandon all plans for reform. In a sense, the PPA agitators, operating within the protection of the AML and of the Association of Reformist Ulama, had induced the French to repeat the mistakes of 1919 and 1936.

All Muslim political parties suffered in the severe French repression of this bloody rebellion, and the various groups looked at the events for lessons. Bourgeois politicians understood the dangers involved in cooperation with Messali Hadj's followers. The PPA, a proletarian and revolutionary organization, definitely discovered the shyness and cowardice of middle-class nationalists.[10] Communists, who had been involved but who were still mostly Europeans, committed themselves to no one but tried, while playing their own game, to work with the various Algerian nationalist parties. But the PPA and the PCA were as far apart as ever.

By the end of the Second World War, Messali Hadj had completely severed his ties with the French Communist Party. A difference of opinion had arisen before the war between the leader of Algerian proletarian nationalism and the Communists, when the latter joined in support of the Blum Popular Front in an attempt to fight international Fascism. This political act led Communists to soft-pedal the question of independence for colonial peoples, a question that did not concern them again until after the war against Hitler. For the moment, they preferred to keep France strong. The Communist press, for example, loudly approved of the dissolution of the ENA in 1937.[11] From then on the latter was the uncompromising enemy of its earlier friends. But the Marxist characteristics of the ENA remained because of the Star's proletarian membership and because of its propaganda techniques. Algerian nationalists had learned valuable lessons from the Communists, a fact that distinguishes this movement from the Istiqlal in Morocco,[12] from the Neo-Destour in Tunisia, and from nationalists in other Arab countries. Tunisian nationalism had middle-class origins, although changes that led the Neo-Destour to break away from the older Destour party gave it a distinctly Socialist option.[13] Bourguiba and the French Socialists were to Tunisia what Messali Hadj and the PCF were to Algeria, but only the latter had truly proletarian origins.

After the war, most of the imprisoned nationalist leaders were beneficiaries of a general amnesty for political prisoners in 1946. By November of that year, the proletarian and middle-class nationalists had split apart. Although Ferhat Abbas did not want to divide the Muslim electorate, Messali Hadj expected a real plebiscite, and there were rumors that he planned to go to Cairo to get the League of Arab States to support the total liberation of Algeria and that he would also go to the United Nations to plead the same cause. In any case, he demanded more than the moderate Abbas during the campaign of the legislative election of November 10, 1946.

The expected did not happen. Officially, some 63.4 per cent of the registered Algerian voters abstained. Of those who went to the polls, only 12 per cent voted for the PPA. Abbas did much better and began to reorganize his bourgeois party, which had become mildly nationalistic after World War II. He took great care to avoid infiltration and subversion from the left.[14] The success of moderate nationalism in Algeria, however, was to be short-lived.

In 1946 the French Communist Party began to support the PPA without demanding control of that organization. From then on, the PPA spread rapidly among Algerians in France. In all extreme left popular meetings throughout France, only the spokesmen of the PPA could be heard. Ferhat Abbas and his followers were accused as traitors and as lukewarm Algerians. Since rules limiting immigration from Algeria into France were largely lifted during these postwar years, the membership of the PPA grew by leaps and bounds.[15] Many Arab and Berber workers in France, of course, returned to Algeria, some permanently, others merely for extended vacations. When they did, they naturally brought with them the revolutionary ideas learned in France. Nationalism grew throughout the colony but especially in Kabylia, a rather poor region of Algeria in which the population density was particularly high.[16] So the party that had emerged out of the ENA, a group of frustrated emigrés, continued to have the characteristics of the parent body. The members were practically all proletarians, and the party was largely composed of Kabyles. But now, as this convinced nationalist organization spread in the colony, even members of the Algerian middle class, who had in the past been moderate in their programs, become more intransigent in their nationalistic demands.[17]

Thus the seeds of the PPA began to grow, especially after

the Second World War, and the partisans spread Messali Hadj's propaganda. Outlawed since 1939, the party continued to live in secrecy, then under the legal cover of the MTLD *(Mouvement pour le Triomphe des Libertés Démocratiques)*, which was created in 1946. The colonial administration could not disband this new party because it was legally distinct and unrelated to the PPA. Activist PPA members who supported the MTLD, of course, worked in secret as they did not wish to spoil the chance of having their program, or at least part of their program, heard at every level of elected governmental agencies. Then, as a result of legislation passed in 1947, a relatively liberal era in the political life of Algeria began, during which the government attempted to work with native political parties.

Reforms that would grant Algerians more of a voice in the government of Algeria had been promised by de Gaulle after the Brazzaville Conference that considered colonial problems in 1944. The insurrection of 1945 and the crude repression inflicted by the French population on the Muslims temporarily stopped all liberal thoughts. By 1947, however, Paris was ready to try again. Enough legislators believed a compromise was possible between France, which was in a difficult position because of her material and moral losses in World War II, and Algerian nationalists. So the law of September 20, 1947, put to rest the policy of assimilation, which had been the continuing policy of France with respect to Algeria since the nineteenth century. The new law was an attempt to give Algerians more autonomy in local affairs. Association, copied from the model of the British Commonwealth, would, it was hoped, replace assimilation, which had completely failed.[18]

The new law satisfied no one in Algeria. Europeans felt they were being sacrificed to metropolitan egalitarian concepts; Algerians were angry because they did not get important political advantages at once. Messali Hadj and his party took a hard line once more, and this time they completely eclipsed Ferhat Abbas and Dr. Ben Djelloul, representatives of a more moderate brand of nationalism. A show of relative political strength first occurred in municipal elections in Algiers in October 1947. The MTLD captured most of the seats reserved for the second college, that is, for representatives of the Muslim electors.[19]

More important, perhaps, was the fact that Messali's MTLD won in the larger centers, while Ferhat Abbas' party, the UDMA *(Union Démocratique du Manifeste Algérien)*, managed to hold its own in smaller townships. These two parties, respectively, got 31 per cent and 27 per cent of the votes cast, and the Algerian Communist Party got 4 per cent.[20] As a result, the nationalist parties obtained a clear landslide in the second college. The colonial administration was to suffer another shock in November and December of 1947, when rural councils were elected throughout Algeria. These councils, or *jama'ah* as they were called, had usually been staffed by official government candidates. Yet in spite of careful supervision by the administration, 28 per cent of the Algerian vote went to nationalists, whom the administration called secessionists. Coinciding with those elections was a rash of terrorism apparently conducted by the MTLD, which accused the administration of electoral fraud. Although the nationalists probably exaggerated and were not above reproach themselves, there was just enough truth in their claims against the administration to push uncommitted Algerians over to the nationalist party.[21] News of electoral frauds, real and imagined, added weight to the arguments of the anticolonial forces and spurred nationalists toward more revolutionary fervor.

Messali Hadj's party, then, had some considerable successes at the polls. But the leader himself was beginning to lose control of his own organization. An impatient left wing, composed almost entirely of younger cadres, wished to pass from the polite world of politics to subversive activities, the more direct means of attaining what they wanted. In December

1947, perhaps because of frustration in connection with the rural elections of that month (the MTLD did not do well), Hocine Ait Ahmed, a Kabyle, created the paramilitary Special Organization (OS), apparently in spite of Messali Hadj's objections.[22]

Ait Ahmed and other young hawks in the clandestine PPA apparently wanted to restructure the MTLD as well as the remnants of the PPA. They wanted to make their party more manageable and, especially, more revolutionary. To accomplish these aims, they had first infiltrated the PPA by creating a network of complicity. By the time they were through, the proletarian nationalist party of Algeria had three distinct levels. On the surface was the legal MTLD, which had presented candidates in 1946 and after, and which had had some limited success. Below the surface were the structures and organization of the PPA that had survived official sanctions taken against the party. In deeper secrecy was the OS, which was meant to direct the PPA and to support the MTLD by sabotage and terrorism. The OS also served to check on the activities of PPA and MTLD members. It was, in a way, a parallel and secret hierarchy which official party leaders could not always control.[23] The connections, of course, were never admitted; in this the OS simply followed a precedent set by the illegal PPA. The object was to avoid the destruction of the legal arm of proletarian nationalism, which even OS members did not desire, since MTLD members elected to office at every level of government could broadcast useful propaganda, even in international congresses. But the attitude of the OS appears to have been one of toleration rather than of full support. Until a revolution could be started, the legal party might be useful.

Thus behind the facade of the MTLD a really revolutionary organization had been set up. Messali Hadj's hold on his own party and particularly on the secret branches of that party was weakening continually. As a beneficiary of the amnesty of

1946, he was a resident of Bouzaréah, near Algiers. He was, however, still excluded from the capital itself. But following the terrorism during the elections of December 1947, he was once more forced into exile, just at the time when the OS was created. He took up residence in France, from where he found it increasingly difficult to keep his followers in line. He was, nevertheless, kept well informed of party activities, and he usually knew what the OS was doing. But he could not control young OS leaders who tended to reject his authoritarian direction. The OS itself was changing.

In 1949 Ahmed Ben Bella, an Arab from Tlemcen, replaced Ait Ahmed as director of the OS. Then, in 1950, the French police in Algeria accidentally discovered the supersecret paramilitary OS. Many of the leaders of that organization were arrested, perhaps to Messali Hadj's relief. Among those arrested were Ben Bella and his accomplices in the hold-up of the main post office in Oran during 1949, a coup that had brought the equivalent of some nine thousand dollars to the party coffers. Much more money had been left in the drawers and on the floor of the post office by the political bandits, but the event was a warning of things to come and symptomatic of the evolution of Algerian nationalism. The year after the hold-up, the participants and many other leaders of the secret arm of the PPA-MTLD were captured after police stumbled upon some OS documents. The accident nearly led to the complete destruction of this organization.

After the police managed to uncover the OS on March 28, 1950, the colonialist newspaper *L'Echo d'Alger* wrote that the investigation had revealed the attempted creation of a veritable clandestine army in the department of Constantine. The *Dépêche quotidienne,* another daily, added that this army had been created on the model of a Resistance network in the territories occupied by the Germans during World War II. The discovery seemed sensational. And yet Marcel-Edmond Naegelen, the governor-general of Algeria, answered a query on May 5 with the following words: "We have put our hands on a clandestine operation . . . [and] we wonder whether we should treat it as child's play or seriously."[24]

The OS was treated seriously and suffered severe blows, particularly in Bône, Oued Zenati, Souk-Ahras, and Condé-Smendou. This was also true in the departments of Algiers and Oran, where OS sections were apparently still in a formative stage. But because it was a carefully compartmentalized secret organization, many sections survived intact, as in Philippeville. By and large, however, leaders were captured and filled prisons. The organization was decapitated, but many local cell members escaped notice and simply waited for leaders to contact them, and for an occasion to reorganize.

OS members who were arrested acted quickly to make the best of a bad situation. They immediately began a hunger strike to win recognition as political rather than criminal prisoners. Such strikes lasted fifteen days in Tizi-Ouzou, fourteen in Oran, twenty-two in Algiers, and thirty-six days in Orléansville. Then, because torture was used to extort confessions and to find out the names of OS members still at large, nationalists found another theme on which to base political propaganda. Most contemporary and neutral observers did not believe the reported incidents of torture. Yet prisoners were not brought to trial unless they had made "spontaneous confessions." In Bône one such prisoner, Henini Salah, told the judge before whom he was arrested: "Give me any policeman, I'll make him suffer the tortures that were inflicted on me and I'll surely bring you back a document signed by his hand admitting that he collaborated with the enemy." Another prisoner reported that he was told, while in a police station, that "even if God comes here, we'll make him confess."[25] The Bône trial was the only one involving suspected OS members ever to be held in public.

Legal parties, including Ferhat Abbas' UDMA and the MTLD, demanded a full legislative investigation to determine responsibilities. Abbas also called on the United Nations to intervene, defining its mission as being "first of all to free peoples from colonial oppression."[26] Justice was carried out, but only by the French colonial administration and behind closed doors. Meanwhile European settlers, who were legally entitled to own weapons of war, armed themselves. The moderate nationalist newspaper *La République algérienne* began to worry about the appearance of *colon* militias, many of which were supported by local administrators. The advent of bands of armed settlers was interpreted as an attempt to "make the Arabs think,"[27] which was probably a correct judgment.

While the press and politicians asked questions, many OS leaders who were not caught in 1950, but who were condemned *in absentia*, took up clandestine lives in the *maquis* (i.e., they went underground). Among them were Boudiaf, Didouche, Ben M'Hidi, Bitat, Ben Tobbal, Boussouf, and the professional bandits of Kabylia, Benaouda, Krim, and Ouamrane. All with the exception of Oumrane, who was killed by treason shortly before the insurrection of November 1954, would reemerge as leaders of the Algerian Revolution. Although the "Arab telephone," the oral news media of an illiterate people, told of the exploits of these fugitives from justice, the administration seemed unable to capture the wanted men. Then, in 1952, Ben Bella and Mahsas escaped from prison in Blida. Zirout and Ben Boulaid broke out of their cell in Bône. All somehow got to Cairo, where they joined Ait Ahmed and Mohammed Khider, both of whom had fled Algeria in 1950. All these fugitives, whether in Algeria or in Egypt, had been in the OS; all were to play important roles in the revolution of 1954. That some of them went to Cairo is important because it helped strengthen Arab influences, which had first been felt after Messali Hadj's 1936 chance meeting with Arslan at Geneva, within the proletarian branch of Algerian nationalism. Of more immediate importance is the fact that ex-OS leaders acquired a safe and friendly sanctuary from which to plan the liberation of Algeria. Egypt had just had a revolution of her own and was sympathetic to revolutionary movements throughout the Arab world, revolutions from which she expected to profit.

Until the police discovered the OS in 1950, nothing was known about that paramilitary organization. By 1952 little more was known, although many suspected members had been thoroughly questioned. Perhaps a few informants were found, but the police were not terribly successful. Nor were they able to infiltrate the clandestine organization in an attempt to penetrate all its ramifications, and the effort was quickly abandoned. Since practically all the OS leaders were known to be in prison or in exile, officials believed the organization too weak to recover. Such calculations did not take into account the determination of the revolutionary nationalists. Late in 1954, however, the attempt to understand and describe the OS more fully was undertaken with more vigor. It was then evident that the beast had not been killed in 1950, and was probably responsible for the events that threatened the French security in Algeria. The renewed search led to a gathering of information on the basis of which it is possible to reconstruct the organizational structure of the OS before 1950.

The OS appears to have been modeled on earlier secret organizations within the PPA. According to an anonymous observer, the PPA had several specialized and clandestine groups as early as 1941.[28] One such group was a nerve center in which tactics were worked out, while a separate group studied the application of such tactics to local conditions. A third group specialized in action that included intelligence work, the education of the young, recruitment and selection of members for the specialized organizations as well as for the party as a whole, and political agitation in generally passive populations. The anonymous writer thought that the illegal and clandestine PPA, with its specialized organs, intended to promote nationalistic agitation without being directly involved. It would urge the people to violence against the French administration without exposing the organization. This plan apparently failed in 1945, when many party members were arrested and held responsible for the insurrection of May 8.

According to the same informant, the secret hierarchy and planning boards were reorganized in 1943. Thereafter the basic cells were composed of four members and one chief. Only the latter knew anyone in the organization besides members of the individual cell. Four cell chiefs met to form a sector, and four sector chiefs met to make up a district. In each case, only the chief of the cell, whatever its level, knew any members of the organization on a higher level. At the top were chiefs of local committees made up of district chiefs. Local chiefs reported to regional committees, then to people on the arrondissement level, and finally to three federations, each of which corresponds to the French administrative division of Algeria into three departments. An executive committee coordinated the work of the three federations on a national scale and did all liaison work between these departmental organizations.

If the report is correct, Algeria was blanketed by a secret organization that was itself buffered by the illegal PPA. This underground group had cells primarily concerned with political action planned by other cells that set tactics and studied the application of such tactics to local situations. The action cells were undoubtedly the most numerous. When the MTLD was created in 1946, it served as additional covering for the secret organizations, which, after 1947, were carefully watched by the OS. Ordinary party members knew nothing. The OS was even more particularly concerned with the setting up of weapons and munitions depots throughout Algeria and with the training of certain carefully screened and selected young natives in military skills. The OS was meant to be the military arm of a revolutionary party.

If the cells of the illegal PPA were carefully compartmen-

CHART 1
PROBABLE PPA UNDERGROUND ORGANIZATION
(1939–1945, VESTIGES TO 1954)

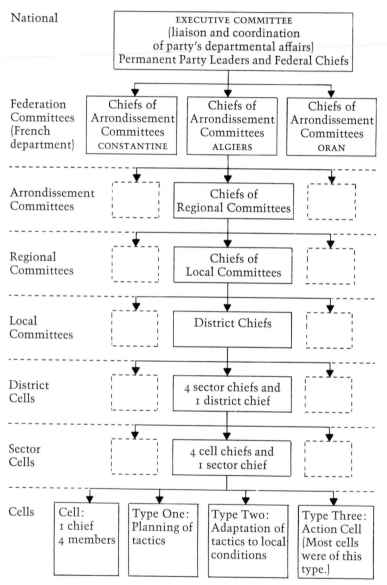

National — EXECUTIVE COMMITTEE (liaison and coordination of party's departmental affairs) Permanent Party Leaders and Federal Chiefs

Federation Committees (French department) — Chiefs of Arrondissement Committees CONSTANTINE | Chiefs of Arrondissement Committees ALGIERS | Chiefs of Arrondissement Committees ORAN

Arrondissement Committees — Chiefs of Regional Committees

Regional Committees — Chiefs of Local Committees

Local Committees — District Chiefs

District Cells — 4 sector chiefs and 1 district chief

Sector Cells — 4 cell chiefs and 1 sector chief

Cells — Cell: 1 chief 4 members | Type One: Planning of tactics | Type Two: Adaptation of tactics to local conditions | Type Three: Action Cell (Most cells were of this type.)

CHART 2
SPECIAL ORGANIZATION (OS) 1947–1950

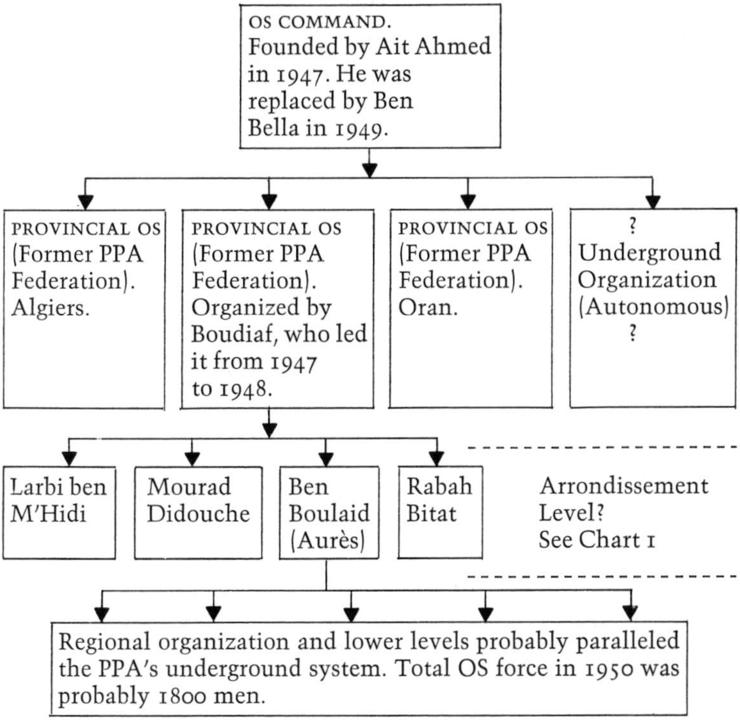

```
┌─────────────────────────┐
│ OS COMMAND.             │
│ Founded by Ait Ahmed    │
│ in 1947. He was         │
│ replaced by Ben         │
│ Bella in 1949.          │
└─────────────────────────┘
```

PROVINCIAL OS (Former PPA Federation). Algiers.	PROVINCIAL OS (Former PPA Federation). Organized by Boudiaf, who led it from 1947 to 1948.	PROVINCIAL OS (Former PPA Federation). Oran.	? Underground Organization (Autonomous) ?

Larbi ben M'Hidi	Mourad Didouche	Ben Boulaid (Aurès)	Rabah Bitat	Arrondissement Level? See Chart 1

```
┌───────────────────────────────────────────────────┐
│ Regional organization and lower levels probably    │
│ paralleled the PPA's underground system. Total OS  │
│ force in 1950 was probably 1800 men.               │
└───────────────────────────────────────────────────┘
```

talized, the OS, when it appeared, was even more aware of the need for secrecy. Thus it is still difficult to assess, geographically or numerically, the extent of the OS between 1947, when it was created, and 1950, when it was uncovered. But available information does show that the OS was strongest in eastern Algeria. Boudiaf, for example, directed the activities of M'Hidi, Didouche, Ben Boulaid, and Bitat in the department of Constantine during 1947–1948. All of these men were leaders; it would be difficult to imagine them in so lowly a position as cell chief on the lowest level. But this is speculation. A known fact pointing to a strong organization in eastern Algeria was the survival of the Philippeville OS sections after

1950. Finally, the terroristic activities that paralleled the election campaigns of 1947 and 1948, quite obviously the work of OS cells, were much more common east of Algiers. Roger Le Tourneau, a leading French specialist on North African history, claims that the numerical strength of the OS in 1950 has been estimated at about 1,800 men. This is probably a good, educated guess, although the actual number of OS members may never be known.[29]

Obsession with secrecy is clearly illustrated in OS documents that were later seized. One of these, entitled *Bulletin d'éducation* and dated August 1949, carried the following advice for OS members:

Imperialism must not be afforded the possibility of subverting us through disguised agents, of infiltrating among us mangy sheep [in an attempt] to cause deviations. One must take away all hope and all attempts to break up our ideological cohesiveness. [This] requires (1) the application of the principle of authority under a centralist format, that is to say, authority comes from the top to the base. Strict discipline is the law for all, directors and directed, chiefs and executioners. (2) The application of the principle of the division of labor, that is to say, of specialization in the [assigned] tasks.[30]

OS documents such as the one just quoted clearly indicate a dependence on Marxist organizational techniques. Such an observation might lead to the facile conclusion that the OS was a Communist front. It was not. It was born within the illegal PPA, whose parent body was the Communist-inspired ENA, but, like Messali Hadj, OS leaders opposed the Communist Party. The PPA forced the exclusion of the PCA from the Second Muslim Congress held at Algiers in 1937. All the other Muslim nationalist parties were represented in this Congress. Later in the same year the PPA refused to withdraw candidates from a run-off election. As a result, a list headed by Ben Ali Boukhourt, a leading Algerian Communist, failed to get enough votes to gain representation.[31] Then in 1945 organized political demonstrations were held throughout Algeria during which Muslims were heard chanting slogans such as "Down with the Communist Party."[32] Stubborn enmity between the native and foreign proletarian parties continued into the period of revolutionary war. The leaders of the OS who were to play such a major role during the revolution systematically excluded members of the Communist Party from their organization. To fight the French, Algerian Communists had to give up all party activities for the duration of the war and join the ranks of the nationalist army as individuals, not as party members (see chapter 15).

The OS, then, was not a Communist institution. All of the Algerian revolutionary organizations inherited Communist methodology from the ENA and its successors, but they also inherited the strong anti-Communism first introduced into the Algerian proletarian party by Messali Hadj. Like him, they were open to Arab and Muslim influences that clashed with atheistic aspects of Communism. They obviously counted on help from Arab nations in their coming struggle against French domination in Algeria. If nothing else, this reflected a good grasp of political realities.

In the early 1950's the OS leaders were in hiding or still in jail. Their influence on political developments in Algeria was consequently minimal. Once more, Messali Hadj and other politicians took complete control of the nationalist movement. While the most extreme nationalists were unable to act, others organized Algerians for political activities that they hoped would lead to independence or at least to more autonomy for Algerians within a French federal system. Messali Hadj, at the head of the MTLD, was especially successful during this period and reached the zenith of his political power in 1952. During that year he stumped the country to enhance his own position within the party and to increase its numerical and financial strength.

Messali Hadj's power was solidly based. His party was firmly structured throughout Algeria, and he was assisted by able lieutenants, among whom were Ahmed Mezerna, a former deputy for Algiers; Hocine Lahouel, the secretary-general of the MTLD, who had been elected to the Algiers city council in October 1947 but who had been deprived of his seat in December of the same year; and Ahmed Ben Amar Boudaa, a delegate to the Algerian Assembly. These men and several others were members of the Executive Board of the MTLD and did most of their work in committees. The standing committees were in charge of Planning, Press and Propaganda, Finance, "Complicity Network," Relations with Mo-

CHART 3
NATIONAL EXECUTIVE: MTLD EXECUTIVE BOARD AND
CENTRAL COMMITTEES*

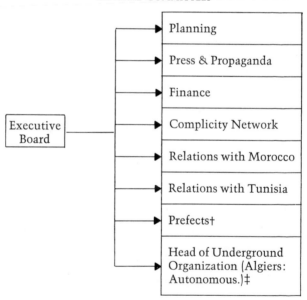

* Geographical organization of the MTLD is illustrated in chart 4.
† Prefects represented either the old PPA Federations (departmental), or each of the MTLD's own provinces or *wilaya*, of which there were 5 in actual operation.
‡ May have been the chief of the OS, although Ben Bella went into exile in 1950, and his successor, if any, is not known.

rocco, and Relations with Tunisia. Also on the Executive Board were "Prefects," one for each of the three Algerian departments, who were ready to replace the French officials whose titles they carried, and a Head of the Clandestine Organization in the Algiers Region. All of these committees and officials had local and regional counterparts.[33]

The MTLD's pyramid was a copy of the Communist Party. It provided a "summit with a disciplined hierarchy capable of carrying the chain of command without interruption from level to level down to the innumerable cells at the bottom." Geographically, the party was divided into five *wilayas* or provinces, thirty-three *dairas* or districts, and over one hundred *kasmas* or sectors. Some local party organizations were named *douars*. This term referred to groups or hamlets. There were even fractions that were parts of *douars* or villages known as *dechras*. At the bottom were the cells. There were, in all, some twelve thousand active MTLD members. According to rumors started in January 1952, there were in addition some secret "Action Groups," recruited first in Algiers but apparently also in Boghari, Tlemcen, and Marnia. There was also some talk of a contraband traffic in arms and ammunitions along the frontiers, especially between Spanish Morocco and Algeria.[34]

Nothing comparable to the OS was created by Messali Hadj, except in a very few localities where Action Groups were established. These differed from OS cells in that they were apparently more closely supervised by the regular party hierarchy. Messali Hadj's great ability was in another area. Because of his oratorical abilities, he rode a wave of popularity during 1952. Beginning in April of that year, he undertook a membership and fund-raising drive throughout Algeria that aroused official attention and led the governor-general to have Messali Hadj arrested. The nationalist leader was ordered to limit his activities to Bouzareah, a suburb of Algiers. But Messali Hadj, who had enrolled 2,000 members at Oued Ze-

CHART 4
MTLD GEOGRAPHICAL ORGANIZATION IN 1950*

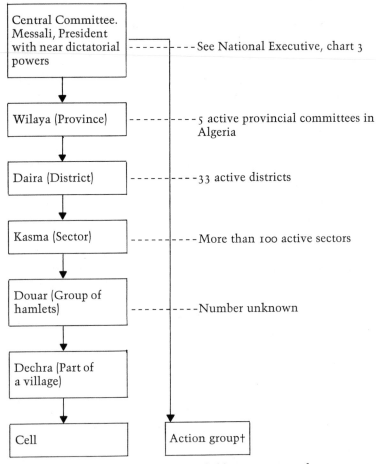

* Total MTLD strength in 1950 was probably at 12,000 members.
† Action Groups were not part of the OS.

nati, 2,500 at Souk Ahras, 6,000 at El Arrouch, and 200 at Phi-lippeville, would not stay still. Brought back to Bouzareah, he quickly set out for Boghari, Reibel, Affreville, Blida, and Orléansville, all party strongholds.

In Orléansville, MTLD-PPA organizers drove members and sympathizers too far. They attacked policemen with clubs and sticks. That turned out to be Messali Hadj's last stop in his campaign to regain control of the MTLD. On May 14, 1952, he was declared undesirable in Algeria and was deported to France, where he was assigned a residence in Niort near La Rochelle. His rise to popularity as Algeria's national leader came to an abrupt end.

Ferhat Abbas, meanwhile, was on a political tour of his own, but he was too reasonable to attract a mass following. He recommended nonviolence, a program that was far less attractive than Messali Hadj's. The latter's advice would inevitably lead to violence in the pursuit of independence for Algeria. Muslims who were all too often on the brink of starvation were simply not interested in compromises.[35]

A third group, politically inactive because it was composed of outlaws, watched in disgust. These were men who had been in the OS and who had long since lost faith in legal courses of action. Fraudulent elections, directed by the administration in the late forties and early fifties, had proven to them the futility of political opposition. They wanted action, revolutionary war. In 1952 these men were still trying to reorganize, but they could find no program. Then during 1953 the monolithic organization of the MTLD began to crack. Messali Hadj, exiled in France, could not control lieutenants who were active in Algeria. His authority over the party was slipping, but the old fighter would not concede graciously.

Messali Hadj's struggle to retain dictatorial powers over his party quickly led to a break within the MTLD. OS leaders were not involved in this factional fight, but they were undoubtedly tempted to go against a leader who had tried to disown them in 1950. In their eyes, Messali Hadj had also sinned when, in 1952, younger cadres had announced Ben Bella's escape from prison in Blida. The leader had refused to give up his ritual siesta in order to celebrate the event. In the same year Messali Hadj had refused to follow advice given by OS members who wanted him to escape from French surveillance in Niort, to leave France, and to continue to lead the MTLD from a friendlier base of operations.[36] Messali Hadj, however, had preferred the relative comfort of France to the uncertainties of a clandestine existence in North Africa or in some other Arab country. All things considered, the young party members who had been in the OS were getting tired of the old leadership, were becoming more insistent in their demands that the party adopt a more radical program and engage in more sensational activities.

It was not the OS leaders who openly challenged Messali Hadj. They had tried between 1947 and 1950 but failed when caught by the colonial police. In 1950, however, men such as Hocine Lahouel and Benyoussef Ben Khedda had begun to fight against the personality cult surrounding Messali Hadj. A few cadres, including Moulay Merbah, tried to impose respect for Messali Hadj among party members; with the leader in France, the opponents quickly gained the upper hand in Algeria. Messali Hadj's unwillingness to compromise quickly led to a definitive break.[37] OS members were not involved in this dispute of personalities that pitted members of the party's Central Committee against Messali Hadj and his supporters.

In April 1953 a party conference was called in Algiers. Messali Hadj, still under enforced residence in France, could not attend. Also absent were the ex-members of the OS. Those who wondered about these absences were told that security was involved. At this party conference a new Central Committee was named. Messali Hadj was appointed a member, but some of his closest lieutenants, including Mezerna and Filali, were not.[38] Messali Hadj objected; the old leader brought the factional fight to the streets in an attempt to gain rank and file support against rebellious cadres. Lahouel was knocked unconscious in the streets of Algiers by Messali Hadj faithfuls.[39] The break appeared to be irreparable.

By and large, Hocine Lahouel led moderate MTLD members who became less and less sympathetic to the older and more radical PPA. They wished to move away from revolutionary programs. The apparent direction of this group was toward more legal means of achieving nationalist objectives. They represented a non-proletarian leadership in the PPA, all of them latecomers to party membership. In effect, Lahouel tried to create a new party and to take all the organization of the old Messalist institution with him.[40] Messali Hadj, with the help of Embarek Filali, among others, fought back. During a conference of the French section of the PPA-MTLD held in Paris early in 1954, Filali spoke of his attachment and faithfulness to the chief who had been "derided [and antagonized] by the Central Committee." The fight was now out in the open.[41]

The rebellious cadres and the supporters of Messali Hadj held their own mutually exclusive party conferences, during which Messalists or anti-Messalists were read out of the party. At a three-day meeting held in a cinema in Hornu, Belgium, Messali Hadj struck all Centralists, as his opponents were known, from membership in his MTLD. The Centralists, in a conference held in Algiers, a more strategic location, made the break final by expelling Messali from the party he had created.

Colonialists rejoiced, seeing evidence of the failure of Algerian nationalism in the splintering of the party that had most effectively challenged French domination of Algeria. Logically, the 1954 split in the MTLD, together with the police discovery and dismantling of the OS in 1950, should have put proletarian nationalism back for a few decades at least. Unfortunately for the colonialists, however, there were too many able OS leaders at large. Such men might have seemed ineffective enough, for they scattered far from the battleground on which they must fight. Yet it was these men—Ben Bella, Ait Ahmed, Mohamed Boudiaf, and others—who reacted most

3 | *CRUA Leaders and Revolutionary Planning*

CERTAINTY ABOUT THE CHRONOLOGY OF EVENTS SURROUNDING several important issues in the Algerian Revolution is difficult to achieve. The history of the founding of the Revolutionary Committee for Unity and Action (CRUA for *Comité Revolutionnaire d' Unité et Action*) is one of the questions about which writers have disagreed. It is evident, however, that the bickering between the two branches of the MTLD, together with the moderate approach of Ferhat Abbas, so irritated some young nationalists that they decided to prepare for direct action. The four members of the so-called external delegation, Ahmed Ben Bella, Mohamed Khider, Mohamed Boudiaf, and Hocine Ait Ahmed, apparently made this decision early in 1954. In the spring of the same year, these Algerian nationalist leaders, who operated from headquarters in Cairo, got in contact with five members of the internal regional delegation, Mustapha Ben Boulaid, Mourad Didouche, Rabah Bitat, Mohammed Larbi Ben M'Hidi, and Belkacem Krim. The four political leaders of the external delegation and the five internal or military leaders formed the Revolutionary Committee for Unity and Action, which was often referred to as the "Club of Nine." The birth of the CRUA was self-announced in a pamphlet that appeared in April 1954. The same brief mimeographed document also scolded the Centralists and the Messalists for destroying the most vital nationalist party.[1]

Another theory suggests that this revolutionary committee was born in Algeria during the fall of 1953 the brain child of outlawed nationalists who had gone underground in their homeland. However, recurrent references in the press to the nine historic leaders and to the Club of Nine tend to support the external thesis. In either case the nine men mentioned above are without a doubt the best known leaders of the earliest stages of the Algerian Revolution.

The group that declared itself the CRUA included men who had long since lost faith in normal political procedures. As former members of the MTLD's Special Organization, they were all radical nationalists. Besides this common bond, however, there were few similarities among them. Some were fugitives, such as Ben Bella, Khider, and Ait Ahmed, all of whom had taken up residence in Egypt, and Boudiaf, who lived in France. Several had remained in Algeria, where they had either escaped notice or were sought as outlaws. This group included Didouche, Ben Boulaid, M'Hidi, Krim, and Bitat.

Although Boudiaf and Krim had been civil servants, only one member of the CRUA ever held official political office. That was Khider, who in 1946 was elected to represent Algiers in the French Chamber of Deputies.[2] None of the CRUA members gained the noted intellectual stature of Ben Badis or Ferhat Abbas, but Ait Ahmed and Boudiaf have since

CHART 5
ORIGINS OF THE FLN

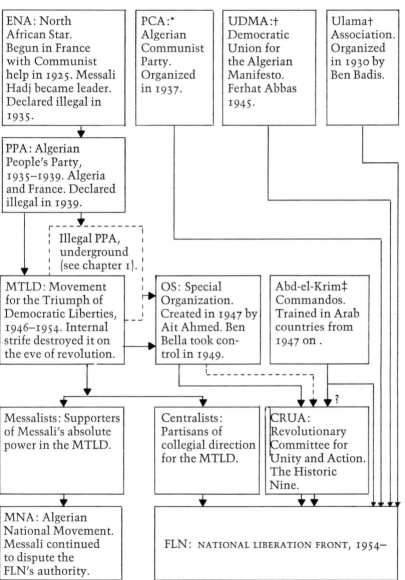

Dotted line shows continuation of underground organization from illegal PPA to FLN.

* Joined FLN in 1956 as individuals (see chapter 15).

† Joined FLN as a group by 1956.

‡ When Commandos, trained because of Krim's activity in Egypt, joined insurgent Algeria is not known. They may have been in on CRUA planning, but it is more probable that they joined after November 1, 1954.

joined the select group of leading Algerian writers. Ait Ahmed, especially, has become an accomplished theoretician and exhibits some of his intellectual prowess in his book *La guerre et l'après-guerre.*[3] In 1954 the nine men were all relatively young; Khider was the oldest at 43, and Bitat, one of the youngest, was only 29.[4] Socially, these leaders represented a cross section of Algeria's Muslim population. Krim and Ait Ahmed came from well-to-do families that could afford to send them to school in Algeria and in France. Boudiaf's family probably had a moderate income; had his parents been poor, he would not have been educated enough to obtain even a lowly civil service job.[5] The other revolutionary leaders represented the lower middle class or extremely poor families. Ben Bella, Khider, and Bitat certainly came from the latter group.

While many of the military leaders who emerged after the outbreak of revolution had been trained in the French army, only four of the original members of the CRUA can be definitely placed in that service. Ben Bella, a sergeant, participated in the Italian campaign during World War II, and received a medal for bravery. Krim was a staff sergeant[6] in 1942, Bitat was drafted in 1939, and Boudiaf was drafted in 1943. All served in the French army until the end of the war. Ouamrane, Krim's aide after the beginning of the revolution in November 1954, was an ex-sergeant. Mohammedi Saïd, another man in the same organization, had an unusual and interesting background: he was a veteran of both the French and the German armies. In 1944 the Germans parachuted him into Tunisia as an agent of the Abruehr, the German counterintelligence organization.[7]

Because the economic, social, educational, and military backgrounds of the members of the CRUA are so diverse, perhaps the best way to discover what drove these men to the political extreme of insurgency warfare is to look at some of the individuals. The best known member of the Club of

Nine was, without a doubt, Ahmed Ben Bella. He was born on December 25, 1916, into a typically poor Arab Muslim family at Marnia, close to the Moroccan border.[8] He was the youngest child in a family of several girls and five boys.[9] The last of his four brothers, his senior by four years, died in 1942. So Ahmed was the last surviving son of a man whom he has described as a good but severe father, especially with respect to the Islamic religion and native customs. He managed to earn his primary school certificate by the time he was thirteen and continued his secondary education until the age of eighteen.

Ben Bella claims to have had numerous contacts with militant nationalists between the end of his formal education and the beginning of World War II. Drafted into the 14th regiment of Algerian Sharpshooters *(Tirailleurs algériens),* he earned a military cross in the Italian campaigns. He returned to Algeria in 1945 during the terrible repression of the Sétif uprising. He immediately joined the illegal PPA and became party director for the Marnia section, an area that lies between Tlemcen in Algeria and Oujda in Morocco. In 1947 he was elected to the municipal council, and in 1948 he was a candidate for a seat in the Algerian Assembly as a representative of the MTLD, which served as a legal cover for the PPA. The 1948 Algerian election was obviously manipulated by an administration that would not accept nationalists in the elective institutions of Algeria.[10] The experience undoubtedly further embittered Ben Bella and many other Muslims. In any case, he was soon transferred to the OS, the supersecret branch of the MTLD.

Ben Bella quickly replaced the Kabyle Hocine Ait Ahmed as director of the OS. It was in pursuance of his new duties that Ben Bella directed an attack on the main post office in Oran on April 4, 1949. He was arrested and jailed the next year for his participation in this robbery, but in 1952 he managed to escape with Ahmed Mahsas, and quickly made his way to

Cairo. There he began plotting the events that would lead to an Algerian war of national liberation.[11]

Participating with Ben Bella in the same hold-up was Mohamed Khider, a Berber from Biskra in the department of Constantine, and the brother-in-law of Hocine Ait Ahmed. Born in 1912, he was also a member of a poor family. He held all kinds of jobs, including a position in a tobacco factory and another as a collector in a bus system. A very articulate though self-educated man, Khider apparently joined the North African Star, then the PPA, while quite young. The administration first imprisoned him for nationalistic activities in 1939. He was released in the general amnesty of 1942 but was forced to reside in the city of Aumale, to which he was confined. He was in and out of prison again in 1945, then became deputy for Algiers in the Chamber of Deputies at Paris in 1946. During his term of office he secretly supported the OS. Indeed, he was the liaison officer between the OS and the legal MTLD. He left Paris for Cairo the day before his mandate expired in 1950 and just after the Algerian police carried out a raid against the OS. Had he stayed in France, Khider would undoubtedly have been arrested for conspiracy with that paramilitary organization.[12]

Hocine Ait Ahmed had founded the OS in 1947, and he was the first chief of this secret and activist branch of the MTLD. He is one of a handful of leading Algerian revolutionaries who came from a well-to-do bourgeois background. His father, a Kabyle of some means, was a colonial native official or *caïd* in the service of the French government. Ait Ahmed, however, joined the proletarian PPA while still in secondary school.[13] Widely read, particularly in Marxist theory, he quickly became a leading light in the Kabyle section of his party. As an important Algerian theoretician, he was the first to call for armed violence. In order to carry out his convictions he created the OS, apparently over the objections of Messali Hadj. After only two years, however, he was replaced as chief of this organization by Ben Bella, an Arab. (This change in leadership was full of divisive implications that were not to become obvious until after the revolutionary outbreak of 1954.) In 1950 the French police uncovered the OS; the following year they closed in on Ait Ahmed, forcing him to flee to Cairo. Both Ait Ahmed and Ben Bella were in Egypt when plans were drawn up for the creation of the Revolutionary Committee for Unity and Action.[14]

Similarly in exile, but in France, was Mohamed Boudiaf, another Kabyle member of the OS, and the first chief of the CRUA. Probably the most secretive member of the club, he was highly regarded for his political sense and organizational abilities. He was born on June 23, 1919, to parents of modest means at M'Sila, south of the high plateau in the department of Constantine. He passed the primary grades of the French school system and followed a two-year complementary course for students not planning to go on to the university. He worked in Constantine and in Djidjelli, on the Mediterranean coast between Algiers and Bône, until he was drafted into the French army in 1943. By the end of the war he was already an organizer in the nationalist movement.

Boudiaf's first ventures in revolution, however, were not successful. In 1943 he attempted to form a nationalist section in Djidjelli but failed when no party was found into which his group could be integrated. While in the army he organized other soldiers into a military section that he wanted to put at the disposal of the PPA in Constantine. Leaders of the party refused to have soldiers in their following, considering such members too dangerous. But Boudiaf persisted, and after the repression of 1945 he became chief of the Bordj-bou-Arreridj section of the PPA. Though small, this city was strategically located halfway between Constantine and Algiers. Boudiaf held the same position in the Sétif arrondissement after 1946. In 1947 he was charged with the task of creating a branch of the OS in the department of Constantine. Under his orders were some of the men who were to originate the most spectacular subversive acts of November 1, 1954. Among his lieutenants were Larbi Ben M'Hidi, Mourad Didouche, Mostefa Ben Boulaid, and Rabah Bitat, all members of the OS and future members of the CRUA. Three years later, as a result of the police crack-down on the OS that sent Khider and Ait Ahmed to Cairo, Boudiaf took refuge in France. From June 1953 until February 1954 he was the chief organizer for the French branch of the MTLD. In 1954 he returned to Algeria, where, while leading a clandestine life, he worked for revolution. Meanwhile, he had been condemned *in absentia* to eight years' and ten years' imprisonment, respectively, by courts in Bône and Blida. Boudiaf was the key liaison officer of the CRUA when orders were given to start a subversive war against French authority in Algeria late in October 1954.[15]

Rabah Bitat, an Arab, was one of Boudiaf's men in 1947 and one of the historic leaders. He was born on December 19, 1925, to an impoverished Muslim family in Ain-Kerma in the department of Constantine. In a moving declaration before a military tribunal of Algiers on March 20, 1956, he eloquently explained why he became a nationalist:

I was a child in the period between the two wars when education was granted in a parsimonious manner. I was nevertheless lucky enough to go to school until I was thirteen years old. We were taught that the Gauls were our ancestors and we were not allowed to speak Arabic, our maternal tongue, even during recess hours. I remember that my father and I were desperate when I had to leave school: the books were too expensive for us.[16]

Like all Muslim children of Algeria, he continued, he had been thrown into the streets at an early age. He became aware of the inferiority that stigmatized him and his kind. He saw that there were two kinds of children, the French and the natives. Gradually he came to realize that the Europeans in Algeria had all the rights, and abused these, while the Algerians had only misery and the obligation to serve in the

French army. He and his generation were drafted in 1939 and sent to the first lines of defense for the "cause of liberty." Having contributed a great deal to the defeat of the Nazis and to the liberation of France, Algerian soldiers expected to be granted Liberty, Equality, and Fraternity. Instead, they got the Sétif repression of 1945, a rude reminder of the horrible reality: inequality would always remain. Bitat continued:

After May 1945 a true abyss was established between the Muslim population and the European population of Algeria. . . . From then on, I was keenly aware [of the fact] that I was a colonized [person]. As soon as the MTLD was created, I took interest in its political program. In 1948 I joined this movement so as to participate in the struggle for a free and independent Algerian nation.[17]

As soon as he became engaged in nationalist activities, Bitat was a wanted man. He was condemned *in absentia* in 1950 to a prison term and to five years of forced exile from Algeria. But he stayed in his native land, taking up a clandestine life. He participated in the founding of the CRUA in 1954 and directed subversive activities in Algeria until the French police captured him on February 23, 1955.

Bitat's experiences could be generalized to explain the experience of a whole people. His words would undoubtedly apply also to the lives of three other members of Boudiaf's OS section in the department of Constantine—Larbi Ben M'Hidi, Mourad Didouche, and Mostefa Ben Boulaid—who were members of the original Club of Nine. They were in Algeria in command of regional activities on November 1, 1954, and after. All three died during the revolutionary war they helped to start: Didouche in January 1955, Ben Boulaid in March 1956, and M'Hidi in February 1957.[18]

Belkacem Krim, another Kabyle, was the ninth historic leader. Born in Dra-el-Mizan in 1911, he was educated in Algeria and in France, so he must have come from a relatively well-to-do family. After the Second World War he joined the AML, the moderate nationalist party led by Ferhat Abbas. He quickly worked his way over to the revolutionary PPA, served in the OS, and was arrested on several occasions.[19] He went underground in 1947, quickly becoming the leader of a group of bandits in the mountains of Kabylia. He was, therefore, in armed opposition to the French administration long before the outbreak of revolutionary warfare in Algeria. By exceptional luck he was never captured or seriously wounded after he became a declared outlaw. As a result, he enjoyed a great deal of prestige among the Kabyles. His personality, however, drove many of his fellow mountaineers to hate him.[20]

Robert Buron, one of the French negotiators who observed Belkacem Krim at Evian, has described him as a small man with the noticeable stomach of so many Mediterranean people. He had thinning hair, brilliant eyes tempered by long and heavy eyebrows, and chubby yet surprisingly young hands, with which he played constantly during negotiations. His voice was amazingly soft, almost musical, and yet the man had authority. Krim was, of course, a natural leader who already had a subversive tool, a band of outlaws, when he became a member of the CRUA.[21]

How these nine men, all of them sought by the French police, most of them escaped convicts from colonial prisons, got together to plot revolution is an interesting tale in itself. It is apparent that those in the Cairo group, particularly Ben Bella, played the leading organizational role. But the others were, of course, key actors. Without Boudiaf's dangerous liaison work between the outsiders and the insiders, the events of November 1, 1954, would have surprised no one. Nor could the coup have been carried out without the leadership of those among the nine who took up commands in Algeria itself, and of other ex-OS elites who were asked to join them shortly before the outbreak of revolution.

The organizational drive that led to the creation of the CRUA was sparked by Ben Bella early in 1954. As a resident of Cairo since shortly after his 1952 escape from Blida prison, he shared the leadership of the local Algerian colony with Khider. Together they won the support of highly placed officials who came to power after the Egyptian military coup of 1952. Meanwhile, events elsewhere in North Africa strengthened the revolutionary faith of the exiles. In Tunisia *fellagha* (outlaws) began an insurrection in an attempt to upset the French protectorate there.[22] In the same year, the deposition by the French of Mohammed V of Morocco provoked the violent reaction of his subjects.[23] The moment could hardly have seemed more propitious for Algeria to join her neighbors to the east and west in a concerted struggle against the French yoke.

Unfortunately, the most outspoken Algerian nationalist party was racked by an internal conflict that threatened to become fatal. The sorry state of the MTLD convinced the men of the OS that their traditional leaders could no longer serve their ambitions. Only armed insurrection would unify the rebel ranks, and time was of the essence. They must strike while the French hand in North Africa was weak and while the popular resentment was at its peak. It was time for Ben Bella and his fellow exiles in Cairo to renew contacts with former OS comrades and to prepare for action.[24]

Boudiaf, too, was pondering the recent events from across the Mediterranean, and his reaction was the same as that of the men in Cairo. At Ben Bella's invitation he left France for Berne, Switzerland, there to meet Ben Bella, Khider, and Ait Ahmed. These fugitive four committed themselves to the cause of armed and open revolution at the first opportunity, and accordingly Boudiaf was sent into Algeria to lay the groundwork. His chief task was to mold into one revolutionary tool the numerous armed bands that roamed Algeria in defiance of the French administration. In addition, he was to contact ex-OS members who would join in their plans.

In March 1954 Boudiaf reentered Algeria. Within a few weeks he accomplished his mission; OS members throughout

Algeria prepared to act, as did the armed bandits of Kabylia and the Aurès region. Fugitive nationalists who had long lived in exile returned from France to their native villages.[25] Then in July of the same year Boudiaf returned to Switzerland for a second meeting with Ben Bella, where they were now joined by Ben Boulaid, Ben M'Hidi, and Mourad Didouche, who were not exiles but had chosen to remain underground in their native land. The insiders reported on their organizational success at home, which was due especially to Boudiaf's intelligence and superior leadership. The five discussed logistical problems, to whose solution Ben Bella had given his full attention.[26]

For some time before the meetings at Berne, a number of Algerians living in Cairo had been actively working and soliciting support for their cause. They received encouragement and material aid from many Arab nations, particularly Egypt, which had long served as a base for the military training of North African recruits. Active in Cairo, besides Ben Bella, was Abd el Krim, who had led a Moroccan uprising in the 1920's and escaped from the French authorities while being transferred to prison in France. Since 1946 he had lived in Cairo, where he devoted himself to the task of recruiting young men from the Maghrib for the future revolution. These youths were placed in various Arab military schools, especially in Baghdad. Such activities were accelerated after 1952 when Nasser took control of the Egyptian government and began to cultivate all elements which might further his pan-Arab dreams.

Abd el Krim was not a member of the Club of Nine, though he undoubtedly helped its members. While the CRUA worked specifically for the liberation of Algeria, Abd el Krim had long since dedicated himself to a larger cause. Working with Habib Bourguiba, the leader of the nationalist Tunisian Neo-Destour party, he had founded the Liberation Committee of the Arab Maghrib in 1947.[27] Ben Bella and the other members of the newly created CRUA clearly did not share this wider vision. Now, in the early 1950's, Abd el Krim's star began to fade. He had been the undisputed master of the North African colony in Cairo, recruiting young men from the entire Maghrib and having them trained in commando tactics in both Egypt and Iraq. Very few of his recruits, however, were to see action in Algeria.[28]

In the long run, the most important facet of Abd el Krim's life may have been his escape from the French in 1946. This incident was a great propaganda coup for North African nationalists, and Abd el Krim remained as an important symbol.[29] But he lost whatever influence he had with high officials in the Egyptian government after Nasser's seizure of power. The Egyptian Special Service took control of the program for the recruitment and training of Maghribi youths.[30] Subsequently, this direction was relinquished to Ben Bella and Khider. The latter devoted himself to the development of an effective revolutionary fighting force, while Ben Bella was concerned with the creation of a general staff to direct the military operations.[31] The Egyptian Special Service assigned several men to assist Ben Bella in his undertaking. It was at this point that Ben Bella approached Boudiaf in Switzerland in March 1954.[32] It is probable that Switzerland was chosen to allow the Algerians to escape the close supervision of the Egyptians.

After the outbreak of the Algerian Revolution on November 1, 1954, official French information agencies went to great lengths to "prove" that the order to begin the insurrection had come from Cairo. The implication was that Algeria's revolution was a foreign import, but this hardly seems the case. Although they welcomed aid from the Arab world and other nations, Algerian nationalists, exiles though some may have been, were entirely responsible for its planning and execution.

At the meeting in Switzerland in July 1954 the Algerians made important decisions. For their purposes Algeria was di-

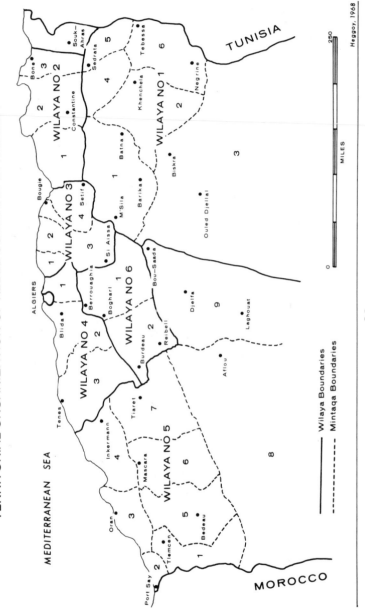

TERRITORIAL ORGANIZATION OF REBEL COMMAND IN ALGERIA

Heggoy, 1968

MEDITERRANEAN SEA

ALGIERS

TUNISIA

MOROCCO

WILAYA NO 1
WILAYA NO 2
WILAYA NO 3
WILAYA NO 4
WILAYA NO 5
WILAYA NO 6

——— Wilaya Boundaries
- - - - Mintaqa Boundaries

MAP I

vided into six *wilaya,* or provinces. Two months later, Boudiaf assigned five "historic leaders" to their respective commands according to these divisions. Wilaya I, which included the Aurès and Nementchas mountains, was placed under the command of Mostefa Ben Boulaid. Rabah Bitat took charge of Wilaya II, consisting of the northern half of the department of Constantine. Kabylia, where the armed bands of Belkacem Krim were already well entrenched, formed Wilaya III under Krim's command. Mourad Didouche was appointed to the fourth, the department of Algiers. He quickly exchanged his post for that of Bitat, who had been assigned to command the largely rural department of Constantine. Bitat, an ambitious man, saw a chance to advance himself through spectacular urban terrorism, while the rather retiring Didouche felt more at ease in a provincial situation. Finally, Larbi Ben M'Hidi took charge of the department of Oran or Wilaya V. Wilaya VI, which included the entire Algerian Sahara, was left without a commander. (See Map 2.)[33]

The ex-OS leaders were moving quickly. They were perhaps afraid that the French police, as in 1950, would discover their organization before they could bring it to fruition. They had, in effect, resurrected the OS and were determined to use it to the fullest. While making preparations for armed action, the CRUA tried to mediate the political dispute between the Centralists and the Messalists. However, an appeal for unity in the cause of a liberated Algeria was not sufficient to resolve the bitter factional quarrel. Lahouel, the leader of the Centralists, was opposed to both Messali Hadj and the CRUA. The Messalists were equally intransigent, and they tried to eliminate all competition, from both the Centralists and the CRUA. Each saw the others as a competitor for sole authority.

Violence mounted as the rivalry continued unabated. A group of Messalists clubbed Lahouel in the rue de la Lyre in Algiers. Soon thereafter they left Boudiaf for dead on the pavement of the same city, and he spent several weeks in a

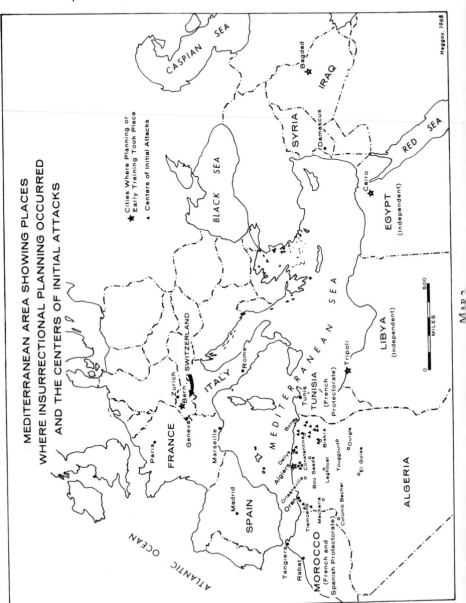

MEDITERRANEAN AREA SHOWING PLACES
WHERE INSURRECTIONAL PLANNING OCCURRED
AND THE CENTERS OF INITIAL ATTACKS

★ Cities Where Planning or
   Early Training Took Place
▲ Centers of Initial Attacks

hospital as a result.[34] Still, the CRUA made every effort to reconcile the split within the MTLD. Mediators were sent to Lahouel and Messali, but neither made any concessions. Some of Lahouel's followers established relations with the Cairo group, but Lahouel himself disagreed with Ben Bella on the wisdom of immediate direct action and did all he could to prevent the start of the revolution.[35] The three-way tug of war continued in print; the CRUA bulletin, *Le Patriote,* advised MTLD members to adhere to neither faction, while Messali's *L'Algérie libre* and the Centralist organ, *Nation algérienne,* railed against each other in competition for the allegiance of party members.[36]

The CRUA pressed on with its military plans. Refusing to take sides between the Centralists and the Messalists, Ben Bella, Khider, and the others continued to organize the most committed nationalists for imminent violence. Having convinced the Egyptian Special Service that the CRUA was ready, Ben Bella in late September or early October asked Boudiaf to give the signal for revolution.

On October 10 a committee of *wilaya* commanders under the presidency of Boudiaf created the National Liberation Army (ALN). They decided that the revolution would commence at midnight on the night of October 31. Although this decision was made in Algiers, it was kept in utter secrecy; no Messalists, Centralists, or moderate nationalists were informed. On October 25, traveling with a false passport in the name of Dridi, Boudiaf flew from Algiers to Geneva and thence to Cairo, where he joined Ben Bella, Khider, and Ait Ahmed. M'Hammed Yazid, an officer of the French Federation of the MTLD, succeeded in eluding the French police on November 2 and joined the group in Cairo a few days later. Also in Egypt, as it happened, were the members of a Centralist delegation that had come to discuss its position with the CRUA. Like so many others, they were caught flat-footed by events in Algeria and immediately joined forces with the

Cairo group. The CRUA had obviously managed a great coup; it had pulled the rug from under the other nationalist leaders. Though Messali was still a formidable rival, he was never to challenge the upstarts successfully. All established political factions, including the PCA and its parent, the PCF, had simply been left behind. Their only choice now was to fall in behind the new leaders or be lost in the surge of forces they could not control.

serve as a teacher among the people in whose name he was killed. Monnerot's assailants also shot his young wife and Hadj Sadok, the *caïd* of M'chounèche. Sadok, a Muslim and a captain in the Spahis, a French native corps, would probably have been spared had he not tried to protect the young French couple; but he reached bravely for a small revolver under his burnous. He was fatally wounded by a burst of submachine gun fire for his courage. Such murders, seemingly wanton and illogical, characterized the long war that had just begun.[2]

The victims had been passengers on a regular bus route near Arris, the small administrative center of the southeastern part of the department of Constantine. Where the road wound through the gorges of Tighanimine, a band of men laid a barrier of rocks. Dressed in leather jackets and khaki pants, armed with rifles and a few submachine guns, they covered their faces but made no attempt to hide as the bus approached. According to the driver, the bandits asked for the *caïd* of M'chounèche as soon as the bus halted.[3] Others claimed that the rebels had simply looked through the windows and chosen Monnerot, the only European male, as their victim. In any case, both Monnerot and his wife were taken off of the bus and forced to remain in the gorges, while the wounded *caïd* was allowed to reboard the vehicle. He died in Arris a few hours later.[4] The bus then emerged from the gorges and the band of about fifteen men disappeared into the countryside.

When the bus arrived in Arris, witnesses of the Tighanimine incident learned the attack was only one of many in the Aurès region. The previous day, there had been an intimation of trouble to come when Jean Servier, a leading French ethnologist, had been warned nervously by previously friendly villagers to leave a small community in which he had been doing research. He had not understood the warning, but now it was he who organized a rescue party for the Monnerots. He commandeered a jeep, luckily the only official car that had not been sabotaged, and left quickly with a few volunteers,

including two Chaouia tribesmen. The young teacher died
before Servier and his men found him. Mme. Monnerot survived, but the terror of this young woman, wounded herself
and left alone with her dying husband, would be shared by
countless others before peace returned to Algeria.[5]

Not all Algerians chose to side with the nationalists and,
indeed, many were as surprised by events as their European
neighbors. In Arris the atmosphere was tense as the chief local
officials prepared for trouble. Open ammunition crates clut-
tered the mayor's office, various types of rifles and some submachine guns leaned against a wall. Brochures, stamped
"Secret" and entitled "Instructions to be followed in case of
an attack on the commune," lay scattered on the desk. A
flurry of activity followed the initial paralysis, and the defense
of the town was well organized when the rescue party returned with Mme. Monnerot and the body of her husband.
Tension mounted. Inflated rumors as well as confirmed reports of violence circulated not only in the Aurès but
throughout Algeria. At a mine in nearby Ichmoul, for example, there was a supply of dynamite and detonators sufficient to destroy all the bridges around Arris. When the
engineer of the mine, who was in Arris, expressed concern, a
report soon spread that the *fellagha,* or outlaws, had seized
this material. In truth, an attempt was made to take the mine,
but the old native watchman fired four shots from an old gun.
This unexpected resistance unnerved the assailants, who
promptly turned tail and fled.[6] At Batna, at the foot of the
Auresian range, rebels attempted to capture an important
stock of weapons and ammunition. The assailants shot and
wounded Lucien Blanche, the French colonel in command of
the garrison, as he drove to his headquarters, and killed two
French sentries as well. The rebels retreated, however, without capturing the arms. They also failed at nearby Kenchala,
where two more soldiers fell.[7]

All during the day of November 1, until the telephone line

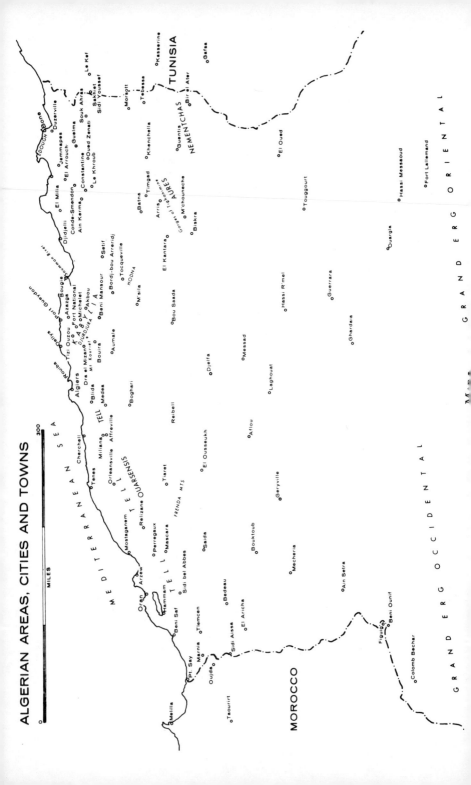

was cut in the evening, news of violence across the country flowed into Arris. Many times the *fellagha* failed, but their activity produced a growing certainty that an organized and widespread resistance to the French rule in Algeria now existed. In the capital the nationalists attempted unsuccessfully to take the studios of Radio Algiers and to blow up gasoline reservoirs in the harbor. Elsewhere in the city two bombs exploded, causing some material damage. Other bombs shook the city of Biskra, on the edge of the Sahara, where the rebels shot a policeman in the legs. Each incident, considered in isolation, was relatively minor, and the *fellagha*'s material resources and tactics proved inadequate for their aims. But the many incidents had obviously been synchronized, a fact that shook the colonial administration.[8]

Officially, and perhaps actually, the events surprised the French government. Even while rebels in the protectorates to the east and west fought against France, Algeria, the heartland of the Maghrib, had remained calm. Here, in these three overseas departments of France, the European community had felt secure because the divided nationalist party seemed powerless against them. But the outburst should have been expected. Algerian society had long been divided into two distinct spheres. On the one hand, the Muslim majority suffered unemployment or underemployment and lacked effective political representation. In sharp contrast stood the European society, a prosperous minority of less than one-tenth of the population, which controlled Algerian institutions.[9]

The economic plight of the native population had not, however, gone unobserved. In October 1954, less than a month before the outbreak, France's Minister of the Interior, M. François Mitterand, had completed a fact-finding mission in Algeria. During his tour he had promised a series of liberal reforms, simultaneously assuring the Europeans that Algeria would always remain French. It was typical of the French administration to consider all native questions in purely economic terms, neglecting entirely the Muslim's pride and self-respect.[10] The Algerians remained unimpressed by the minister's proposals, unaccompanied as they were by any hint of political reform. The nationalists tended rather to see the promised reforms as a sign of weakness. Perhaps colonial officials saw a warning in Moroccan and Tunisian events, some thought, or Paris wished to counter discontent before it led to political protest.

Wretchedly poor themselves, the Muslims saw wealthy Europeans daily. A political gap paralleled this economic discrepancy as one European vote equaled as many as eight Muslim ballots. The natives could not be expected to accept their inferior status indefinitely, and Algerian leaders had long demanded that their people be given equality with the French. While there existed an inherent danger of revolution in such an unjust society, few men saw the problem clearly. Virtually no Europeans admitted the possibility of rebellion, despite the open fighting in both Tunisia and Morocco. There had, nevertheless, been warnings. In the June issue of *Fédération 1954*, for example, an editorialist declared that if nothing were done to alleviate the lot of the natives revolution would surely develop. Even this writer, however, proposed only social or economic changes. "Maffias are being organized," he wrote, "that are led by persons scornful of Franco-Muslim solidarity or by incoherent specialists who attempt to demonstrate that the past inexorably determines the future." Without social and economic reforms for which France must pay, the author concluded, native revolt would soon come.[11]

Because of persistent rumors, Governor-General Léonard called the Commissioner of Arris to Algiers just a few days before the outbreak. When asked for his opinion, the administrator assured his superior that all was calm. And so it seemed. Still, certain clues suggested otherwise. A police report contained a rumor that something important was planned for November 1. This document even referred to a certain Revolutionary Committee for Unity and Action. Fur-

thermore, the administration knew that workshops for manu-
facturing bombs existed throughout Algeria. Finally, the
prefect of Tlemcen had reported that some young Algerians
were training for war at Tamnanam, near Oujda, in Morocco.[12] These ill omens were not heeded by a complacent
administration that ignored even the detailed information in
its files.

A series of incidents along the Tunisian border during the
summer and fall of 1954 should have warned the authorities.
On June 2, for example, French gendarmes were attacked
at the Bir-el-Ater security post in the Tenoukla pass. The
fellagha, presumably Tunisians, wounded one policeman. Official reaction to the incident included the arrest of six inhabitants of Sidi Abia, near Tebessa, who had harbored
outlaws several times late in June. Then in mid-August the
bandits forced a Muslim merchant at El-Miridj, in the Morsott
district just north of Tebessa, to pay a ransom of 50,000 francs.
These were not isolated incidents, and it was not clear
whether all these acts were perpetrated by Tunisians alone or
whether unknown Algerians shared responsibility for the
political banditry.[13]

The French officials considered the problem important
enough to justify a meeting between Governor-General
Léonard in Algiers and Resident-Minister Jean de Hautecloque from Tunis. When the two met in Constantine, Hautecloque was clearly worried, but Léonard was unimpressed. He
returned to Algiers, where, on October 26, he publicly announced that "Algeria has nothing to fear from the infiltration of *fellagha*" from Tunisia.[14] The highest representative of
France in Algeria simply closed his eyes to the numerous incidents involving both Algerian and Tunisian bandits in search
of weapons and funds on either side of the border. Léonard's
failure to interpret these events correctly indicates that the
events of November 1, 1954, did surprise the Algerian administration and indeed most inhabitants of the colony.

On that day some 56,500 French soldiers occupied Algeria.[15]

This force barely sufficed to garrison the country effectively; the government had withdrawn many units to meet the more urgent demands of the Indochinese War. Although this Asian struggle ended some three months before the outbreak of revolution in the central Maghrib, the French had not yet redeployed their armed forces. In Algeria there were three military divisional centers—Algiers, Oran, and Constantine—with the general who commanded the 10th military region (Algeria) acting as the interarmy commander. He received orders to maintain law and order in the colony, particularly in the Aurès, where the insurrection of November 1 was especially violent.[16]

The French forces that faced rebellion in Algeria had been reduced not only by the demands of the Indochinese War but also by continued unrest in Tunisia and in Morocco. The Tunisian situation had smoldered for years although never more than some 2,500 *fellagha* engaged in insurrection.[17] These outlaws operated in small groups of 15 to 30 men, struck at will, and made up in mobility what they lacked in numbers. They kept the French authority off balance and naturally received the support of Bourguiba's Neo-Destour, the Tunisian nationalist party whose leadership had long since decided to use all means at its disposal. To achieve independence in Tunisia the Neo-Destour wanted to force the French government into negotiation, and to this end they used civil disobedience, diplomatic pressure on France wherever and whenever possible, and the terrorism perpetrated by the *fellagha*. They planned to use guerrilla warfare if all else failed but never had to resort to this extreme. However, the use of terrorism on a scattered and less intensive level finally induced the French to seek a negotiated settlement. The French government revealed its changed attitude by announcing Pierre Voizard's appointment to replace Resident-Minister de Hautecloque in September 1953. Policies of repression gradually gave way to an active search for moderate Tunisian

interlocutors; the French continued to refuse to deal directly
with the outspoken nationalists of the Neo-Destour. As might
have been expected, the tempo of *fellagha* terrorism increased,
as did the political and diplomatic pressure of the Neo-
Destour. France could not avoid this party. Therefore, in June
1954, the newly elected Premier Pierre Mendès-France accepted the necessity of talks with the Neo-Destour. On July 31,
1954, he announced that France was ready to grant Tunisia internal autonomy, and soon thereafter the talks began. The
Premier disarmed his opposition in France and reassured Europeans in Tunisia by appointing P. Boyer de la Tour, the commanding general of French armies in the Tunisian regency, as
resident-minister. The talks would be supervised by an advocate of law and order. Mendès-France also won approval for
his policy by limiting the objectives of the proposed talks to
internal autonomy and by traveling to Tunisia, where he announced his decision in the company of General Alphonse
Juin, a leading *colon*. Although Bourguiba did not abandon
his own objective of eventual complete independence, he was
impressed.

The outbreak of the Algerian Revolution in November 1954
made the Franco-Tunisian talks more difficult than anticipated. An independent Tunisia would serve Algerian nationalists as a safe sanctuary; on the other hand, the French feared
that an autonomous Tunisia might be difficult to control and
still might harbor the neighboring rebels. While the talks
dragged, terrorism continued; the *fellagha* refused to surren-
der their weapons. But by the end of December 1954, the authorities had disarmed these irregular soldiers. Thereafter,
even the fall of Mendès-France from power could not stop
progress, and Tunisia became autonomous on June 3, 1955.
Autonomy, however, was but a brief way station on the road
to independence.

While Tunisians were achieving internal autonomy, Moroccans, who also engaged in large-scale civil disobedience

and occasional acts of insurrection, were winning full independence. All of these North African developments were in-
terrelated; the outbreak of revolution in Algeria certainly
affected the French decision to complete the Tunisian and the
Moroccan negotiations. In short, continued difficulties in
Morocco and Tunisia after the outbreak of the Algerian Revolution forced France to decide whether to fight all over North
Africa or to limit the defense of a crumbling empire to the
central Maghrib.

In Morocco Sultan Sidi Mohamed precipitated the crisis in
December 1952 when he used the feast of the throne on the
twenty-fifth anniversary of his ascension to reaffirm his will
to be independent yet to continue in cooperation with
France.[18] This caused a wave of civil disobedience and riots
that eventually led to the lynching of several Europeans in
Casablanca. The French authorities, in turn, arrested the nationalist Istiqlal and Communist leaders suspected of inciting
the people to acts of violence. By August 1953 the Sultan had
followed the politicians into exile; the French, on August 20–
21, had managed a *coup d'état* and proclaimed Sidi Mohamed
Ben Arafa El Alaoui, the deposed Sultan's cousin, as the new
ruler. The change failed to end the unrest. Instead, the deposed ruler became a martyr, and opposition to French rule
continued to grow. Eventually, facing the realities of the situation, France negotiated for the restoration of Sidi Mohamed
and granted Morocco independence in March 1956. Spain followed suit, relinquishing control of most of her share of
Morocco in April. The Moroccan developments, in turn, rad-
icalized Tunisian demands, and, by March 20, 1956, Tunisia
also achieved full independence from France. Now Algerian
nationalists had not one, but two potential and safe sanctuaries in the Maghrib.

Much earlier, when serious negotiations between France
and Tunisia began, the French government had determined to
balance compromise in Tunis with a tough stance in Algeria.

"Algeria," Premier Mendès-France announced on November 12, 1954, "is not Tunisia." There would be no concessions, no compromises.[19] While the French had protected Tunisia and Morocco, they had, officially at least, made Algeria an integral part of France itself. Having suffered a series of humiliating defeats in their colonies, the French people would not accept failure again. Therefore, the government in Paris responded to the events in Algeria with harsh words and strong resolutions, but not always with commensurate actions.

The first military task was to relieve the Aurès region, a center of rebel action incidentally located close to the Tunisian frontier. The first reinforcements, a parachute battalion composed largely of veterans of the Indochinese War, landed at Bône on November 2. Meanwhile Batna, Khenchala, and Biskra became mustering points. Armored units managed to reach Arris, but the smaller centers of European settlement had to be supplied by helicopter for several days. Foum Toub, near Timgad, nearly fell into rebel hands and remained completely cut off for three days. Throughout the Aurès the French relief troops made only slow progress because bridges had been destroyed and roads were blocked by fallen telephone poles or trees. In the words of a French official in Batna, the rebels aimed to "turn the whole region into an impregnable citadel that two extremely mobile divisions could not reduce."[20]

If the rebels' plan seemed grandiose, considering their numerical weakness, the French response was ill adapted to local conditions. Time and time again the *fellagha* outmaneuvered superior French units, whose transport vehicles were of no use in the rugged Aurès range.[21] The Forces of Order nevertheless succeeded in establishing fortified centers and in beginning comb-out operations of the kind already used in Indochina.[22] In these operations French forces surrounded a designated area with a *cordon sanitaire,* closed in, and searched all inhabitants and structures for incriminating evidence. As a rule, however, the rebels either blended into the population or slipped away in a terrain so rugged that it has been compared to the surface of the moon. Aliens among the local tribesmen, the French troops were helpless against those who knew every hill and gully.[23]

On November 15 the French opened a psychological warfare campaign. Throughout the Aurès light army planes scattered propaganda tracts announcing that "soon a terrible calamity will befall the rebels. Then French peace will again reign."[24] These brief documents clearly threatened Algerians, warning them that France would eventually punish the guilty. Nevertheless, the pamphlets failed to convince the Chaouia tribesmen, the Berber people of the region, many of whom had never seen a French administrator and most of whom had only seen a policeman or tax collector once a year or less.[25] Now, when French power was unable to provide adequate protection, they remained skeptical. For the present the natives were most impressed with the French failure. They adopted a wait-and-see attitude which irritated the nationalists as well, although it became evident that the Chaouia would join the rebels if only they could convince themselves that the latter had a chance to win.

As announced in the first propaganda tracts, the first security zones were created on November 21, and officials invited the natives to leave their homes and resettle within these designated areas.[26] There, presumably, the French could protect the innocent while the army would have a freer hand to operate in the vacated regions. From the French point of view resettlement was a sound policy. It could hardly be equally attractive, however, to those who had to leave their homes and who were not convinced of the benefits of the French presence in their country.

On the appointed day not more than 2,000 people out of an estimated total population of 250,000 resettled in the security zones. Interestingly enough, the American journalist Michael

K. Clark, whose sympathies were clearly with the colonialists, reported counting 239 families or about 2,000 souls. *Alger Républicain,* a Communist newspaper that supported the nationalists, counted only 80 families. In any case, virtually no men aged 18 to 35 appeared among the refugees.[27] Although some of the able-bodied men were undoubtedly working in France, most had presumably joined the rebels, had simply refused to leave their homes and lands, or were still not committed to one side or the other.

Meanwhile the operational orders for the active French troops were still very conservative. Soldiers received orders to shoot only after provocation. Only local policemen, presumably acquainted with the population of their region, were to conduct interrogations of suspected nationalists. Democratic scruples prevented the French government from engaging in wholesale repression of innocent and guilty alike, but at the same time it was imperative to search out and punish the rebels, a difficult task.

The government earnestly attempted to afford European settlers and neutral or Francophile Muslims adequate protection from nationalist exactions. Somehow, the effort nearly always fell short of needs. On November 1, 1954, some 56,500 French soldiers in Algeria faced, at most, several hundred rebels; Le Tourneau suggests 400.[28] Even under these conditions, nevertheless, the French army disposed of an insufficient number of men to comb out 900,000 square miles of Algerian territory, or even the tenth of that area which is inhabited. Its numbers were therefore increased time and time again, until by February 1955 the total of French soldiers rose to 83,000. On May 19 of the same year the government in Paris ordered the force increased to 100,000, with still more to come, and by April 1956 approximately 250,000 French troops occupied Algeria.[29] Even this was not enough, although intelligence officers estimated that the National Liberation Front (FLN), which had replaced the CRUA, now consisted of 8,050 regulars and approximately 21,000 auxiliaries.[30] The rebels remained as evasive as ever, mingling with the population at large.

It seems preposterous that the modern French army could not crush these ill-equipped irregulars whom it outnumbered ten to one. But in this new type of combat, in this guerrilla war, the unknown adversary fought on his own terms, combining a strategy of defense with offensive tactics. He would stand and fight only under the most favorable conditions and when a good escape route existed. Otherwise, he simply filtered through the French forces, fading into the back country far from roads and other facilities. Against such an opponent the European army was severely hampered by the same modern equipment which armed it so well for a conventional conflict.

Those Frenchmen who had served in Indochina quickly perceived the nature of these inadequacies, but the rebels held the initiative and forced the French to fight their kind of war. While the modern army ponderously adjusted to the new conditions, the nationalists spread their doctrines and enlarged their operations. French troops demanded new equipment, more men, and more funds, while the government in Paris, weak and financially overextended, could not meet these new requests. Military morale plunged and bitterness was widespread. "Never, from 1954 to 1958," a high officer complained, "did the army obtain the means in men or in materials which it asked of the government. The means were always inferior to the needs of the army."[31] Even if there had been no economic problems, however, the ministerial instability that plagued the Fourth Republic would have prevented a consistent and firm military policy in Algeria.

In 1954, faced with a rebellion in Algeria, Premier Mendès-France countered with a two-sided policy. First, the Premier declared, Algeria was France and would remain an integral part of the fatherland. The murderous rebels, a criminal few, would be severely punished, but the repression would be just, and the innocent would not suffer. Second, the government intended to implement the 1947 Statute.[32] This statute, originally intended to give Algeria home rule and to increase Muslim participation in the administration of the country, had been rejected because it touched on the status quo, which was favorable to European settlers.

The rebels could hardly be expected to react favorably to a planned reform along the lines of an old program dusted off for the occasion and balanced by promised repression. The 1947 Statute fell short of the nationalist demands and, in view of the history of Algeria between 1947 and the end of 1954, it seemed inadequate. In any case, the government of Mendès-France did not survive to carry out his Algerian program; his cabinet was swept from office in February 1955, and he was replaced by Edgar Faure. The new Premier immediately announced that he would make no important policy changes with respect to the Algerian question.

The Algerian policy, then, was still one of repression tempered with reform. In an effort to meet the worsening situation in Algeria, Faure also requested and was granted special powers. Again, he simply followed the path laid out by his predecessor. Meanwhile, the French army continued to strengthen its position south of the Mediterranean, although the effort seemed futile. The nationalist strength grew steadily as the French, hampered by ministerial instability, bumbled on. Nevertheless, the French apparently resolved to stay in Algeria, and the National Assembly displayed its determination by proclaiming a state of emergency in the colony on March 31, 1955.

In July 1955 the French Chamber of Deputies extended the Algerian state of emergency for six more months. Life for the rebels became more precarious, and some of the fighting rebels might have become discouraged, but the nationalists had increased their popular support despite the efforts of the French to thwart them. In the Algerian Assembly sixty-one Muslims, most of them creatures of the administration or so-called *beni-oui-oui* delegates, dared openly to reject any policy that leaned toward the integration of Algeria into France. An appalled and irritated administration reacted by adjourning the session of the Assembly. It was too late; the opponents of the French administration had carried the day. The Faure government limped on until January 1956, when it gave way to a new cabinet under Guy Mollet, a Socialist.

Neither Mendès-France nor Edgar Faure had succeeded in regaining the initiative that the native nationalists had seized on November 1, 1954. The Algerian question now fell into the hands of Premier Mollett, who commenced by outlining his triptych policy even before he officially took office. He called for a cease-fire in Algeria, to be followed by an election and negotiations about the future of the colony. Meanwhile, a new *loi cadre* would be devised.[33] The Mollet program offered nothing new to the Algerians. In addition, some basic problems had to be solved before the new government's policies could be worked out in detail. The military situation was particularly pressing. The French army had been largely ineffective in its effort to stamp out the rebellion; it did not adapt itself quickly enough to the nature of the struggle and had little contact with the population. The enemy remained imperfectly known.

When the organized violence began in November 1954, it was not at all clear where the responsibility for the uprising lay. The MTLD, the most vocal of the nationalist groups, naturally fell under suspicion; the police rounded up many of its known leaders. After it became obvious in due course that these men were not directly responsible, that in fact they had been entirely unaware of the planned rebellion, the French police continued to detain them in order to prevent the MTLD from turning the current disorder to its own ends. On November 6, as the police sought the party chieftains in both Algeria and France, the government ordered the MTLD dissolved.

Operation Bitter Orange, the code name of this ill-advised though seemingly logical police action, caused members of the MTLD to suffer an injustice that may be excused on the grounds that the authorities knew practically nothing about the leadership of the insurrectional movement. This original error was soon compounded, however, and French prestige among the Muslims suffered accordingly. In an effort to extort confessions of complicity and the names of accomplices in the uprising, the police tortured their innocent prisoners. With their legs and hands bound to long boards behind their backs, the accused men were immersed in bathtubs filled with water until they nearly drowned. After prolonged sessions of this kind many signed prepared confessions, only to deny them when the prisoners were later brought before courts of law.[34]

News of the imprisonment and torture sessions could not be kept from the press. Operation Bitter Orange became a disaster for the French administration. The MTLD also suffered severe losses both of its imprisoned leaders and of the many rank and file members who promptly rushed to join the new revolutionary forces. In Cairo the CRUA soon reflected the broadening of its base of support by giving way to the National Liberation Front (FLN).[35] It was to this new organization that most of the embittered victims of Operation Bitter Orange flocked upon their release. Both France and the traditional nationalist elements within Algeria lost to the political upstarts led by the Club of Nine.

Meanwhile, the steady surge of the nationalist cause was counterbalanced by the decline of Messali Hadj, who still lived in exile in France. He had tried to capitalize on the situation by creating the *Mouvement National Algérien* (MNA) and by claiming for his new offspring the responsibility for the rebellion in Algeria. Messali implied, although few observers believed him, that he created his organization in early November 1954, although the FLN was not born until May of 1955. Clearly, the FLN, and before it the CRUA, had seized the initiative, and the new leaders had pulled the rug from under the feet of Messali and of all the other nationalist parties.[36] Even the French could no longer control the course of events. The leaders of the infant Algerian revolution had not only taken matters into their own hands but would hold on until well into 1956. Exactly when the FLN was born—whether in November 1954 or in May 1955—is inconsequential. The same leaders who organized the National Liberation Front also created the National Liberation Army (ALN), which certainly existed on the first day of the revolution. By mid-1956 nearly all the leading Algerian personalities would join the FLN. The outstanding holdouts were, of course, Messali Hadj and some of his die-hard followers. Most of the old leader's faithful disciples lived in France, but a few struggled in Algeria, where they fought the FLN as much as the French authorities.[37]

5 | The Spread of Revolutionary Nationalism

BETWEEN MARCH AND OCTOBER OF 1954 MEMBERS OF THE CRUA held several secret meetings in Switzerland and Algeria. These gatherings revealed two tendencies in the leadership of Algerian revolutionary nationalism. One section, composed of exile political and diplomatic leaders, would soon struggle with the second, the "internal" or military chiefs, for supreme authority over the revolution. Ben Bella led the exiled nationalists who operated from Cairo, a clique of "external" chiefs who enjoyed the support of most Arab governments, and especially that of Egypt. A second cluster within the CRUA, composed of nationalists who remained in Algeria, generally followed the direction of Mustapha Ben Boulaid and Belkacem Krim. These men commanded two key areas, the Aurès and Kabylia, and, because of their effectiveness, won respect and influence over their colleagues. Until the eve of the rebellion Mohamed Boudiaf acted as the liaison between the two wings of the CRUA. He joined the external group after the October 10, 1954, meeting in Algiers, during which Ben Boulaid, Bitat, Didouche, Krim, M'Hidi, and Boudiaf decided that their revolution would begin on October 31.

On this first day of the uprising about 400 followers of the CRUA participated in the insurgency against the French establishment. Other estimates indicated as many as 2,000 or even 3,000 militants, but these are clearly exaggerated figures.[1] The contribution of the CRUA leaders lay mainly in their development of unity and cohesion rather than in their organizational creations. They had infused preexisting structures with a new sense of purpose and cooperation. Their division of Algeria into six *wilaya,* for example, simply copied the territorial organization devised by the MTLD immediately following World War II. In forming the National Liberation Army (ALN), the CRUA simply merged several disparate elements, bands of fugitives from French justice and, according to government sources, groups of professional bandits. (In all fairness, it should be noted that most of the outlaws had run afoul of the authorities because of nationalist convictions.) The coalition also attracted units of traditionally dissident Kabyles and Chaouias.[2] As a result, most of this nationalist force was concentrated in the two mountainous regions of Kabylia and the Aurès, where those who resisted French authority had always found refuge. The CRUA, then, contributed most by taking control of a strange, motley group and turning it into one subversive tool. All sections of the ALN took orders from the CRUA leaders, and all received cadres from the old OS. Individual sections could work separately both tactically and strategically, however, although each operated within rigidly defined geographical areas.[3] Clearly, the CRUA had given direction to convinced nationalists and other established opponents of the French imperium in Algeria.

MAP 4

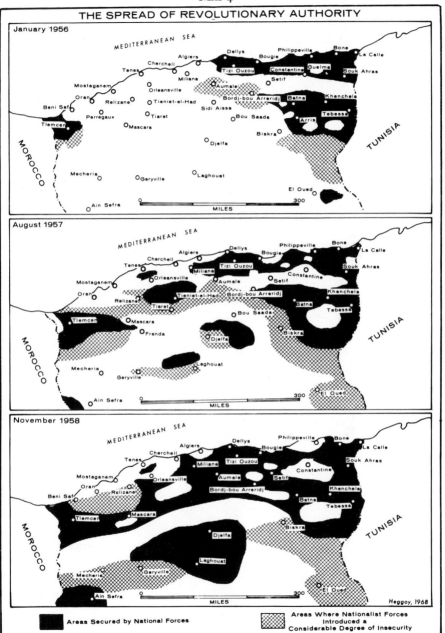

THE SPREAD OF REVOLUTIONARY AUTHORITY

January 1956

MEDITERRANEAN SEA

Dellys
Philippeville   Bone
Algiers   Bougie   La Calle
Cherchell
Tenes   Tizi Ouzou   Constantine   Guelma
Miliana   Setif   Souk Ahras
Orleansville   Aumale
Mostaganem   Bordj-bou Arreridj   Khenchela
Oran   Relizane   Tieniet-el-Had
Beni Saf   Sidi Aissa   Batna
Perregaux   Tiaret   Bou Saada   Arris   Tebessa
Tlemcen   Mascara   Biskra
Djelfa

Mecheria   Laghouat
Geryville

El Oued
Ain Sefra   300
MILES

TUNISIA

MOROCCO

August 1957

MEDITERRANEAN SEA

Dellys
Philippeville   Bone
Algiers   Bougie   La Calle
Cherchell
Tenes   Tizi Ouzou   Souk Ahras
Miliana   Constantine
Orleansville   Aumale   Setif
Mostaganem   Khenchela
Oran   Tieniet-el-Had   Bordj-bou Arreridj
Relizane   Tiaret   Batna
Tlemcen   Bou Saada   Tebessa
Mascara   Djelfa   Biskra
Frenda

Mecheria   Laghouat
Geryville

El Oued
Ain Sefra   300
MILES

TUNISIA

MOROCCO

November 1958

MEDITERRANEAN SEA

Philippeville   Bone
Dellys
Algiers   Bougie   La Calle
Cherchell
Tenes   Tizi Ouzou   Souk Ahras
Miliana   Constantine
Mostaganem   Aumale   Setif
Orleansville   Khenchela
Beni Saf   Oran   Bordj-bou Arreridj
Relizane   Batna
Tlemcen   Mascara   Tebessa
Biskra
Djelfa

Laghouat
Mecheria   Geryville
El Oued
Ain Sefra   300
MILES

TUNISIA

MOROCCO

Heggoy, 1968

■ Areas Secured by National Forces

▨ Areas Where Nationalist Forces
Introduced a
Considerable Degree of Insecurity

Various pressures forced the chiefs of the CRUA to take direct action. As former members of the extinct OS, their fear of discovery by the police or other pro-French elements gave them a sense of urgency. This is what Jacques Soustelle called "bad memories of the OS."[4] In addition, the historic nine rejected what the authorities might refer to as legitimate political protest; they felt certain that the only course open to them was that of an "Indochinese discussion," a guerrilla war that would continue until France tired and granted independence to Algeria.[5]

Political factors also influenced the decisions taken by the CRUA. Ahmed Ben Bella's credentials as a pan-Arabist, and as an active nationalist who had been imprisoned for a daring deed of violence against the French regime, impressed leaders in the Egyptian government, who consequently offered enthusiastic support. Other Arab governments also cheered the prospect of a free and independent Algeria. Finally, the international situation seemed favorable for immediate action; many French troops had not yet left Indochina, and, closer to Algeria, the Moroccans and Tunisians were in open rebellion. A new spirit of resistance was spreading throughout the Maghrib.

Despite other pressures, however, the most urgent need for immediate action arose from the situation inside Algeria itself. Here, the split within the MTLD and the continued attempts on the part of the more moderate Algerian leaders to settle their differences with the French weakened the nationalist cause. A war of liberation seemed essential to force these elements to unite against the French and to compel the uncommitted masses to take a stand for their country, their race, and their religion. The men of the CRUA foresaw that armed insurrection would, by its very nature and its consequences, force all nationalist groups to unite under their banner. Events would justify this opinion.[6]

The Club of Nine assessed the Algerian situation correctly.

Aware of the gravity of the discord within the country, they also perceived, however, that the ideological conflict was largely confined to the upper echelons of the nationalist ranks. Ben Bella and his friends could count on wide support from the rank and file of the MTLD and the other parties, while the passive but generally dissatisfied Muslim masses would surely be sympathetic spectators. Their opinions proved correct when, after the outbreak of the rebellion, members of the MTLD, the UDMA, and the Association of Reformist Ulama flocked to join the new National Liberation Front, the direct descendant of the CRUA.[7]

The armed militants, or National Liberation Army as they called themselves, were ill equipped. They lacked weapons, ammunition, uniforms, safe bases of operations, and indeed even regular systems of command and communications. Their first order of business was, therefore, to organize properly and acquire needed supplies, safe bases, and supply routes.[8] On the local level the organization of this "army" that declared war on France began only a few weeks before the outbreak of rebellion. Mustapha Ben Boulaid, for example, began only in August 1954 to convert the nationalist group he had long commanded in the Aurès from a political to a military unit.[9] He emerged, nonetheless, as one of the most successful early commanders in the revolutionary army, and few of his peers were as well prepared for war.

Insurgency and revolution was at first a rather frustrating experience for these armed militants under the CRUA. With a few exceptions their projects of November 1, 1954, and of the weeks that followed, failed. The colonialists took heart from the fact that the Muslim masses did not rush to the rebels' support. Most, as in the Aurès, remained uncommitted, waiting to see if the nationalist fire would really burn more than a few weeks or months. But in the department of Oran, for example, some natives spontaneously provided the intelligence that permitted the French army and police to destroy several terrorist cells.[10] Early intelligence also enabled the French to dismantle a rebel group near Blida, where the nationalists had planned to model their organization on the rebel underground in the Aurès.

During the months following the first series of insurrectional acts, the guerrillas carried out their most spectacular attacks on the colonial establishment in the rugged Aurès region. When the French reacted by seeking out the enemy, the rebels refused to stand and fight. They roamed the countryside, attacking when and where they chose, blocking roads and felling telephone poles. On the rare occasions when they were forced to fight, spirited engagements ensued. The administration's basic problem continued unchanged: the rebels could strike at will while the French were reduced to a purely defensive position. They were able only to protect the innocent as best they could and to try to guess the nature and location of the next rebel attack. Those portions of the Muslim population not under direct protection remained vulnerable to terrorization by the nationalist bands. Through the use of complicity and terror, the ALN won over village after village. Heads of families, if uncooperative at first, were forced to take part in some subversive project. Once compromised, they became fugitives from French justice and were obliged to take shelter in the ranks of the guerrillas. Their anonymity was preserved by the frightened silence of those villagers who remained uncommitted.

Several French analysts have claimed that the methods of the Algerian rebels were learned in Viet Minh prisons.[11] Since many Muslims who served with the French expeditionary force in Indochina were captured by the enemy, the allegation may be true. Such North Africans could have learned lessons taught by Mao Tse-tung and other Communist philosophers of partisan warfare. Whatever the truth of the claim that Algerian nationalists simply applied Viet Minh methods, some Frenchmen began to seek answers to their Maghribi problems from a study of the Indochinese War of National Liberation. But few, if any, of the Algerian prisoners of the Viet Minh emerged as leaders in the FLN-ALN. Nevertheless, the methods of the Algerian nationalists did resemble those used by the Communists in Southeast Asia.

The tactics used in Indochina, then later, on a lesser scale, in Tunisia, and finally in the Aurès, proved just as successful in Kabylia. In the Beni Ouacif tribal area on the slopes of Mount Kouriet, for example, a group of forty to fifty rebels instituted a reign of terror over the civilian population. By the time the French authorities responded by sending in troops, the bandits-turned-partisan fighters had the Beni Ouacif villagers well in hand. Their ever present friends or relatives lived everywhere among the people. It is evident that many Algerians implored the French to provide them protection, but no one dared to come forward and point out the guilty ones.[12] To denounce them was to court certain punishment and probable death.

A similar situation existed in the Djurdjura Mountains, another section of Higher Kabylia. When French soldiers made their first visit there, in late 1954, the inhabitants were apparently not convinced nationalists. On the other hand, they expressed no Francophile feelings; they knew little about the French. The Beni Ouacif had at least known Frenchmen, as many tribesmen had traveled to France in search of jobs that were not available in Algeria, but even the Beni Ouacif tribes had had few contacts with French officials in the colony itself. As a result, they shared the attitudes of their neighbors in the Djurdjura Mountains. If assured of protection, they were willing enough to help the French, but even France could not guard every Algerian, especially in such remote and rugged areas.

In Kabylia, as elsewhere, the French army tried to uproot the rebel bands by organizing temporary concentrations of military forces for the purpose of encircling predetermined areas. The encircled territory would then be thoroughly searched in operations known as *ratissages* (rakings). The authorities could not keep this kind of operation secret for long, and the rebels nearly always had ample time to leave before the French buckled their *cordon sanitaire*.[13] Alternatively, the irregular soldiers of the ALN hid their weapons and reverted to civilian dress, merging imperceptibly with the general population. The French troops, whose activities were limited by the government's decisions, were constantly frustrated by the impossibility of picking out the guilty guerrillas from among the population at large.

In order to protect their supporters among the Muslims, the French would have had to institute permanent occupation, both civil and military, of those areas infected by nationalism. Unaccustomed to guerrilla warfare, however, most French commanders simply did not gear their efforts to occupation.[14] In spite of growing evidence to the contrary, the government continued to think that a police action would suffice to reestablish peace and order. In spite of the French faith in *ratissages*, the technique proved ineffective. After a search, the soldiers left the area to participate in another similar maneuver elsewhere. The local population was left once more to its own devices, subject to the exactions of the rebels.

Those soldiers who had fought in Indochina or who had read Galliéni, Lyautey, or other great colonial military strategists soon perceived the true nature of the Algerian war. Even before the end of 1954 some saw the necessity of extending their duties and authority to political realms. The ALN fought for the minds of men, not for territory; to win this conflict the French military establishment would also have to fight "in the crowd." But the government of France moved slowly.[15] The great colonialist Lyautey had stressed the necessity of pacification efforts that closely coordinated military, administrative, and psychological functions. Paris, not recognizing the existence of a war in Algeria, put the military under civilian control and kept the army from establishing direct contacts with the population. The army was thus obliged to operate in a void against an unknown enemy whom the civil administration protected.[16]

This situation naturally led to a conflict between the French civil and military authorities in Algeria, to a revival of a typical nineteenth-century French phenomenon involving competition for control over Algerian affairs. Until the fall of the Second Empire soldiers of the *Service des Bureaux Arabes* ruled most of Algeria. The Third Republic relegated military administration to the southern or Saharan territories while the more densely populated northern tier of the country became three French departments ruled, in theory, as any other equivalent administrative unit in France. These changes pleased the European settlers, who had long demanded that they be given all the rights of French citizenship. The colonial situation had nevertheless remained for Muslims, who were subjects, not citizens.[17] Never completely forgotten, the military-civilian conflict reemerged. Soon after the outbreak of revolution some of the vocabulary and policies of the nineteenth-century conquest of Algeria also reappeared. But in 1954 and after, France did not fight a war in Algeria. French soldiers engaged in a police operation, then in pacification. In using this word, the French reverted to nineteenth-century colonial terminology.

The Special Administrative Sections (SAS) system was conceived as a temporary but necessary expedient. The SAS were first led by officers who had previously served in the Sahara or in the *Service des Affaires Indigènes,* a Moroccan organization similar to the *Service des Bureaux Arabes.* The French had created the SAS out of necessity, to administer communes created by a belated political reform designed to give Algerians more local autonomy. By 1957, when the government finally promulgated this reform, the nationalists had done too much damage to French prestige and established fear too firmly in the minds of Muslims; no Algerians would agree to serve France in the new institutional framework.[18] Since European civil administrators also failed to appear in sufficient numbers, the government had to turn to the army. Officers then added civil administration to their normal military duties and thereby eliminated the military dependency on civil officials for all important intelligence. This solution, however, was not suggested until 1956, or applied until 1957. By then many French military leaders had become bitter in their attitudes toward their own government.

In late 1954 and throughout 1955, the French soldiers resented the failure of their government to develop quickly a successful antiguerrilla policy. The legal protection afforded the rebels by French laws compounded their bitterness. Since, officially at least, no state of war existed in Algeria, captured rebels, even those caught with weapons in hand, were turned over to civilian authorities for normal criminal proceedings. Most of the prisoners sought and received good legal counsel and often received only light sentences. Officers and men could also be called to court as witnesses. From November 1, 1954, until the creation of military tribunals in June 1955, French courts handed down a capital sentence for only one Algerian nationalist. From June to September 1955 the military courts, created to relieve pressure on the normal judicial institutions caused by the revolution, handed down one hundred death sentences, all of which the nationalist prisoners appealed.[19] As a result, the first two executions of men condemned by the military tribunals were not carried out until June 1956. The Algerian reaction to that event helped precipitate the Battle of Algiers. The courts thus tended to interfere with the army's normal routines, creating misunderstanding and hostility toward the government. It is perhaps understandable that soldiers sometimes carried out justice summarily in the field.[20] It was easier to account for a dead guerrilla than to become involved with a magistrate.

Excesses such as the hasty execution of prisoners by busy soldiers provided perfect propaganda for the nationalist forces. The guerrillas profited also from the delays forced on the French army by the slow pace of justice. The rebel propagandists claimed that many, if not most, of the prisoners taken in the first few months of the war were innocent of any nationalist connections.[21] This was often the case. True members of the ALN, moreover, did not hesitate to avail themselves of all the protection and legal aid which French criminal law allowed. At the same time they demanded recognition as enemy soldiers, hence as prisoners of war rather than as criminals.[22] In so doing they simply continued their war against France. They were not in the least concerned about the contradiction between their use of legal protection as provided for criminals and their demand for the status of prisoners of war. The rebels made propaganda even as they tied up the French courts. On both counts they furthered the Algerian nationalist cause.

Meanwhile, the ALN continued to circulate revolutionary and Francophobe doctrines in Algeria. The rebel strategy was quite simple and resembled in operation the spreading of an oil spot on a blotter. Almost invariably the guerrillas first seized control of remote villages where the French hand lay very lightly or where some natives had actually never seen a European official.[23] It was not difficult to persuade such people, Muslims who were completely removed from the mainstream of colonial Algeria, to support the nationalist cause. In some areas the rebels simply filled a power vacuum.

Having come to a village, the rebel leaders would draft the young men into the ALN. Each draftee represented a family and was quickly made to participate in some subversive project. Having assisted in the murder of a pro-French notable, for example, the young recruit became an outlaw. Even though he might have acted under constraint, he was guilty and had implicated his entire family in rebellion against

France. Their fear and alienation would grow as the French tried to hunt him down and punish him. The Algerian nationalists understood the ways of the traditional society within which they operated; they comprehended the depth of family ties and of other group allegiances, and they exploited this knowledge.

The importance of the group in Kabyle society can hardly be exaggerated. The *çoff* determines for the individual member all matters of politics, while the family, village, and clan control most other aspects of life. In this patriarchal system all sons marry to help continue the family group; all daughters are wed according to the male parent's wishes, usually at the early age of twelve or thirteen and often in order to further existing group alliances. Cooperation among members of a whole village or clan is typical of the Kabyle approach to certain tasks—the building of houses or roads, the weeding and harvesting of grain or olive crops—and exemplifies the importance of various groups. Individuals and families work on such projects freely, although custom has, in effect, made this work mandatory. The frequency of emigration, usually to France in search of work, further demonstrates the vital role of the group. An individual Kabyle feels free to leave his wife and children for months, or even years, because he knows his male relatives who remain in the village will defend not only his family but also his local rights to specific uses of communally held lands. Away from home the migratory Kabyle worker will usually live frugally or even poorly so that he may send a greater portion of his earnings to his family. Perhaps the most striking example of the importance of the group in Kabyle society, however, involves the behavior of *çoffs*. An offense against any member of a *çoff*, or against its membership as a whole, must be avenged on a member of the offender's *çoff* or on that group as a whole.[24]

Like the Kabyles, the Chaouia have *çoffs*, and, with a few rather minor variations, the family and the clan are the focal points of organized life in the Aurès.[25] Kabyle and Chaouia wives never become true members of the husbands' families. They can be repudiated almost at will and usually have little or nothing to say about important decisions or politics. Yet these Berber wives can achieve a degree of influence if they give birth to sons. Sons, when they reach manhood, gain a voice in family and community affairs; they can, then, express their mothers' wishes on public or family questions. Although their legal position allows them no official voice, and although they rarely get any formal education, the women manage somehow to play important roles in the defense of traditional Berber values and customs.

The role of the emancipated Algerian woman has been celebrated by Frantz Fanon.[26] But the traditional women probably better served the revolution, even long before the insurrection began.[27] They did so by resisting all attempts by the French to penetrate native society; together with other atavistic forces, these women kept many Algerians from becoming naturalized Frenchmen.[28] They wailed when their men were drafted and encouraged them to desert;[29] they mourned when men left to seek work in Algiers or in France but rejoiced and celebrated when the men returned to the village. They rarely approved of foreign women who married into Berber society. Their influence cannot be denied, and their resistance to change must have been effective.

The rebels who became soldiers of the ALN understood their own society. Many of the dissidents and "bandits" who roamed the Aurès and Kabylia were army deserters living among the people, who protected them from an unfriendly and foreign administration. Having drafted young men into their own ranks, compromising these individuals, and through them, the families, clans, and *çoffs* of the young recruits, the rebels also made full use of the feeling of guilt by association. Combining psychology and terrorism to great effect, they fanned fear of reprisals from the French troops into an abiding hatred of France and a spirit of revolutionary nationalism.[30]

Having seized the minds of a local populace through a spreading circle of complicity, the nationalists were ready to begin anew in nearby villages. The oil spot grew as village after village fell under their control. The ALN was unable to exclude the French army from the communities it had won over, but the French presence had no effect on the rebels' control of the populace. Even young shepherds of twelve years or less served as sentinels. Incriminating evidence had usually disappeared by the time the troops reached the scene, and French soldiers saw only a peaceful village whose remarkably quiet population showed its sympathies only by its silence. As the war progressed, the soldiers often entered empty villages, all the inhabitants, warned in good time, having been ordered by the ALN to hide in the forest. Because they knew they were in unfriendly territory, the French would merely search the buildings and then return to the safety of their barracks. If the guerrillas enjoyed a relative safety in their villages during the daylight hours, they ruled as absolute masters at night. In this way they created in a few months the bases of operations which they had lacked at the start of the rebellion. These bases were at first removed from the roads on which the modern French army depended. The mobile partisans, however, could easily reach these routes to strike small convoys or patrols, only to disappear as soon as reinforcements approached the scene of ambush.

The rebels' oil spot strategy was the application in reverse of Lyautey's plan for the French conquest of North Africa.[31] As a colonial soldier and administrator, Lyautey had been forced to combat anarchy in Morocco during the late nineteenth and early twentieth centuries. The way to end opposition to French penetration, he had suggested, was to concentrate the troops in the settled areas, from which a *"paix française"* could be imposed in widening circles. Provided that sufficient centers could be established and adequately garrisoned, the whole of the Maghrib could be pacified. It would of course be necessary for all parts of a colony to be within easy reach of such a garrison. Lyautey envisaged a limited use of military power to help France win over traditional leadership and to enable the colonial administration to apply policies designed to facilitate the economic development of affected regions.[32] Unlike the rebels, the colonial officer began in urban centers, and he did not combine his oil spot strategy with the use of terror. Because they were fighting an enemy who was much more powerful than themselves, the Algerian nationalists in 1954 and after used terrorism as a matter of policy. Although some French officers undoubtedly used terrorism, France itself could not base policies on the use of such methods. For this reason, and because the French fought an enemy who did use terror, it is questionable whether the French could have applied the oil spot technique as easily as the rebels. In any case, the government reacted too slowly, and when the French army finally adopted a similar plan (*quadrillage* and the creation of Special Administrative Sections), it was too late; the guerrillas had already adopted the reverse of Lyautey's plan with great success, and they continued to do so. As the rebels went from victory to quiet victory, Mendès-France and his successor Faure tried in vain to apply the 1947 Statute. In 1954 and 1955, however, Algeria demanded much more drastic measures.

The French failure to effect reforms in Algeria before the situation there became crucial cost dearly in terms of local popularity. By and large, the natives had lost faith in the government of France even before 1954. Electoral frauds and other legal injustices had caused additional resentment, thus preparing the Muslims to listen sympathetically to nationalist propaganda. The rebel ALN, particularly those of its leaders who could point to some local success against the established administration, found many men willing to take a stand against the French. Generally speaking, the ALN had little difficulty in acquiring the support of the population.

A certain basis of popular support is, of course, absolutely essential to a guerrilla movement.[33] To gain this allegiance was, of necessity, the first self-imposed task of the ALN. The ground had been well prepared by the blunders of the French.[34] Further, the guerrillas saw no need to persuade a majority of the masses; in any community the ALN could afford to be satisfied with the active loyalty of as little as twenty per cent of the people. The remainder could be controlled with ease.[35] Given the widespread disaffection among the Muslims, the needed twenty per cent were easily won over; it remained only to eliminate the small group that favored the French presence in Algeria. To this end the most outspoken Francophiles were murdered. Their followers then fled the country or switched their allegiance, usually with plenty of attendant publicity.

Using these techniques, the nationalists saw their numbers increase steadily during the first twenty months of the rebellion. Their ranks swelled in spite of poor organization, disunity at the top, and other internal difficulties.[36] As the revolution began, the guerrillas were solidly entrenched only in the Aurès mountains; from there, however, they steadily extended their sway. The first and most spectacular advances were made in regions similar to the Aurès in poverty, remoteness, and the dearth of European settlers and officials. Most of Kabylia, for example, was converted into a rebel bastion by the end of 1954. It was here that Belkacem Krim, a member of the CRUA, and his lieutenant, Amar Ouamrane, maintained nine troublesome bands. Though short of troops, Major General Paul Padres, commandant of the garrison in Algiers, nevertheless committed 4,000 of his best men to Kabylia less than two months after the outbreak of the rebellion.[37]

Meanwhile, two large-scale comb-out operations in the

Aurès failed to produce the expected results. *Violette* and *Véronique,* as the maneuvers were named, neither contained the rebels nor forced them to the surface. The violence spread from the Aurès to the Nementcha range by February 1955; intelligence reports of that time mentioned two well-armed nationalist bands in the area, close to the Tunisian frontier. Other bands were active at Jemmapes and at El Milia, to the north, between Constantine and the coast. Additional outlaw groups sprang up at Amor Djebar, near Souk Ahars, and in the Edough Range just west of Bône.[38]

The tremendous wave of revolutionary support led the ALN to attempt more daring attacks. On January 9, 1955, for example, some thirty guerrillas fired on Sengalese soldiers in a garrison at Michelet, in the higher reaches of Kabylia. They were apparently led by Ouamrane, Belkacem Krim's second in command. The oil spot also crept toward the capital. There was a rash of agitation around Dra el Mizan, about seventy miles east of Algiers. The insurgents were already well established in the triangle between Azazga, Tizi-Ouzou, and Port Gueydon before the end of March 1955. Worse still, from the French point of view, there were already signs of better organization in the rebellion by the fourth month.[39]

The early disorganization could easily be understood if the FLN had begun its life in late January[40] or in May 1955.[41] But the best informed observers believe the political arm of Algerian nationalism was created on November 1, 1954, just as the ALN swung into action.[42] Effective organization within the disparate group collected by the CRUA was not achieved at once; by the fourth month, however, some clear patterns were beginning to emerge.

Well aware that it could not operate without the support of a certain segment of the population, the ALN thus set out to win over the Muslims through the application of procedures already described. Once having secured the allegiance of an area, the rebels had then to assure the continuation of this loyalty. To this end the ALN followed its initial success in each locality with the establishment of a cell of the Political and Administrative Organization (OPA for *Organization Politique et Administrative*). On the village level the OPA served as the direct representative of the FLN, just as the armed bands of the surrounding countryside formed local units of the ALN.

As befitted the purposes of such an organization, the members of the OPA were civilians. They were charged with the collection of funds, administration and justice, and all tasks which were not purely military but were essential to the rebel cause. They provided every possible assistance to the armed bands of the ALN, and were, of course, under their protection. It was the presence of these cells within the population that prevented the natives from providing intelligence to the French Forces of Order. It was the OPA that disseminated FLN propaganda on the local level, provided guides for transient military units, and supplied the revolutionary leaders with reports on which to base political and military strategy. It was, in short, the backbone of the nationalist movement.[43]

Although they were successful in spreading rebellion and insecurity throughout most of Algeria, the rebels remained divided against themselves. It was not always clear whether ultimate command of the movement belonged to the military or to the political leaders. In certain areas fierce contests for power developed among supposedly dedicated revolutionaries. Finally, the misfortunes of war deprived the nationalist cause of some of its best leaders even before the ALN and the FLN had fully organized themselves and agreed on their respective spheres of activity. Despite these weaknesses, the guerrillas were so successful that Governor-General Jacques Soustelle, the chief representative of France in Algeria, was prompted to complain early in 1956 that there were not enough French soldiers to reassure the population.[44]

The rebels paid dearly for their successes. They lost 3,000

partisans between November 1, 1954, and February 1956. In the same period the French lost only 550 men.[45] Among the dead nationalists was at least one of the historic leaders, Mourad Didouche; he was killed a few short weeks after the start of the revolution.[46] Didouche had been the commander of Wilaya II (North Constantine Province), and his death was a severe blow to the rebels. He was replaced by Youssef Zighout, who was also destined to die in combat. Ben Boulaid, another member of the Club of Nine, was killed on March 27, 1956. He had been captured in February of the same year.[47] Still another historic leader, Rabah Bitat, the first rebel commander of Wilaya IV (Algiers Province), was captured in Algiers on March 16, 1955.[48] While Bitat's arrest was a blow to the nationalists, it impeded their progress for only a short time. Bitat held fast, even under torture, and his organization in the department of Algiers was not disturbed.

It was apparent that rebel losses, particularly those in the middle echelons of the nationalist structure, were always quickly replaced. In any case, the OPA cells were too numerous to be eliminated. If one group was suppressed, another quickly sprang up in its place. The entire success of the rebel cause was based on its great strength and tenacity at this grassroots level.

One of the chief functions of the OPA cells was that of propaganda. The guerrillas had been active in this field from the very start of the revolution. Occasionally, as on the first day of the rebellion, the ALN handled its own public relations. The cells of the OPA, however, soon assumed the major responsibility for propaganda. The most constant and important among its many themes was a bitter reply to the paternalistic racism which all too often had typified the colonial administration. Many tracts attacked those French laws which were so ill adapted to Algerian customs and conditions, proposing to replace them with a new revolutionary code.[49] Although the revolutionary ideology was still largely undefined in 1961, it promised a better day to the Muslims. The nationalists played on the Muslims' deep resentment of their national underdevelopment and their position as a colonized people.[50] The guerrillas' use of psychological techniques dictated that pride should become the single most important theme in their propaganda. This theme formed the basis of the first revolutionary tract.

This first tract appeared in various parts of Algeria on November 1, 1954. It was the work of the ALN leaders and it reveals a certain political immaturity and a lack of a firm program. There was nothing explicit in this short declaration addressed to the Algerian people.[51] It simply said:

Algerian people:
Reflect on our humiliating, colonized condition. Under colonialism, justice, democracy, and equality are but bait and dupery. To these misfortunes must be added the bankruptcy of the parties claiming to defend you. Side by side with our brothers to the east and to the west, who are dying that their fatherlands may live, we call upon you to reconquer your freedom at the price of your blood.
Organize your action beside the Forces of Liberation, to which you must give aid, comfort, and protection. To take no interest in the struggle is a crime; to oppose this action is treason.
God is with the fighters of just causes, and no force can stop them now, save glorious death or National Liberation.
Long live the Army of Liberation!
Long live independent Algeria![52]

On the same day, or perhaps later,[53] the FLN distributed a lengthier handbill that proposed a political program but, like the war itself, carried all the earmarks of an improvised movement. After a brief review of Algeria's political situation, both internally and externally, the authors went on to announce the goals of the FLN. Describing themselves as young leaders, they explained that the FLN had come into being to prevent further disunity among Muslim nationalists. Speaking for the new organization, the authors claimed, "We are independent of the two clans that are competing for power." Messalists and Centralists, and other nationalists as well, would be welcome in the new party, which had taken the only honorable course —open war against the French rulers of Algeria. In the fight for independence, the document proclaimed, the Algerian people were laggards; other colonized nations were already fighting to achieve their freedom. Finally, it announced, the FLN would restore the sovereign democratic and social Algerian state in the context of Islamic principles and of North African and Arab unity. Within this "restored" state, however, all fundamental liberties would be respected without distinctions of race or belief.

On the whole, the November proclamation was vague except with regard to the struggle at hand. The immediate object was to clean house in the revolutionary movement by eliminating all vestiges of corruption and reformism. The second task was to organize all the "healthy energies of the Algerian people" and to liquidate the colonial system. With respect to foreign policy, it was the chief aim of the FLN to bring Algeria into the international spotlight. The United Nations was regarded as the logical platform on which to argue the nationalist case.

The final portion of this tract was addressed to the French government. On the assumption that the mere outbreak of violence heralded the approaching collapse of the French regime in Algeria, the rebels demanded the start of negotiations which would lead to independence. Such an ultimatum was incredibly arrogant in the light of the disunity and numerical weakness of the nationalist ranks at the time. Like the proclamation of November 1, the entire rebel insurrection was an *ad hoc* affair. Stirring oratory took the place of clear goals.

Having thus issued a challenge to France in both word and deed, the FLN was obliged to tighten its organization for the struggle ahead. The achievement of internal discipline duly became the primary concern of the FLN for the first twenty months of the rebellion. Simultaneously, they seized the military initiative and continued to hold it while the French came only slowly to recognize the challenge and the nature of the struggle in which the nationalists compelled them to engage.

6 | Revolutionary Institutions and Organization

THE INSTITUTIONS OF ALGERIAN REVOLUTIONARY NATIONALISM were created while the ALN and the FLN fought for the independence of their country. The rebels' organization was thus characterized by pragmatism; it was, in essence, determined by the exigencies of the struggle. Wherever possible, the guerrillas borrowed from older organizations. The MTLD, for example, had divided Algeria for its own purposes into five provinces, each of which was subdivided into zones, regions, and sectors.[1] These geographic divisions, with a few changes, were adopted by the CRUA, then by the FLN. The directors of the rebellion also incorporated many of the organizational methods which Messali had previously borrowed from the Communist Party. The French government and the colonial administration provided many more structural models for the insurgents to copy. From the latter, for example, the rebels took the territorial units known as *douars*. A *douar* usually covered the area of two, three, or more villages whose inhabitants were of the same tribe. A smaller unit was the fraction, a small area encompassing part of a *douar*. While the nationalists succeeded in hastily building a framework suitable to their needs, their accomplishment was based in great measure on imitation and adaptation.[2]

Structurally, the rebel organization was tied to the geographic division of Algeria along the lines established by the MTLD. The territorial units were, in descending order, provinces, zones, regions, sectors, *douars*, and fractions. The provinces, or *wilaya*, as they were called by the nationalists, were divided into zones, which might number from five to eight. The smaller divisions, especially the *douars* and the fractions, corresponded to the natural units in traditional Muslim society.

From November 1, 1954, until August 20, 1956, the insurgents built continuously on their foundation, a combination of pragmatism, Muslim proletarian party organizations, and Communist methodology. During the same period the FLN and the ALN were also able to create an extraordinary surge of popular nationalism. As a natural corollary to the new spirit of revolution, they gained control of large segments of the native population. The new leaders fought among themselves, however, and quarreled bitterly with other revolutionary parties, such as the *Mouvement National Algérien* (MNA), which shared the objectives but followed different leaders. The French, meanwhile, sought in vain effective policies with which to contain and destroy the revolutionary movement.[3] The confusion and weakness of the French is underscored by their failure to take any advantage of the discord in the rebel ranks.[4]

The French administrative and military divisions took no account of the nationalist territorial organization of Algeria. They divided their military forces into three divisions—

Algiers, Constantine, and Oran—each of which was sub-divided into zones, sectors, subsectors, and *quartiers*. This territorial organization did not coincide with the ALN's geo-graphic structures, as the French author Jacques C. Duchemin has clearly illustrated in the following chart for Algiers province:

French Army	ALN
Algiers Army Corps	Wilayas III, IV and VI
1) North Algiers Zone (ZNA): Algiers-Blida	Wilaya IV, Zones I and II
Algiers Sahel Sector Bouzareah Sub-Sector	Algiers Autonomous Zone
2) West Algiers Zone (ZOA): Orleansville	Wilaya IV, Zone III
3) South Algiers Zone (ZSA): Medea	Wilaya IV, Zone II (south) Wilaya III, Zone I (west) Wilaya VI, Zones I & II
4) East Algiers Zone (ZEA): Tizi-ouzou	Wilaya III, Zones I, II and III

Rebel leaders knew what the French territorial organization was, and could use this intelligence to create problems of au-thority for the enemy commanders. The French officers, how-ever, could never be quite sure whether the armed men just beyond their territorial limits of authority were colleagues from a neighboring sector or nationalists. The consequent difficulties for the defenders of the colonial regime were turned to the benefit of their enemies.[5]

A rebel colonel had supreme military and political au-thority over the FLN-ALN organization on the provincial level. Each of the colonels was assisted by three majors, of whom one was responsible for political affairs, one for mili-tary affairs, and the third for liaison and intelligence. Using officers of lower rank, this organization was repeated in each of the provincial subdivisions down to the sector.[6] In each of the rebel zones, for example, a captain commanded with

CHART 6
REBEL LEADERS AND THEIR TERRITORIAL AND
ADMINISTRATIVE JURISDICTION

National Leadership was Collegial and
in Exile (Cairo, Tripoli, and Elsewhere)

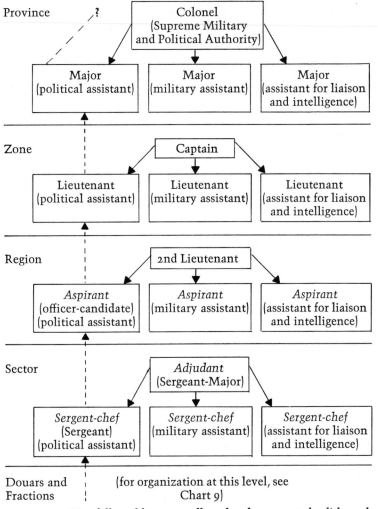

Province

Colonel
(Supreme Military
and Political Authority)

Major
(political assistant)

Major
(military assistant)

Major
(assistant for liaison
and intelligence)

Zone

Captain

Lieutenant
(political assistant)

Lieutenant
(military assistant)

Lieutenant
(assistant for liaison
and intelligence)

Region

2nd Lieutenant

Aspirant
(officer-candidate)
(political assistant)

Aspirant
(military assistant)

Aspirant
(assistant for liaison
and intelligence)

Sector

Adjudant
(Sergeant-Major)

Sergent-chef
(Sergeant)
(political assistant)

Sergent-chef
(military assistant)

Sergent-chef
(assistant for liaison
and intelligence)

Douars and
Fractions

(for organization at this level, see
Chart 9)

Line followed by taxes collected and moneys to be disbursed.

the assistance of three lieutenants. Second lieutenants directed the affairs of the ALN on the regional level; they were aided by *aspirants,* a French term applied to officer candidates between the ranks of second lieutenant and company sergeants major. At the lowest command level, the sector, *adjudants,* or company sergeants major, were in command. They were assisted by three *sergent-chefs,* a rank which has no American equivalent but whose duties were similar to those of the lowest ranked sergeants in the United States military.

In the above hierarchy one element, at least, appears to have been adapted from the Communist system.[7] This was the political assistant to the colonel at the provincial level and to the captain and the others at the lower steps in the chain of command. The duties of these men resembled those of a Bolshevik commissar. Other aspects of the ALN's system appear to have been copied from the French military. The most obvious examples are the ranks of *aspirant* (officer candidate) and of *adjudant* (company sergeant major). The basic similarities between the ALN and the French army, such as the designation of ranks, may be seen at a glance; there were many others of a more subtle nature.

The ragged bands of irregulars who initiated the rebellion against the French rule in 1954–1955 were gradually transformed into small, disciplined army units. Observers in 1956 were already remarking their similarity to the French model. The basic units appeared quite early in 1955; these were squads *(groupes)* of ten men under one sergeant, and platoons *(sections)* of three squads and two officers, a total of 35 men. It was not until the summer of 1956, however, that the ALN was able to present itself at company strength. The ALN command created companies only under the most favorable of conditions. Three platoons and five officers, or a total of 110 soldiers, was a rebel company at full strength.[8] Rebel battalions apparently existed only on paper, although each province supposedly had several such units. One of the rare appear-

CHART 7
ALN ORGANIZATION: A COMPANY

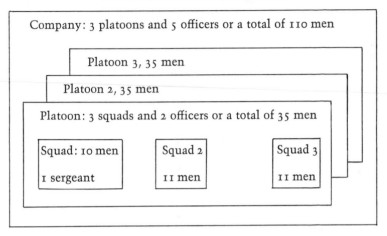

Company: 3 platoons and 5 officers or a total of 110 men

Platoon 3, 35 men

Platoon 2, 35 men

Platoon: 3 squads and 2 officers or a total of 35 men

Squad: 10 men	Squad 2	Squad 3
1 sergeant	11 men	11 men

ances of battalions was in 1957, when a few of them appeared near the Tunisian and Moroccan borders, where sanctuary on foreign soil was close at hand.[9]

It is hardly surprising that the terminology and organization of the ALN were clearly copied from the French military system, since practically all those guerrillas with previous military training had seen service under the French flag. The ALN even adapted French training manuals to its own needs. The adaptations were designed to make the manual comprehensible to the men of the ALN, many of whom were illiterate. A copy of the modified manual, incidentally, was found on Ben Boulaid's body at his death.[10] The result of these adjustments, however, was rather poor.

Men who had previously served France could be found at all levels of the rebel ranks. According to one French journalist, for example, the "bandit" who ordered the shooting of *Caïd* Saddok near Arris was a veteran of the French army. The victim aroused his killer's rage, the author reports, because he wore a military cross awarded for service in Indochina.[11] Several of the historic leaders, among them Ben Bella, Bitat, and Boudiaf, had seen service in World War II. Other revolutionary commanders had likewise passed through the French ranks. Bensalem, the commander of the second battalion of the ALN in the Souk-Ahras region, for example, revealed to a reporter from the *Manchester Guardian* that he had been a career soldier in the French army for fourteen years. He had waited eighteen months after the rebellion began to join the FLN.[12] Cherif Mahmoud, the assistant to Colonel Ait ould Hamoudia, who is better known as Amirouche, was a deserter from the French forces.[13]

An anonymous professional soldier was interviewed in 1956 by Peter Throckmorton of *The Reporter.* The soldier had served with the Free French in World War II, he said, and was still with the French army when he was wounded at Dien Bien Phu. While recovering from his injuries in a hospital near Paris, he was told that his village in Algeria had been bombed. He left the hospital, deserted from the army, and joined the rebel forces in his native land. Arnold Beichman, a correspondent for *Newsweek*, spoke with an ALN officer during the summer of 1956. This man, Tahar, the commanding officer of the 4th rebel battalion, had in 1954 been an officer in the French army, which he had served since World War II. He had deserted to join the nationalists at the start of the revolution. Twice captured by the Forces of Order, he had escaped to return to his command.[14] Not all ALN officers were former French soldiers, but the veterans of that army certainly held key positions in an organization which badly needed trained cadres.

The regular rebel army consisted of elites, who have been favorably compared to the French paratroopers. Interestingly, the latter were most feared by the ALN, which went to great lengths to avoid combat with them. The rebels fought willingly against other French units, however, especially when they could take advantage of local conditions.[15] By mid-1956 there may have been as many as 20,000 or 25,000 regular rebel soldiers, known as *moudjahidin*. These combatants were supported by local auxiliaries of irregulars and by the Political and Administrative Organization (OPA).

These irregulars, or *mousseblin*, were veritable subversive militias. They sabotaged roads, felled telephone poles, and damaged the property of European settlers. The *mousseblin* also helped to transport wounded guerrillas and served as guides for any ALN units in their territory. Above all, they provided the rebel army with intelligence about enemy troop movements. Since they wore no uniforms, the *mousseblin* could circulate freely and observe the activities of the French. On the whole, they confined their activities to their own villages, which they rarely left except for short expeditions under cover of darkness, or when they were drafted into regular units of the ALN. *Mousseblin*, as units, rarely participated in battles, although they might be called upon to help in particularly violent engagements near their homes. They did receive military training, however, and they provided an invaluable source of manpower.

Another group of locally based irregulars were the *fida'iyin*.[16] These soldiers were highly specialized terrorists who usually joined the regular ALN when they fell under suspicion and it was inadvisable to continue as civilians. The *fida'iyin* made their presence felt through arson, bombing the homes of suspected Francophiles, and other forms of attack on those who opposed the nationalist cause.[17] Frequently they destroyed schools, which, in operation, stood as symbols of the French presence. Local officials of the colonialist regime were also their frequent targets; those natives who served France were particularly vulnerable and, from the nationalist point of view, desirable victims. The first Muslim killed in the revolution was the *caïd* of M'chounèche. Not only was he a native bureaucrat of the French regime, but he was doubly damned in the rebels' eyes for his pride in being a former captain of the French army. More often than not, then, the *fida'iyin* employed their terrorist tactics against fellow Muslims. In this capacity these men were the tools by which the FLN and the ALN assured their continuing control over the people. In the most direct sense they were at the command of the OPA, the political arm of the revolution, whose cells controlled each village.

Neither the *moudjahidin* nor the irregular *mousseblin* and *fida'iyin* could operate without a certain amount of popular support; such is the case in all guerrilla wars. In the Algerian insurgency, however, the officers of the ALN were very proud of the fact that rebel colonels with a maximum of 1,500 men could compete successfully with 20,000 to 30,000 French soldiers. On military maps the French general and the nationalist colonel each commanded a zone of approximately the same size.[18] When we remember the difference in the strength of the forces opposing each other in these zones, the importance of the popular support of the guerrillas becomes very clear. Were it not for the tacit, if not always active, support for the nationalist cause among the local people, the sheer numerical superiority of the French would have assured them of victory.

When the revolution began, the top of the FLN's organizational pyramid was in Cairo. Its outstanding leader was Ben Bella, whose authority was both political and administrative. At this loftiest level it was the task of the FLN to define and execute the policies of the nationalists, to secure foreign support both inside and beyond the Arab world, to raise the necessary financial support, and to procure the required material for the combatants. The last function was particularly designed to benefit the ALN, which began its struggle as a poorly equipped ragtag band. At its inception most of its members were armed only with knives and hunting rifles. A few had secured military weapons, which had been bought at great cost in Tunisia or Libya, or had been salvaged from the battlegrounds of World War II. A few weapons and other items of equipment had been stolen from the French. The earliest rebel attacks on French army units had as their principal purpose the seizure of arms and munitions.[19]

In order to supply the ALN with weapons, ammunition, and other military necessities, the FLN had to buy or solicit gifts of this type of material. Once these items were obtained, there remained the difficult question of their transportation into Algeria itself. An elaborate system of supply was established that began, of course, in Egypt, and then passed through Libya and Tunisia across the Algerian border. Aside from the difficulties of concealment and transportation in the war zones, serious problems were posed by Tunisia, which was under French occupation until 1956. Even Libya was not a safe haven for the nationalists, as French secret agents could easily cross the frontier from Tunisia. In December 1955 Ben Bella himself was almost killed by such an agent;[20] on February 11, 1955, Ben Boulaid was arrested in Tunisia near the Libyan border as he was on his way to a meeting with Ben Bella.[21] As these examples show, the Algerian nationalists had many obstacles to overcome. Not the least of them was the rudimentary state of their own organization.

The supply network described above began as a very humble operation. The ALN's agents and supporters in Cairo and Tripoli, however, soon proved that they were not to be taken lightly. Initial errors and irregularities soon faded, and regular shipments of weapons and munitions began to reach their destinations in Algeria. Such consignments usually went by a southern route from Libya into the Algerian Sahara or through central Tunisia into the Aurès mountains in the department of Constantine. This camel-borne contraband was eventually supplemented by maritime freight. Ultimately, the guerrillas received up to one thousand weapons per month.[22] This was more than they lost on the field in any comparable period of time. Engagements with the French resulted in some cases in a net gain of weapons and equipment.

Under the direction of Ben Bella an adequate supply system was instituted by the end of 1955. At that time the rebels had several arms depots in northern Libya, and there were also transshipment points in Tripolitania. As was to be expected, a certain percentage of these secret consignments failed to reach their destinations. Many caravans were intercepted by the French, but a sufficient number continued undetected to justify the continued use of this network. The rebels continued to supply themselves in friendly countries and to direct their shipments into Algeria. Until late in 1957, at least, this contraband was profitable for the FLN-ALN.[23] The rebels, it should be noted, had great difficulty in recruiting cadres for this network. Without Egyptian help, the ALN could never have obtained adequate logistic support.[24]

The entire FLN-ALN organization suffered from a lack of discipline and central authority. In theory the colonels who held supreme political and military power in the provinces were subordinate to the collegial leadership of the FLN. The highest authorities of the FLN issued their directives from Cairo and from a second base in Tripoli. In fact, however, the colonels, whose commands were remote from the highest authorities, tended to act as provincial warlords. This was particularly true in those provinces commanded by ambitious men. It was not until after the creation of the *Conseil National de la Révolution Algérienne* (CNRA) and its executive board, the *Comité de Coordination et d'Exécution* (CCE), on August 20, 1956, that the revolution had a well-organized central authority. Almost four years of rebellion passed before the nationalists made serious preparations for a political future; the *Gouvernement Provisoire de la République Algérienne* (GPRA) was formally established on September 18, 1958.

The years prior to the creation of the GPRA were marked by a bitter division between the distant chiefs of the FLN in Cairo and other capitals and the "internal" colonels and other leaders who directly engaged in the struggle. The depth of the quarrel was evident by the summer of 1956. The internal leaders made pointed reference to the fact that, in their opinion, the interior leadership took precedence over those who issued orders from desks in Cairo and Tripoli. As seen by the colonels, the FLN was little more than a logistic institution whose function it was to supply the ALN with the equipment it required.

The difficulty of communication between the interior and the exterior further confused the situation. Several provincial chiefs, including Ben Boulaid and Rabah Bitat, were caught by the French while trying to reach other revolutionary leaders.[25] Finally, competition for the office of colonel within certain provinces helped to make the situation nearly chaotic.[26] When Ben Boulaid was sent to prison, for example, he was replaced by Bachir Chichani. The latter was killed by his own successor, Laghrour Abbes, on November 1, 1955. Abbes bowed out three weeks later when Ben Boulaid escaped from prison on November 22. Then, when Ben Boulaid died in March 1956, his brother Omar tried to take his place. Chaos ensued until Amirouche, acting as representative of the top FLN leaders, reorganized Wilaya I and appointed Cherif Mahmoud, a deserter from the French army, as colonel in the Aurès.[27] Amirouche's mission in the Aurès showed that on occasion the FLN had authority over the officers of the ALN.

With so many internal problems the survival of the rebellion is truly surprising. It is possible that the centralization of power in the hands of the colonel commanding each province explains this survival. In any case, very little is known about the structures of the FLN above the level of the *douar* or below the external level represented by the groups in Cairo and Tripoli. As in most subversive situations, much of the available information is based on the work of the intelligence units of the counterinsurgency forces.[28] It appears that in Algeria the political assistant at the levels of sector, region, zone, and province was concerned with the affairs of the FLN in his area, and simultaneously acted as a commissar within the ALN.

The political assistant is one of the most interesting officials in the rebel organization. As a soldier, he was a propaganda officer whose duty it was to keep alive the revolutionary faith in each militant. Since those who had the courage to volunteer to join the ALN were clearly dedicated to the success of the rebellion, his duties on behalf of the party were perhaps more demanding. In addition to his political responsibilities the political assistant was in charge of the financial affairs of his sector, region, zone, or province. These financial matters were closely related to his political duties. At the *douar* level taxes were collected by the administrative assistant, but were quickly turned over to the political assistant. The taxes and other funds collected at a lower level were channeled by the political assistant to the higher ranks, where they might be disbursed for weapons, munitions, and other supplies. The fees collected from members of the FLN followed the same path and were not distinguished from other types of revenue. The same official was charged with the disbursement of the funds that were returned to him from above. Because of his position as tax collector and as paymaster, the political assistant constantly ran the risk of being caught by the French at any time with more money on his person than he could easily account for.

Nor were these his only problems and duties. The commissar or political assistant at the sector level was also responsible for the organization and smooth operation of the party's OPA cells at the *douar* level and, where possible, at the fraction level as well. It was through these smallest units that the FLN spread its tentacles even to the most remote Algerian communities. Because they represented the nationalist rebellion directly to the rural peasants, these cells were the essential factor in the success of the FLN-ALN.[29]

It was the primary duty of the OPA cells to undermine the French administration at every level, gradually replacing it with officials and institutions of the revolutionary party.[30] This task was made easier by the relative lack of French officials in the most inaccessible regions of Algeria. Many of these areas, while of course theoretically under French control, were in fact administrative vacuums into which the rebels moved without difficulty. Wherever the European settlements were strong, however, the appearance of the OPA cells created extremely difficult conditions for the local Algerians. Here, two administrations existed side by side, the second clandestine but very effective. People to whom the colonial administrators referred as Muslim citizens were held responsible to both systems, and they soon found the situation to be utterly insupportable. The OPA, for example, habitually ordered the Algerians to destroy their identity cards, which French law required them to carry at all times. Once having obeyed this directive, a native was liable to a fine and a prison term. Failure to cooperate with the OPA, on the other hand, invariably resulted in drastic punishment such as mutilation or death. Punishment meted out by the nationalists was occasionally justified on religious grounds; for example, Islam's teaching against alcohol. Basically the same argument was used when the FLN decided to boycott the use of tobacco—a French government monopoly—and tried to impose this directive on all Algerians. In any case, the Muslims, when forced to decide between French and nationalist orders, found their choice unpleasant, but very few hesitated for long.

The local shadow government of the guerrillas was invariably under the authority of a committee of three, composed of a president, a political assistant, and an administrative assistant. The political assistant, in charge of the local FLN organization, popular education, and psychological action, was often aided by three other officials, who were in charge of security, the policing of the civilian population, and supply problems. The administrative assistant of the committee was in charge of the administration of the *douar* or, where applicable, the fraction. Much of the OPA's work, of course, involved psychological warfare and propaganda, but there was a quantity of administrative work as well.[31]

The committee of three represented the revolutionary party, the FLN. According to criteria presented in the statutes of the FLN, its members divided the population into various groups for purposes of administration and control. There were three categories of party membership. The most dedicated were the militants, who were expected to be on call at all times for any duty the party might require. The second group consisted of those who, while less devoted, attended all party meetings and paid their dues; they were known as adherents. Finally, there were sympathizers, who simply paid dues. Adherents were recruited from among the sympathizers, militants from among the adherents, and the FLN cadres were chosen from the militants. Many, if not most, of the militants served as irregulars in the *mousseblin* or *fida'iyin*. Adherents and sympathizers were occasionally required to work. Although unarmed, they could cut telephone poles or dig ditches across highways.

The FLN operated through its local branches, to which all sympathizers were admitted. But, unknown to the rank and file, the adherents and militants were assigned to cells of six members, which with two other cells formed a group. Each five groups were united in a section.[32] The base cell could easily be compared to a military squad while the groups were similar to the ALN's platoons, although 18 rather than 35 men were involved. Sections with 90 members resembled the companies of the ALN, which included 110 soldiers. It seems unlikely that the similarities in the organizations of the FLN and the ALN were accidental. In any case, the FLN apparently

CHART 8
FLN ORGANIZATION: THE RURAL SECTION

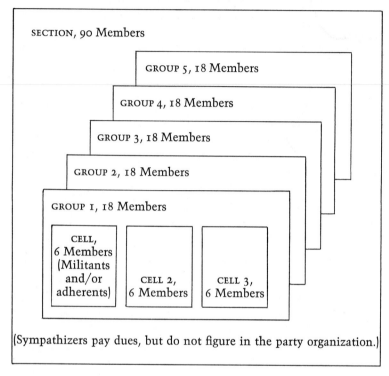

SECTION, 90 Members

GROUP 5, 18 Members

GROUP 4, 18 Members

GROUP 3, 18 Members

GROUP 2, 18 Members

GROUP 1, 18 Members

CELL, 6 Members (Militants and/or adherents)

CELL 2, 6 Members

CELL 3, 6 Members

(Sympathizers pay dues, but do not figure in the party organization.)

dominated the local administrations, just as the military dominated the political at the higher levels of the nationalist hierarchy.

In an effort to create at least a semblance of popular and democratic government, the guerrilla leaders developed local people's assemblies, the members of which were elected by all the men of the *douar* over the age of eighteen. Such assemblies, however, were created only when the local FLN chiefs were firmly in control of the population. The president of such an assembly was, by right, a member of the committee of three, and the candidates for its other offices were nominated by the party. The people's assemblies were in fact the FLN's puppets, and the party kept a firm hand on the strings.[33]

In the name of these assemblies taxes were collected on income and property; however, taxes were collected even where such institutions had not been created. This revenue served to swell the party's coffers, as there was no distinction between government and party above the level of the *douar*. At the highest echelons this fusion was reflected in the fact that there was no separation of civil and military authority within Algeria itself. At each level all power, both political and military, was ultimately concentrated in the hands of the commanding officers, be they lieutenant, captain, or colonel. The political assistants were entrusted with many tasks, but in case of conflict the final decision lay with the military commander. It was to support this political and military system that the taxes on income and property were levied and collected. Apart from these revenues the party collected dues and gifts from its militants, adherents, and sympathizers.[34] Such was the efficiency of the party's financial apparatus that the common citizen paid for almost the entire nationalist struggle.

To all appearances the party and the people's assembly in each *douar* or fraction were independent of each other. Because the revolution was primarily a political struggle, however, the administrative officers at the base were generally subordinate to the political functionaries.[35] While the people's assembly was theoretically the responsibility of the administrative assistant in the committee of three, the political assistant could work through party channels and dictate the policies of that body. The authority of the political assistant was further enhanced by his direct control over three subordinates in charge of security, the civil guard, and supply. These three men directed the local auxiliary forces, and could order terroristic actions.

The people's assembly was composed of five members.

CHART 9
BASIC FLN RURAL ORGANIZATIONS

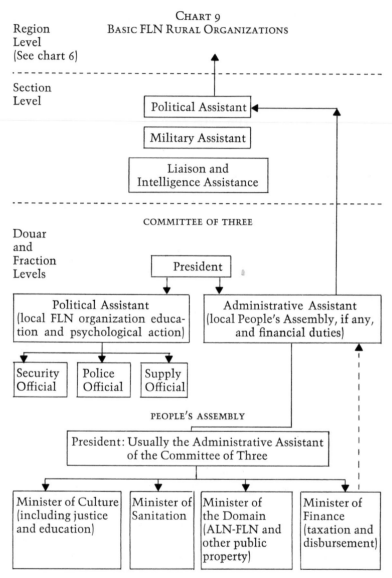

Region
Level
(See chart 6)

Section
Level

Political Assistant

Military Assistant

Liaison and
Intelligence Assistance

COMMITTEE OF THREE

Douar
and
Fraction
Levels

President

Political Assistant
(local FLN organization education and psychological action)

Administrative Assistant
(local People's Assembly, if any,
and financial duties)

Security
Official

Police
Official

Supply
Official

PEOPLE'S ASSEMBLY

President: Usually the Administrative Assistant
of the Committee of Three

Minister of Culture
(including justice
and education)

Minister of
Sanitation

Minister of
the Domain
(ALN-FLN and
other public
property)

Minister of
Finance
(taxation and
disbursement)

------ Line of money flow if the president of the people's assembly is not
the administrative assistant of the committee of three, but another
member of that group.

First, of course, was the president, a member also of the committee of three. Below him were four ministers, of whom one was responsible for culture, defined as to include justice and education; a second served as clerk and sanitation officer, a third administered the domain and the rebel police; and the fourth was a financial official in charge of taxation, disbursement, and economic planning.[36] The taxes collected locally flowed first into the hands of the financial official, then moved on to the administrative assistant in the committee of three, and thence up through the ranks to the political assistants at the levels of sector and region. From there the revenue was turned over to treasurers—accountants of the zones, who were responsible to the political assistant at their own level. The funds customarily were deposited in bank accounts in fictitious names. Through foreign branches the money could be used abroad to purchase weapons and other supplies that would eventually find their way back to the sectors or *douars*.[37] The people's assembly, of course, was not involved in this, but the political assistant and his auxiliary troops were very much interested and involved.

Some of the weapons were distributed to the irregular soldiers, but the auxiliaries, acting under the authority of the political assistants of the committee of three, were entrusted primarily with the task of supplying arms to the regular troops of the ALN.[38] They received the shipments from OPA cells in adjacent areas; in turn, they either transmitted the consignment to other OPA branches, or delivered it to the local units of the ALN. The network of OPA cells was indispensable to the FLN; in company with the committee of three, the people's assembly, the local FLN organization, and the organized irregulars in the *douars* and fractions, it served as an essential cog in a great revolutionary machine.

Since Algeria is primarily an agricultural country, the institutions of the revolution were necessarily adapted to a rural milieu. There are, however, several large cities, important both as industrial centers and as large concentrations of population. The FLN was not willing to concede control of these cities to the French. The party fully intended to cultivate the fertile nationalist soil to be found among the urban Muslim masses, and metropolitan OPA cells were created for this purpose. Here, too, the FLN pursued its policy of creating a shadow administration to undermine that of the French. Without taking physical occupancy the guerrillas used and extended their control over the population to remove all actual power from the hands of the French officials.

In an urban setting, however, the rebels were in a much more difficult and dangerous position. Here they were in direct opposition to a well-entrenched colonial administration, whose extensive modern equipment could be used to full effect. The ALN was unable to operate in these large urban areas where there were French mustering and supply centers. The OPA was therefore obliged to lean heavily on its irregulars, particularly the *fida'iyin*, who often operated alone.[39] These factors led to certain organizational modifications. The rebel organization in the Belcourt section of Algiers may be taken as an example.

In Belcourt the basic cell of the FLN was composed of one chief, one tax collector, and one or more propagandists. No attempt was made to separate the rebel governmental administration from the party organization, and there was a much greater decentralization of authority than was the case in the rural areas. The Belcourt OPA had a subsector, two districts, four subdistricts, eight groups, and sixteen cells. A terrorist commando was attached to each of the eight groups. At the district and subdistrict levels the OPA apparently enjoyed the services of European Communist advisers. Such, at least, was the situation in 1956. But the key officials were the Algerian chiefs of the commandos. These chiefs, who directed the FLN's urban terrorism, were political commissars, the equivalents of the rural political assistants in the committees

of three. At the group level the chief, the tax collector, and the propaganda official were joined by a liaison chief. His was an especially essential function because the Belcourt OPA operated in the area of the Halles Centrales, the metropolitan center for the distribution of vegetables, fish, and meat. This produce came from all parts of Algeria and from abroad, and the rebels made full use of this fact. In one way or another many truckers became messengers, and the Halles Centrales served as a hub of nationalist liaison.[40]

The entire organization of the OPA in Belcourt involved perhaps one hundred men. Other sections of Algiers presumably had similar organizations, although none was as important. In any case, Belcourt was an autonomous district responsible to the autonomous zone of Algiers. Geographically, the city should have been included in the fourth *wilaya* or province, but Algiers' status as an autonomous zone reflected the special situation of that city and the particular problems that the capital posed for the guerrillas. The insurgents created a different type of autonomous zone in the territories near the Tunisian and Moroccan frontiers, for example, the zone of Souk-Ahras. There the principal difficulty was one of logistics; weapons purchased abroad and destined for the interior had to pass through this zone. Apart from these few rural areas, however, the majority of the autonomous zones were located in the cities. Because of their unique problems, these zones were granted extensive authority in local matters. Decentralization was the insurgents' answer to these special problems in security.

An important additional difference between the rural and the urban cells of the OPA involved party relations with the trade unions, which were instruments of the FLN. This complicated subject deserves to be treated separately, but for the purposes of this chapter, suffice it to note that the rebels forced urban workers to pay more than the rural workers in taxes, party dues, and union dues. Only urban workers paid union dues. Finally, again for security reasons, the urban participants in the revolution had nothing resembling the rural people's assemblies.[41]

The FLN and the ALN, with their vast and complex chains of institutions at every level, worked steadily for three inter-related goals. For the purposes of the revolutionary struggle, they aimed to subjugate the Algerian masses to the FLN. Education, propaganda, terror, and organization were but the means to conquer the minds of men, and through these men to wear down the French will and power to resist. Second, in order to sustain the struggle, gifts had to be solicited, taxes and dues collected. Third, it was necessary psychologically to prepare the population for the war against France and for its role in the future independent state of Algeria.[42] Through the rural and urban cells of the OPA, the local fronts, and the trade unions, the nationalists succeeded in their attempt to gain the loyalty of hundreds of thousands of Muslims from every walk of life.

7 | *Some Motives for Support of the FLN-ALN*

Documented information on the rebel organization during the first twenty months of the revolution is hard to come by and difficult to use. By and large, it is necessary to rely on later accounts, particularly those of officers of the French Special Administrative Sections (SAS), which were created in 1956. By the end of 1957 these officers had drastically reduced the effectiveness of the OPA. In the process they had discovered a great deal about the rebel organization, and their reports are of great interest to scholars.[1] Another important source of information on the nationalists' institutions is the political platform of the Soummam Conference of August 20, 1956, which was printed in the contemporary issues of *El Moudjahid*. This document has been widely quoted in studies of the Algerian question.[2]

Another fascinating aspect of the revolution concerns the

motives of those who joined the nationalist movement. The information available on this subject is clear and almost unmanageably extensive. Many Algerians, of whom the majority are illiterate but excitable men, can hardly express themselves on the subject; asked why they joined the ALN, they often simply shrug their shoulders in reply.[3] Others joined because a brother, son, or cousin had done so, or because a relative had been a victim of French repression.[4] Still others claimed to have volunteered because Arabs and Berbers were not allowed to own hunting rifles while many Europeans legally possessed weapons of war. Resentment of this particular inequality was very strong among the Berbers.[5]

The right to own a rifle was hardly sufficient reason to risk life and limb in the cause of nationalism and independence. This legal discrimination, however, was one facet of the much larger issue of the Algerians' dignity and pride. The Kabyles gladly tell a folk story which illustrates this point.[6] A Kabyle man, according to this homily, owns a wife, a dog, and a gun. He can dispense with the wife and, if need be, do without the dog. But to have no gun is to have no honor. Western observers have been amazed by the sacrifices willingly made by Berbers in order to obtain a weapon.[7]

Pride, then, was an important element in the motivations of the rebels and their supporters. They resented their inferior legal, economic, and social status vis-à-vis the European settlers in their country.[8] Berber and Arab pride suffered constant insult in daily life. For example, with the exception of high-ranking Muslim officers in the administration or army, Algerians were excluded from certain beaches. The Hotel St. George, long the most prestigious in Algiers, was open to "clean" Arabs and Kabyles, but there was always some uncertainty or uneasiness. In certain restaurants the European customers ate in excellent style while those few Algerians who could afford to patronize those establishments were served at uncovered tables in the poorest locations.[9] There were a thousand and one small irritations of this kind, individually unimportant but collectively insulting.

The gratuitous insults were, of course, simply some of the secondary manifestations growing out of the major impulse that was, quite simply, the colonial situation. In Algeria a ninety per cent Muslim (Arab or Berber) majority was dominated by a ten per cent minority of a different religion and culture. In spite of sporadic efforts to the contrary, the French had failed to establish any institutional arrangements that offered hope of eventual removal or mitigation of the dominant-subordinate system that affected the social, political, and economic realities of the country. After more than a century of French rule in Algeria, the Europeans were still the favored conquerors and the Algerians the defeated subjects. The only alternative was for the Algerians to become Frenchmen. The chauvinistic implication of such a solution was the most severe insult to Muslims, who rightfully thought they had a valid culture and civilization of their own.

It was possible for an Algerian to be assimilated into the society of the European settlers. To do so, however, he was obliged to reject his own culture and to become a European in every sense. Even conversion to Christianity was not a guarantee of acceptance. An Arab pastor, the Reverend Mr. M. A. Boukhechem, was refused a room in an ordinary hotel in downtown Algiers just after World War II.[10] The occasional Algerian who earned a degree from a prestigious French university was not assured of social or economic success in his own country, although he could usually attain these in metropolitan France. The most liberal and enlightened French father, if he lived in Algeria, might oppose the marriage of his daughter to a youth of an alien culture, for the most natural and understandable reasons. A young Algerian, however Westernized, could hardly be expected to accept such a judgment; pride was again involved. Many of the ALN soldiers who were interviewed by European journalists cited broken romances of this kind as their reason for personal rebellion.[11]

As one might gather, there were very few mixed marriages in Algeria before the revolution, and those few were much criticized by the Muslims.[12]

Many of such unions as existed involved educated and Westernized Algerians, such as Ferhat Abbas. Habib Bourguiba, the president of Tunisia, married a French woman. But these *évolués*, as they were known, composed a tiny fraction of the Maghribi population. Furthermore, the Westernized North Africans were a troubled group, French by education but Muslim in their deep attachment to their families, which were generally not Westernized to the same extent. In addition, the colonial system created real problems for the educated Algerian *élites*. Their opportunities for careers in the professions, for example, were severely limited.[13] Many felt that, having educated them, France had abandoned them. The most Westernized Algerian naturally hesitated to take French citizenship, even when encouraged to do so. On the average, only thirty-five Muslims did so each year.[14] The majority of the *élite* clung to their culture and their inferior status. In their bitterness many saw Algerian autonomy as the only solution to their dilemma.[15] Autonomy and independence were only a step apart.

Economic factors also contributed to the unrest. The Algerian masses were poor, and as many as sixty per cent were officially classified as indigents. In comparison the Europeans enjoyed the standard bourgeois comforts, and many were wealthy. This contrast, although to a large extent a result of conditions beyond the control of the colonial administration, lent itself to exploitation by the nationalists. As in Kenya, where the Mau Mau revolted largely because of the land questions, the European *colons* of Algeria owned a percentage of the productive farm lands greater than their proportion to the population.[16] The Algerians lived on the less desirable properties, farming them in the traditional manner with consequently pitiful harvest.

While the benefits of French medicine allowed the birth

rate to soar to 2.8 per cent in 1954, the underdeveloped economy of Algeria provided little nourishment for these new mouths. Yearly increases in opportunities for education and employment did not keep pace with the rise in population.[17] By 1954, for example, only 302,000 Algerian children, 14.6 per cent of the total number, were in school. Ten years earlier, only 110,000 children, or 8 per cent, had been in school. Yet, in spite of increases in the percentage enrolled, too many had no opportunity to get an education. Even though the national economy was based on agriculture, only 112,000 men earned a living as agricultural laborers in 1954. This meant that they worked at least 180 days a year; wages, of course, were low. There were, however, an additional 400,000 to 1,000,000 unemployed agricultural laborers.[18]

In the industrial sector of the economy the situation was equally bleak. In 1954 there were 133,110 unemployed unskilled laborers and 172,000 employed. Of the latter, 84,000 were only partially employed. Among the Algerians who worked regularly were an additional 68,000 Arab or Berber skilled workers and minor functionaries, and some 12,000 technicians. Virtually no managerial positions were held by Algerians. While the Algerians accounted for 95 per cent of the unskilled and 68 per cent of the skilled laborers, they made up only 17.6 per cent of the technical and 7.2 per cent of the managerial ranks in the colonial economy.[19] Since most Arabs and Berbers had large families, they were, as a group, very poor. Many sought survival by emigrating to France, where work was more plentiful. This emigration was so significant that checks sent back to Algeria by Algerians working in France accounted for more money than was paid out in wages by the whole agricultural sector of the colonial economy.[20] Still, unemployment and underemployment were an enormous problem for the non-Europeans. The situation was not improving as the revolution broke out late in 1954.

To the thousands of Algerians to whom starvation was a

very real threat, the promises of the FLN offered hope and a sense of purpose. A poor farmer might well clutch at the chance of being given a piece of the European settlers' lands. Among an illiterate people, oral traditions had great influence. Many of these tales kept alive the bitter memories of the seizure of tribal lands by the early French colonists. The local Berbers were aware, for example, that the lush orange grove of an Alsatian settler near Camp du Maréchal stood on tribal lands confiscated after the revolt of 1870. Again, the colonial system was at the root of the problem, although Kabyles who lived in the area saw the situation in a much more personal way. Perhaps the failures of the past could be avenged by a successful rebellion in 1954. In the mountains of the Djurdjura many a Kabyle was ready and willing to take the gamble. As the French fumbled along through 1954 and 1955, and as the uniformed men of the National Liberation Army circulated through Kabylia with apparent impunity, the Kabyles' resolve grew firmer from day to day.

The ALN offered a salary to members of its regular units. Each *moudjahid* received ten new francs, about two dollars, per month. His wife received twenty francs a month from the FLN if she lived in a rural area, fifty if she lived in a city. There was an additional allocation of twenty francs per child left at home by the volunteers in the regular army.[21] In the face of widespread unemployment this monetary reward may have attracted some recruits. It seems unlikely that these wages lured many men to volunteer, however, since one franc (twenty cents) was enough to buy a loaf of bread at government-supported prices but not enough for a pack of cigarettes.

The payment of salaries certainly made it possible for some men temporarily to abandon their families. Most of these rebels, however, had already committed themselves to the nationalist cause for other reasons. The majority of the early volunteers in the ALN and the FLN were not from the ranks of the destitute; they came from all walks of life and their reasons for joining the rebel camp were as many as the men themselves. Many took great risks and received no recompense, for only the regular guerrillas were paid. The *mousseblin* and the *fida'iyin*, who remained in their own villages, for example, were expected to support themselves and to pay taxes and other dues to the revolutionary movement. The same, with a few exceptions, applied to the members of the OPA and other FLN organizations. Many of the revolutionary officials were unpaid.

Proletarian by any standard except those of an underdeveloped country, many who volunteered for early service in the ALN were middle class by the Muslim standards of Algeria. Among these "bourgeois" recruits, who, nonetheless, were proletarian in terms of their political creeds, were French-educated professional men. As a group these were people who had been educated in French schools and who had broken with their own society and traditions but, having done so, were deprived of self-fulfillment in the new world of a European colonial society.[22] Algerian intellectuals complained that, in effect, France had led them to the middle of a ford and abandoned them, had left them at the mercy of less generous colonial settlers. Above all else, these intellectuals were very much aware of their own subordinate position in the colonial society.

Among the intellectuals who joined the insurgents were some men who had previously served as the leaders or as the middle cadres of the MTLD. Not all the leaders of this party were well educated, however; in fact, most of the early recruits were poorly educated former MTLD-PPA-OS members who were usually blue-collar or minor white-collar workers. All of them, like the nine men of the CRUA, were disillusioned nationalists who had become convinced that a purely political struggle would never bring independence to Algeria.[23] According to Belkacem Krim, one of the historic leaders, the whole revolution was simply a reaction against "motionlessness."[24] Ben Bella argued in much the same way, condemning the nationalist parties as much as the colonial system.[25]

As the war progressed and as the French Forces of Order continued in their failure to eliminate the ALN, more and more Algerians joined the regular or irregular units of the revolution. Others simply showed their support by becoming dues-paying members of the FLN. Most of the masses contributed in one way or another. By the fall of 1955 the uniformed rebel units had repeatedly shown themselves in villages throughout the country. This display, together with effective propaganda, convinced and even exhilarated many of the ignorant peasants. The long-awaited deliverance from the rule of the infidel, it seemed, was at hand. To join the rebellion was a chance to reenact the epic deeds of heroic forefathers. The insurgency also answered the basic needs of the people for vendettas and *razzias*.[26] The young especially were aroused to action by stories of feats of rebel bravery and daring.[27] After the fall of 1955 the ALN always had more volunteers than it could use.[28] Materiel, not manpower, was what the rebels needed most.

In order not to lose the support of the young would-be soldiers, the ALN or FLN usually gave them a brief but intensive course in propaganda. Officers then directed the new converts into irregular units of *mousseblin* or *fida'iyin*. Here the political education of the young partisans continued while they learned military skills. The *fida'iyin* especially had many chances to show their devotion to the cause by risking their lives in acts of urban terrorism.[29] If lucky, they eventually graduated into regular units of the ALN. When needed as regular soldiers, they would be fully trained guerrillas of proven convictions and ability.

To a great extent the security of a revolutionary organization depends on secrecy. This did not pose a great difficulty as long as the ALN-FLN depended on units of bandits or nationalists sought by the French for political crimes. But once the door to the ALN was opened wider, as it was after November 1, 1954, secrecy became more difficult to maintain. As an increase in manpower was absolutely essential, the rebels recruited first from among the ranks of the preexisting nationalist proletarian party, the MTLD. Only later did they recruit from the population at large.[30] Still later the ALN-FLN sent young recruits to their sanctuaries in Tunisia and in Morocco. There they were able to train the men and keep them out of the hands of the various French institutions of counterrevolutionary education.[31]

During the first several weeks of revolution, to avoid denunciation and the possible destruction of whole bands, the ALN quickly learned to combine propaganda, recruiting procedures, and outright terrorism. Some French writers have gone as far as to say that many members of the OPA served the nationalists only out of fear.[32] There can be no doubt that terrorism paid the rebels handsome dividends. This was especially true because the French army also used terrorism; the Algerians were more willing to forgive their fellow Muslims for their terrorist tactics than the alien rulers.[33] Nevertheless, the FLN could not have built its organization by terror alone. Propaganda with a grain of truth accomplished wonders. Pierre Bourdieu's analysis is probably the best available:

> To deny that the revolutionary war had its basis in an objective situation is to refuse to admit its true character and to deny the real reason for its existence. To claim that the war was imposed upon the Algerian people by a handful of ringleaders who resorted to compulsion and trickery is to deny the fact that the struggle was able to draw on strong popular sentiment for its vital strength and purpose, a sentiment inspired by an objective situation.[34]

Rebel propaganda was naturally based on unpleasant incidents that had, in one way or another, affected most of the Algerian population. Zohra Driff, for example, became a nationalist when her brothers were arbitrarily killed after weeks of cruel treatment at the hands of the French soldiers in makeshift prisons.[35] Still another was unjustly arrested and no one looked after his animals while he was away. Other complaints were more fundamental or at least more generalized. There was a widespread feeling of having been fooled too long by French administrators and politicians. There was also, of course, the uneasy feeling of shame of being a colonial people and thus inferior to the European conquerors.[36]

During the early months of the revolution Algerian peasants and workers were generally afraid to join the activities of the FLN-ALN. While most were sympathetic to the rebels, they recalled at the same time the many unsuccessful revolts of the past with the high toll in lives and the consequent repressions. The latest and bloodiest of these prerevolutionary uprisings had occurred in 1945 and had led to the death of up to 50,000 non-Europeans.[37] The memory of that event died slowly. So when the CRUA called the people to arms in November 1954, the vast majority of Algerians adopted a wait-and-see attitude.[38] Though the Muslims' grievances were numerous, most Algerians preferred to take no action until it became evident in their eyes that the FLN had a chance of success.

The early confusion and ineptitude of the French army gave the National Liberation Front time to win over the doubtful peasants. Moreover, as Bourdieu pointed out, the French forces unwittingly helped the rebels by creating a feeling of identity among the Algerians:

[The] general attitude of suspicion, the methodical searching of cars whose passengers are wearing the veil or *chechia*, the identity checks, the arbitrary arrests, the daily vexatious measures (to cite only the minor ones) are all examples which illustrate the existence of racial discrimination and which force all members of the dominated caste to become aware of their opposition to the dominant caste and their solidarity with the other members of their own caste.[39]

Thus after the outbreak of the revolution, Arab and Berber grievances were multiplied by the severity of the ensuing countermeasures of the government. It was now evident to many that constitutional means were utterly inadequate to realize their goals.[40] Using a clever mixture of propaganda and terror, the rebels offered a possible solution.[41] The FLN-ALN took advantage of every useful facet of the colonial situation, thus giving the Algerian masses strong motivation to share in the coming struggle. Rebel propaganda agents exploited the uneasiness of the colonial proletariat, their feeling of being second class citizens; they reminded Muslims of their religious pride and their distaste for infidel rule; they insisted on pointing out the seemingly hopeless economic situation. At the same time, the nationalists allayed the Algerians' fear of defeat by showing off ALN soldiers in full uniform and by exaggerating the brilliance of rebel military activities. By mid-1955 the initial skepticism of the populace had been replaced by pride, faith, and a hope for the future.[42]

8 | France Takes the Initiative: Institutional Reforms in Algeria (1956)

SOME WRITERS, GENERALLY THOSE OF IMPERIALIST SYMPATHIES, have pointed out that organizations of approximately the same size launched the Algerian rebellions of both 1945 and 1954. Why was it, they asked, that, while five days sufficed to reestablish order in 1945, the second uprising was still gaining strength nearly two years after the outbreak of hostilities?[1] The October 1956 issue of the *Bulletin du Comité de l'Afrique Française,* a colonialist periodical, suggested an answer. The original French mistake, the editorialist remarked, lay in the failure to suppress the terrorism at its very inception in 1954. While the Algerian government hesitated, underestimating the strength of the opposition, the rebels bent every effort to develop, strengthen, and extend their movement. They achieved these goals, the author continued, mainly by finding important accomplices outside the French sphere,[2] in areas of the colony badly controlled by the colonial administration.[3]

Although there is some truth in this generalization, it ignores some important differences that existed between the two rebellions. The 1945 uprising, for example, was largely limited to the Sétif region: other portions of the country were affected to a lesser extent. The insurgency of 1954, though limited to the Aurès in terms of effective subversion, encompassed the whole Algerian territory in terms of organization. There were attempts at sabotage everywhere in Algeria. Moreover, the French troops of World War II were available for repression in 1945; nine years later, however, there were hardly enough men to garrison the country properly.

In the first months after the commencement of hostilities, the Forces of Order carried out their campaign against the guerrillas without any clear objective. They were not offcially at war, and more often than not they were required to serve as policemen, not soldiers. They had, of course, no police training. Their enemies were deadly shadows, experts in evasion. If in uniform, the rebels were hard to find and usually could not be captured. The relatively small regular guerrilla force was supported by a vast army of irregulars in civilian dress who could not be distinguished from peaceful members of the local population. The resulting confusion and indecision sharply reduced the effectiveness of the Forces of Order. The lack of strong political leadership in Paris only added to the dilemma.[4]

In due course French military policy in Algeria was officially defined. The soldiers received orders to guarantee the security of the frontiers, to protect all inhabitants, and to destroy the OPA and the *maquis* units of the ALN. These orders reveal in their simplicity the essential weakness of the French position. Shorn of initiative, the Forces of Order merely reacted to each thrust of the guerrillas. Precious time was lost as the French struggled to adapt their techniques and equipment to a new kind of conflict. Their only instructors were the veterans of the Indochinese War and their own hard-earned experience in Algeria. A more basic weakness of the colonial regime, indeed a weakness which proved fatal, was the lack of a doctrine for which the French troops would willingly fight.[5]

The failure of the French military establishment to develop an ideology resulted partially from the hesitation of the colonial administrative and political leadership. Having failed to interpret correctly the signs of danger before the outbreak,[6] the same civilian leaders were slow to grasp the gravity of the situation and to adopt a firm policy after November 1, 1954. Obstinately, the government sought to solve the Algerian problem by applying old remedies. Throughout 1955, for example, its counterrevolutionary efforts were based chiefly on an attempt to enforce the application of the 1947 Algerian Statute,[7] a program of reforms that would have dismantled the mixed communes and created new departments on the metropolitan model. The Arabs and the Berbers would have been granted a larger voice in the colonial government, and Algerian women would have gained the right to vote.[8] Even in 1947 the Statute had met with opposition from both settlers and Algerians;[9] the latter disliked the reforms because they did not go far enough, and the former opposed any change. Nevertheless, had it been applied in 1947, the Statute would undoubtedly have secured the allegiance of some Algerians.[10] In 1954, however, the government overlooked the fact that anticolonial forces, in Algeria as well as elsewhere in the non-Western world, are apt to increase their demands in geometric progression, especially once a revolution is in progress.[11] In effect, then, the resurrected program offered too little too late.

An overhaul of the ponderous administrative and political system in Algeria was essential. In 1954 this system combined features copied wholesale from the French model and exceptions designed to adapt the European method to local peculiarities. In theory Algeria was composed of three overseas French departments, but these were much larger than any of their metropolitan equivalents. It is interesting to note, too, that a customs inspection was required of all travelers between the French mainland and the Algerian provinces, despite the official view of Algeria as a part of France itself.[12] In this respect, at least, Algeria remained a foreign possession. The three North African departments had, in addition, a degree of local economic autonomy not found anywhere else in France. Finally, Algeria alone was administered by a governor-general, a kind of super-prefect without parallel elsewhere.[13]

A more fundamental difference between metropolitan France and her Algerian departments was mirrored in their respective electoral systems. In metropolitan France there was only one electoral college. In Algeria there were two, one for the Europeans, naturalized Algerians, and members of sixteen special and rather restrictive categories of Muslims, and a second for the bulk of the native population. In 1944 there were 450,000 voters in the first electoral college and 1,500,000 in the second. In the first college were approximately 32,000 Algerians who were members of the special categories of Muslims mentioned above, although between 50,000 and 60,000 might have qualified; many evidently preferred to remain members of the second college.[14] By 1947 the first college had 464,000 voters who were all considered French citizens (Europeans and naturalized Algerians) and 58,000 Muslims. Some 1,300,000 voters were registered on the rolls of the second college. During the same period, there were about 922,000 Europeans and 7,860,000 Muslims in Algeria.[15] Essentially, the first electoral college represented Europeans and the second the Muslims; as a result, one European vote was roughly equivalent to eight Algerian ballots. Since few Algerians became naturalized Frenchmen, the European domination of the first college was never threatened. The Algerians' political power was further weakened because native women were never granted suffrage.[16]

In 1954 each college elected sixty members to the Algerian Assembly, an institution that had no equivalent anywhere else in France, but sixty Algerian delegates and their sixty European colleagues met separately. Finally, to ensure European predominance in this dual body, the bylaws of the Algerian Assembly stipulated that the governor-general could require a two-thirds majority on any issue that came to a vote. Otherwise, an absolute majority within each half of the Assembly sufficed.[17] The balance of power was close yet definitely in favor of the settlers; thus the *colons* succeeded in their effort to resist practically all reforms affecting the political structure and the administration of Algeria.

European control was as well established on the municipal level as in the Algerian Assembly. Those communes that contained no settlers were ruled directly by the government through appointed *caïds*. Next came the so-called mixed communes in which the small minority of Europeans ruled themselves while most Algerians remained under the authority of the *caïds*. Third were the full communes, which were modeled on the metropolitan system but in which the minority of full French citizens were completely dominant over the Algerian majority. The existence of three types of communes added to the administrative confusion.

In 1945 there was some discussion in official circles of a plan of territorial reorganization. Communes, arrondissements, and departments, most of which had no connection with economic or social realities, were to be replaced with something more rational. Nothing came of this proposal, however, except a few experiments on the municipal level in some scattered areas where appointed *caïds* were replaced by elected municipal councils.[18] Although it did not affect their power in the least, the *colons* criticized even this limited experiment.[19]

After the outbreak of revolution all the planned reforms suddenly gained new importance. The rebellion was largely blamed on underadministration. It was agreed in 1954 and after that the departments of Algeria were simply too large, both territorially and in terms of population. As a result, the administration of the colony had lost contact with the Algerians. The problem was to wrest away from the nationalists those people over which the FLN-ALN had already gained control. Although this goal could not be achieved by purely military means, soldiers were to serve in place of civilian administrators who were not available.

From the very start French army officers were deeply involved in the administrative reorganization of Algeria that was hastily ordered after the outbreak of revolution. The system of Special Administrative Sections (SAS), for example, was created after a model set up by a dozen French officers who were sent into the Aurès during the spring of 1955. These military men had previous experience as administrators in North Africa; some had served as soldier-administrators in the Moroccan Native Affairs Department, while the others were recruited from a similar institution that controlled the indigenous peoples of the Algerian Sahara. Their mission in 1955 was to do whatever might be necessary to gain the confidence of the Shawia, the people of the Aurès.[20]

During the first year of the insurgency a lack of intelligence badly hampered the French army in its efforts to combat the ALN. Such information, the soldiers felt, should have been furnished by the civil administration. But in the Aurès, as in many other underadministered rural areas, the colonial government had no contacts with the population, hence no intelligence to communicate to the army. The resulting recriminations led many soldiers to bitterness against their own government and, more constructively, to seek alternate solutions to the problem.[21] The military forces, for example, could take over the administration of the country, thereby obtaining the desired contacts and intelligence.

In 1955 the officers of the SAS were assigned two tasks. First, they were to reestablish contact between the government and the people. To this end they were to get to know the people in their charge whom they would organize socially, politically, and economically. They were to seek out leaders who might serve France and, of course, to watch closely those who might intrigue with the nationalists. Second, they were to gather intelligence; relevant information might be free or bought. They were to guard against being deceived by double agents or by informants seeking personal vengeance. The informants were to be protected from any publicity that might make them targets for rebel reprisals. Finally, any important information was to be communicated at once to the officers' military superiors.[22] The work of the twelve officers in the Aurès had no appreciable effect until mid-1956, when colonial offcials decided to establish as many SAS centers as possible. By the end of that year 452 such centers had been created, of which 250 were in operation.[23]

Until the idea of the SAS system was more fully developed, older institutions were used to speed reforms in Algeria. One such institution was that of the Rural Administrative Sections (SAR). According to Governor-General Soustelle, who replaced Léonard at the end of January 1955, 200 SAR centers had been created before he took office. By the middle of the same year Soustelle had added 50 new units.[24] SAR units were concerned with economic development only. An official decree of September 26, 1955, established the SAS system, which was designed to speed economic, political, and administrative reorganization at the municipal level.[25] The SAS system was clearly a more useful tool for pacification, and it subsequently spread to all threatened regions.

While the SAS officials were soldiers, usually captains or

lieutenants, their duties became progressively less military and more administrative. They performed some military tasks, but their primary function was to replace civilian officials who had fled Algeria after the events of November 1954. Many other officers filled new positions created during the revolution in an attempt to meet the problem of under-administration.

During 1956 French policy in Algeria continued unchanged and was based on the application of the Algerian Statute of 1947. Lacoste, the successor of Léonard and Soustelle, pursued the struggle to regain control over the disaffected Algerians. As resident-minister, he took over the duties of the defunct office of governor-general by decree on February 15, 1956. The next day another decree transferred responsibility for Algerian affairs from the Interior Ministry to the Office of the President of the Council of Ministers. A month later the reform program was given teeth when the Assembly of Deputies in Paris voted special powers for the government of Algeria.[26] These powers permitted the resident-minister to suspend laws as he saw fit and to rule by decree. Thereafter a series of promulgations began to change the structure of the whole country.

An early decree sought to attract more Arabs and Berbers into government service, both in the administration and in the state-controlled industries. On March 17, 1956, the government annouced that Algerians would be recruited on a contractual basis for government work. Hitherto, in applying for official positions very few Algerians had succeeded in competition with the better educated Europeans.[27] The government hoped to weaken the rebel cause by associating as many Arabs and Berbers as possible with the French regime. Progress toward this goal was slow, nevertheless, especially at the highest echelons. In 1955, for example, there were eighteen prefects in Algeria, all European; three years later there were nineteen prefects, two of them non-European. Although certain diplomas were still required of the holders of some offices, on November 16, 1956, it was decided that tenure might in some instances replace the diplomas. Thus Algerian offcials of the second or even the third highest classification might be assigned to positions of the first rank. The first two North African prefects were appointed soon thereafter, but, as new appointees, they were sent to recently created posts while their European colleagues were moved to better positions. Consequently, Algerian officials often felt they had been sent into exile.[28] With change, then, arose some new problems. In any case, however, it was clearly impossible to continue to relegate indigenous civil servants to auxiliary functions and expect to defeat the FLN.[29]

Those Arabs and Berbers who served in the Algerian government naturally tended to support the French in their struggle with the guerrillas. The new employment policy also constituted a three-pronged attack on the situation of the Muslims in Algeria. First, by increasing the number of Algerian civil servants, the government not only spread its influence but took a step forward in the struggle against the low income and widespread unemployment that plagued the natives. Nor was it simply a matter of creating new jobs. The second effort was thus to raise Algerian employees to managerial and executive positions, long the preserve of the Europeans.[30] Third, the legal minimum wage for agricultural workers was raised. Algeria had been previously divided into three zones, each of which had its own salary scale. In Zone I salaries were raised by 180 to 525 francs per day; in Zones II and III the raises brought the minimum wages up to 480 and to 440 francs respectively.[31] (Although the percentage increases were great, the new daily wages were still less than one dollar in the second and third zones, and the work, of course, was seasonal.[32]) Other parallel reform measures were the reorganization of free medical assistance, which had been disrupted by the rebellion, and the abolition of sales taxes on certain foods, sugar for example.[33]

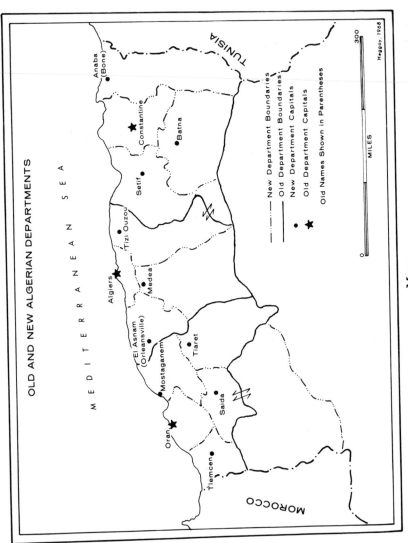

OLD AND NEW ALGERIAN DEPARTMENTS

MEDITERRANEAN SEA

TUNISIA

MOROCCO

Anaba (Bone)

Constantine

Batna

Setif

Tizi Ouzou

Algiers

Medea

El Asnam (Orleansville)

Mostaganem

Tiaret

Saida

Oran

Tlemcen

——·—— New Department Boundaries
·········· Old Department Boundaries
● New Department Capitals
★ Old Department Capitals
( ) Old Names Shown in Parentheses

0   MILES   300

Heggoy, 1968

MAP 5

Perhaps the most important changes were the territorial reorganization ordered on June 28, 1956, and the final abolition of the *communes mixtes* on the following day.[34] In theory these mixed communes, hated by the Algerians, had been eliminated in 1947; they survived, nonetheless, and in 1956 there were still writers willing to defend them.[35] In any case, there now appeared on the map of Algeria 12 departments carved out of the original three. A department was the unit over which a prefect's authority extended. Subprefects directed the arrondissements, of which there were 20 at the end of 1955 and 71 a year later. Finally, 333 full communes *(communes de pleine exercise)* and 79 mixed communes disappeared to be replaced by 261 full communes and 1,200 common law communes. Because the two-college system was abandoned at the municipal level, except in the 261 full communes, Algerians theoretically gained a great deal more control over their own destiny. But the two-college system remained at the higher levels.[36] Thus the rebels could still claim that the Arabs and Berbers continued to be only second class citizens. At the lower level the effect of the new unified college was greatly weakened when the FLN-ALN applied terror to prevent the Algerians from cooperating with the French regime.

On paper the new reforms had many virtues. According to law each of the 1,200 common law communes was to elect a mayor or special delegates as soon as possible. Hundreds of SAS units were established to facilitate these elections and the installation of a new administrative system that would bring the government closer to its constituents. A start was made toward assuaging the widespread unemployment and poverty, and toward rectifying the underadministration of the interior. By the time these measures were drawn up and executed, however, a majority of the Algerians had swung into the nationalist camp. While most refrained from open rebellion, their sympathies clearly lay on the side of their guerrilla compatriots. Members of the ALN-FLN were no longer regarded as *fellagha* (outlaws) by the common people, who now spoke of the rebels in neutral or friendly terms.

According to Germaine Tillion, many family chiefs, members of the *jama'ah* (local assemblies), spoke of the guerrillas as outlaws until April 1955. Then the term *hodjadj*, plural for *hadj* (a pilgrim to Mecca), became more common. The new title was not only one of respect but also had religious meaning: the rebels were engaged in a holy war. Eventually terms meaning "those of the mountains" and "ours" were applied to nationalists,[37] a fact that may reflect the FLN's desire to avoid religious terms. The evolution of this terminology clearly points to a swing in Algerian opinion toward support of the nationalist movement by the spring of 1956. In other words, the rebels had achieved a spectacular political success before the French were able to take steps to draw many Algerians away from their nationalist sympathies.[38] On March 16, 1956, however, when special powers were granted to permit the Algerian government to rule by decree, the French were ready to take the initiative.

previous occasions. Until June 1955, for example, there had been no official recognition of the state of war in Algeria. Instead, politicians had talked vaguely of a vast police action. As a result, captured nationalists were tried in the civilian courts of the French judicial system. In June 1955, however, the government acceded to a demand by the *colons* that military tribunals be created to remove the guerrilla prisoners from the dockets of the overcrowded regular courts. The government maintained a legal fiction, nevertheless, by insisting that the rebels were not to be treated as prisoners of war and that the decisions of the military courts should be reviewed by civilian judges.[2]

Gradually but relentlessly the leading European activists in Algeria prodded the French authorities toward harsher policies with respect to the nationalist prisoners. The *colon* street demonstrations of February 1956 were but the most spectacular in a series of events designed to intimidate the Paris administration. Activists also demanded that the rebels be fought and prosecuted with more vigor, that the military be given more authority. The *colons,* whose predecessors had fought against military rule in Algeria, were faced with special conditions created by the insurgency, and they were now willing to have military administration at least for the Algerians at large. In June 1956 the government capitulated again. Although less than three months earlier a majority in the Chamber of Deputies had declared itself opposed in principle to capital judgments for Algerian prisoners, the government allowed Hamida Zabana and Abdelkader Ferradj to be shot.[3]

Meanwhile the FLN-ALN continued to propagate their doctrines and to gain new converts. They took full advantage of the inevitable lapse of time between the formation of French policy and its application. After the creation of the military tribunals, for example, an entire year passed before the execution of the first guerrilla prisoners. The first SAS officers were sent into the Aurès in the spring of 1955, but another year passed before the institution enjoyed any degree of success. During 1955 and 1956 almost every advantage achieved by the colonial forces was countered by a nationalist success. The creation of military tribunals in June 1955 was followed by a business strike ordered by the FLN; most Algerian storekeepers participated. Difficulties on the civilian front increased as military necessities forced the restriction of movement by ordinary citizens. Although elected Algerian officials protested these measures, such restrictions only further united the non-Europeans against the French.

In the fall of 1955, on the day of the formal inception of the SAS system, all the Arab and Berber representatives in the Algerian Assembly walked out in protest against integrationist policies designed to bring Algeria into a closer union with France.[4] The "sixty-one," as these representatives were called, dared to speak of "the Algerian national idea." Although there were many administrative creatures or *"beni-oui-oui's"* among them and although many of these men held no sympathy for the FLN, their support for a basically nationalistic concept must be seen as a sign of rebel influence among these politicians. Then in December of 1955 all the members of the UDMA (Union Démocratique du Manifeste Algérien) who had been elected to any office resigned their positions. Simultaneously, these followers of Ferhat Abbas declared themselves in favor of the creation of an Algerian democratic and social republic.[5] The program of this hitherto moderate organization was now barely distinguishable from that of the radical FLN. This change in emphasis reflected the fact that the FLN was winning over the educated Algerian *élites* even as the French army was depriving the ALN of the military initiative.

In the realm of international diplomacy the rebels made an important breakthrough even before they were forced to take a purely defensive attitude in their own country. In September 1955 the General Assembly of the United Nations decided, by a slim margin of one vote, to put the Algerian question on its agenda.[6] The Assembly thus voted against France, which had maintained that, since Algeria was legally a part of France, the Algerian conflict was an internal matter over which the UN had no jurisdiction. Despite the reverse they suffered on the Algerian question, leaders of the French government took firm steps to meet the challenge at hand: martial law was imposed on most of Algeria, and then the special powers were voted for the resident-minister in March 1956. Events were forcing the French to abandon the euphemistic description of their military efforts in Algeria as a police action.

Resident-Minister Lacoste did not wait long to use the new powers granted him by the Deputies in Paris. After signing various decrees designed to improve the living conditions of Algerians, he dissolved the Algerian Assembly on April 11.[7] He and his advisers wished to enact a reform program quickly so as to win popular support, especially among Arabs and Berbers. But the dissolution was, in a way, an admission of failure. A primary objective of the FLN was the destruction of the existing political institutions. By dissolving the Assembly the government thus admitted that it could not work with Algerian politicians and that it would have to find more docile representatives. The nationalists had already undermined another colonial institution. Late in 1955 the rebels had threatened to punish any Algerian who brought a complaint to any French court. The order had reduced the number of cases to such an extent that French judges were only semi-employed.[8]

The economic reforms that Resident-Minister Lacoste decreed under his special powers after March 1956 presented a different problem to the FLN. The new laws increased the minimum wages for the Algerians, and provided that they should have better opportunities to obtain higher paid jobs and even executive positions in government and industry. The FLN thus found its strength and its propaganda challenged by these new laws that might have satisfied many of its lukewarm supporters. Reacting violently, the Front announced that any peasant who profited from the agrarian reforms would be considered an enemy of the people. Those Algerians who might have been tempted to accept positions in the newly created municipalities were threatened with death.[9]

From the French point of view, then, it became more essential than ever to reduce the FLN-ALN to inactivity. To this end more troops were assigned to Algeria; by the end of April 1956 their numbers reached 400,000.[10] This infusion of military might, together with the special powers voted in the previous month and the subsequent measures of reform, began to swing the balance in favor of the colonial power. Yet the nationalists were to score another great political coup during the next month.

On April 22 Ferhat Abbas, Abderahman Kiouane, Ahmed Francis, and Tawfik el Madani officially rallied to the FLN in Cairo. Madani was one of the best known religious leaders in Algeria, a high official in the Ulama Association. The other three were prerevolutionary leaders in what had been the moderate nationalist groups. Ferhat Abbas himself was virtually peerless. Only Messali Hadj had as good a claim to the title of father of Algerian nationalism. But by 1956 Messali Hadj had been largely discredited by the younger leaders in his own party who had broken away to form the CRUA and then the FLN. Ferhat Abbas, as leader of a broader and less dogmatic party, had not suffered such a loss of prestige. His public conversion to the Front was thus an important success for the men who had started the Algerian Revolution; it strengthened their claim to be sole spokesmen of Algerian nationalism. Now only Messali Hadj and some of his old guard were still left outside the FLN.

In the rest of North Africa the political climate seemed to favor the nationalists. First Morocco[11] and then Tunisia[12] were granted independence. The latter had used the granting of Moroccan sovereignty to bolster its own claims to freedom. The Algerian nationalists were quick to follow suit. After Tunisia, with the blessing of France, began to rule itself late in March, 1956, the FLN propagandists pointed to what they called an illogical situation. With both the eastern and western wings of North Africa now free, why should the central Maghrib alone be kept in bondage?

French colonialists had been aware of the possible repercussions of Moroccan and Tunisian independence. Not only would the FLN gain a propaganda advantage, but they would most likely gain bases on foreign soil from which the ALN might safely mount operations against the Forces of Order in Algeria. In addition, the Front would now have supply routes both safer and more convenient than those going through Libya into the Sahara south of Constantine province. The logic of the *colons* and imperialists was not sufficient, however, to prevent the granting of independence to the two nations. More practical considerations forced the hand of the French—the country was not prepared to fight in Morocco and Tunisia while she was deploying close to 500,000 troops in Algeria. Since each of the protectorates had its own national liberation army poised for action, there was a real danger of enlarging the military operations in North Africa.[13] This possibility was avoided by French recognition of the independence of the eastern and western Maghrib.

The Algerian rebels were of the opinion that their independence would follow that of Tunisia and Morocco. The government refused to consider this notion, however, and remained steadfast in its legal claim that Algeria constituted part of France itself. It was also obliged to take into account the wishes of more than one million Europeans who lived in Algeria. The sentiments of the army also constituted a crucial factor. The French soldiers, especially the professionals, reacted in a more complex and emotional manner than the political leaders. Their army, they felt, had been defeated in Indochina because the civilian leaders in Paris had stabbed it in the back.[14] French military honor required a success to vindicate the earlier failure. No compromise would be made with the FLN-ALN. Indeed, a French solution to the Algerian question would have to be imposed.

By mid-1956 events in Algeria appeared to point to a solution that would satisfy the soldiers and veterans. This impression was reinforced during the fall of that year when the army seized the *Athos,* a ship that had taken on a cargo of weapons and ammunition in Alexandria. Although the capture occurred just outside Moroccan territorial waters, these supplies were obviously destined for the ALN.[15] Soon thereafter, on October 26, Ben Bella and four important nationalists were arrested in Algiers. All four were aboard a plane owned by the Sultan of Morocco. This plane, captained by a French pilot, made an unscheduled landing in Algiers, where soldiers, acting without prior authorization from the Prime Minister, seized the four leaders. The pilot had been talked out of his flight plan by military authorities in Algeria. The government in Paris was thus presented with a *fait accompli,* as well as some embarrassing prisoners and diplomatic questions.[16]

France paid dearly for these two successes. While insisting that the Algerian question was an internal problem, she had reached into international waters and air space to combat her enemies. The entire French position in this matter was thus greatly undermined, and the FLN gained sympathy and prestige even while it lost a shipment of weapons and some vital chiefs.

These incidents also made it more evident than ever that the nationalists enjoyed important foreign support. The Front now scored another important propaganda success when the French compounded their error by becoming involved in the Suez crisis. By joining in an expedition against Egypt the French army hoped to strike at the source of the Algerian rebels' chief supply of arms. In addition, the FLN-ALN might have suffered an irreparable loss of prestige if Egypt, their most important ally, had been decisively beaten.[17] Such a loss might well have disillusioned the guerrillas and discouraged them in their dreams of national independence. Disaster ensued for France and her allies, however, when the United States and the Soviet Union joined in a common effort to exert diplomatic pressure on the aggressors. When the European armies were obliged to leave Egypt, Nasser found his prestige greatly enhanced. His North African supporters shared in his glory. In the long run, the FLN-ALN lost its military struggle but won the political war which the CRUA started in 1954. Hitherto uncommitted Algerians joined the nationalists and shed their fear of French power. Among the masses the FLN was winnning the psychological struggle.

These nationalist propaganda successes were paralleled by a greater intensity of subversion. Late in 1956 the rebels managed to commit approximately 3,900 subversive acts in one month, a high point for the war.[18] Thereafter the number dropped gradually to less than 1,200 acts during February 1958. In the same period rebel military strength continued to grow, although much of it was based on foreign soil and was therefore not very useful for actual combat in Algeria itself. The ALN probably reached its maximum power early in 1958, and then declined during the balance of the war. These gains, however, were largely offset by the enormous build-up of French manpower. As a result, nationalist subversion attained its greatest intensity in late 1956, rather than at the climax of the rebels' strength.

Also in 1956 the guerrillas moved from success to success on the international scene. Largely because of events within Algeria, the Front achieved one of its primary goals, to attract international attention to the Algerian problem. The capture of the *Athos* and the arrest of Ben Bella helped further to bring the entire struggle to the attention of the international press and foreign governments. Other important factors were the rallying to the Front of such popular and respected middle-class politicians as Ferhat Abbas, and the independence of Morocco and Tunisia.

These diplomatic advances, strangely enough, appear to have been balanced by a simultaneous weakening of the Front's internal strength. While the nationalists had clung to the initiative for the first two years of the rebellion, they were losing their momentum by 1956. With the installation of Robert Lacoste at the Gouvernement Général in Algiers, the French took on a new decisiveness and began to enact the reform program that slowly gave France the advantage over the FLN. Clearly the turning point came when the Chamber of Deputies granted special powers to the resident-minister in Algiers.[19] The rebels naturally examined the policies of the Lacoste administration with great care in order to counteract each new thrust as effectively as possible. As the SAS system became alarmingly successful, its officers became the targets for rebel bullets. In the summer of 1956 the FLN called a leadership conference in the Soummam valley. Its purpose was evidently to resolve internal differences, and also to devise new programs and propaganda to undermine the reforms offered to the Algerians by the new colonial administration.

10 | The Soummam Congress

WHEN THE ALGERIAN NATIONALISTS FIRST BEGAN THEIR STRUG-
gle against the colonial regime, they defined their objectives
only in vague and general terms. Their primary goal was independence, of course, and they declared their intention to
achieve it by defeating the French army. But by design or oversight, the men of the CRUA did not elaborate on the program
that they hastily produced soon after the November outbreak.[1] During the next twenty-two months there arose a
swelling demand for a more carefully worded and detailed
platform. The soldiers of the ALN, among others, asked about
the reasons behind the struggle. Subordinate political officials
of the FLN requested that the purpose of the insurgency be
defined.[2] Last but not least, the mounting strength of the
French pointed up the obvious need for a detailed nationalist
manifesto.[3] The revolutionary leaders finally responded. On

August 20, 1956, most of the commanders who had not sought political asylum abroad gathered near Akbou in the Soummam valley.[4]

Only internal leaders met at the Soummam Congress.[5] The external chieftains, including Ben Bella, Boudiaf, and Khider, had been informed that the meeting was to take place on July 31. Plans changed, however, and while a delegation of exiled nationalists were waiting in Tripoli for final confirmation of the new date, the meeting was held on August 20. By design or because of serious military pressure created by numerous French "seek and destroy" operations throughout the country, word to enter Algeria never reached the external representatives in Tripoli.

From the very beginning of the revolution, there had been two conflicting theories within the ALN-FLN. One group insisted that the vital struggle must be waged within Algeria and that consequently the external delegation could only serve to contribute diplomatic and logistic support. The opposing faction, led by Ben Bella, was of a different opinion. As early as the spring of 1954 these men had planned the creation of an external group that would, while operating from friendly foreign territory, constitute the real directive body of the national revolution. Even in the earliest days of the struggle, then, the ranks of the "historic chiefs" were split between adherents to the external theory and the internal clique headed by Belkacem Krim and Ramdane Abane.[6]

From reports of the Soummam Congress, and from documents taken later from the captive Ben Bella, French and European observers learned of the struggle between the interior and exterior factions of the ALN-FLN.[7] Whether by accident or by intent, the absence of the exiled leaders from the meeting in the Soummam valley allowed the internal commanders to seize direction of the war. This turn of events did much to nullify the effect of the French seizure of Ben Bella, Boudiaf, Khider, Ait Ahmed, and Lacheraf from a Moroccan airplane on October 22, two months after the meeting.[8] As all of these men were leaders in exile, the leadership of the internal delegation continued unweakened by this act of international brigandage.[9] Thus the factional split might well have weakened the nationalist camp, but it had no such discernible effect. In fact, the nationalist movement continued to grow after the Soummam Congress, and this growth was largely due to decisions taken at the Congress itself.

The seizure of the revolutionary apparatus by the internal leaders can also be viewed as a victory of the Berber Kabyles over their Arab corevolutionaries. Krim and Abane, both Kabyles, rose to the very apex of power at the expense of the Arab Ben Bella. This change was reinforced by the arrest of the latter. In a sense, the Kabyles were taking their revenge for the Arab take-over of the OS in 1949.[10] But although the Soummam Congress revealed to all the long-hidden rivalry between these two factions, its chief importance lies entirely elsewhere.

The nationalist guerrillas and their followers in the population at large gained new confidence from the fact that the Congress met within Algeria despite the overwhelming military strength of the French forces. Also, the delegates at the Congress constituted the first meeting of the CNRA (*Conseil National de la Révolution Algérienne* or National Council of the Algerian Revolution). This was no mean achievement for a movement that claimed to represent a nation but had not yet created a government or even a shadow cabinet. The CNRA next met in Cairo a year later but accomplished practically nothing because of political in-fighting. In December 1959 the Council met in Tripoli, where it created a provisional constitution for Algeria and gave official status to the FLN party. It was the Soummam Congress itself, however, that established the first revolutionary institutions for Algeria.

Of first importance was the creation of the CCE (*Comité de Coordination et d'Exécution* or Executive and Coordinating

Committee), the executive body that henceforth directed the
entire movement between full meetings of the CNRA.[11] The
Congress also gave official recognition to the political and
military organizations that had evolved during nearly two
years of insurgency (see chapter 6). The platform drawn up
by the Soummam delegates served as the nationalists' most
effective source of propaganda for the balance of the revolution.[12] It also outlined the use of terrorism, which quickly led
to the development of the Battle of Algiers, an important
chapter in the history of the war.

That the Soummam Congress met in Algeria was in itself
useful to the rebel propaganda. They had, in fact, managed to
hold a meeting in spite of the tremendous counterinsurgency
effort undertaken by the French, who must therefore have
been weak or incompetent. According to some observers the
meeting represented an attempt to pass into another phase of
revolution, to progress from secret to open action. Revolutionary doctrine declared that this was the moment for the
rebels to conquer a base from which "legal" authority had
been completely expelled. They failed to do so, however, and
French writers consequently tried to turn this fact to their
advantage. Authors such as Michel Déon argued that the FLN
had tried to make the world believe that the Soummam
Congress had taken place on a nationalist base of liberated
territory; when this deception failed, claimed Déon, the nationalists then created the provisional government in Cairo.[13]
Since both sides were using the issue for purposes of propaganda, it is difficult to arrive at an impartial conclusion.

The French Psychological Action Service may have had
better luck in its attempts to exploit the split between the internal and external leadership of the rebel camp. After 1956,
for example, the Service published numerous tracts exposing
the life of ease led by *émigré* leaders in Cairo and elsewhere.[14]
It is again difficult to assess the effectiveness of these tracts. It
is undoubtedly true that the soldiers of the ALN, who risked

their lives daily, felt little loyalty to those leaders who had taken refuge abroad. There were more immediate commanders, however, who shared the dangerous life of the guerrillas within Algeria, and it was these leaders who in fact controlled the revolutionary movement after the Soummam Congress. There can be little doubt that the ALN troops and the supporting cast of FLN officials knew this. The French propagandists nevertheless bent every effort to exploit and deepen the rift between the Cairo group and the internal leadership, with some success, it seems. An incident concerning the financial affairs of Ferhat Abbas is one example of their effectiveness. Abbas had allegedly received a gift of twenty-five million francs from an American named Kemal, to be used to aid Algerians who were suffering as a result of the war. Ben Bella accused him of pocketing the gift, and the Front asked Abbas to account for the funds.[15] It must be admitted, however, that both men were members of the external delegation. On the whole, the nationalists did a rather good job of suppressing the divisions within their ranks during the war.

The Soummam platform itself made important points with regard to this internal conflict and to propaganda. The question of a split was not openly presented; indeed, the document contained only the most general self-criticism on this score. The statement chided the movement for a tendency toward regionalism and also reproached certain unidentified leaders for their abuse of power. Throughout its platform the Congress stressed the collegial nature of the nationalist leadership. In the same vein the delegates emphasized the need to convey the impression that a unified command existed for all of Algeria.[16] This command, however, was not defined.

The subject of propaganda, on the other hand, was discussed at some length.[17] After an analysis of the French efforts in this field, in which the French statements were termed false and designed to depersonalize the Algerian people, the manifesto explained in detail how the ALN-FLN was to combat the French propaganda. First, every precaution should be taken to ensure the safety of guerrilla refuges, in order to reduce the number of prisoners taken by the French. Nothing should be done in these refuges that might attract the attention of the enemy. Second, responsible nationalist leaders should always be on hand when the Forces of Order ravaged a community. These rebel cadres should nurse and comfort the suffering population, interpret those depredations to the inhabitants, and above all maintain the political presence of the Front among the local citizens even under the most adverse conditions. In short, the rebel cadres had to show the Algerian people that the ALN was their army, an army fighting to reconquer their lost dignity and national independence.

A third objective of the insurgents' propaganda was to contradict the military picture painted by the French publicists. The press service and political commissars of the FLN were instructed to publicize the sacrifices made by the troops of the ALN. By a constant insistence on the courage and revolutionary fervor of the rebel soldiers, the nationalist strategists hoped to fortify the morale of the masses. The speakers at the Congress and the authors of the platform were confident of the high prestige enjoyed by the nationalist combatants. In the fall of 1956 their evaluation was probably correct (see chapter 7). In any case, the members of the FLN-ALN would need to preserve and enlarge this esteem.[18]

In order to nurture popular support for their movement, the rebel propagandists should always be ready to attack the claims of the French. They should, for example, challenge the "myth" that the maintenance of French prestige in the world required the continued occupation of Algeria. On another front they should struggle to counteract the repressive measures, enforced by the French army, that were seriously affecting the Algerian population in many ways. The Soummam platform depicted these restrictions as an attempt to wear down the Arab and the Berber peoples and thereby force them to abandon their hostility to the colonial regime. Most important, all the counterpropaganda of the nationalists was to be based on truth. Since the facts would ultimately be revealed for all to see, it was best to avoid undue optimism and to be completely candid about the hard struggle to come. This insistence on truth was itself propaganda, as was the entire platform. The disproportionate military advantage of the French forced this reliance on propaganda, a fact the rebels themselves recognized.[19]

The platform nevertheless included much wider aims as well. The insurgents received in the Soummam program their first sophisticated political blueprint, something the movement had hitherto lacked. Its authors outlined revolutionary institutions, tactics, strategy, and objectives.[20] Despite many deficiencies the document went a long way toward defining all the nationalists' policies and doctrines. Generally, it called for a weakening of the Forces of Order sufficient to prevent a French military victory. An additional objective was the destruction of the colonial economy from within by sabotage, in order to disrupt the normal administration of the country. France itself should be subverted economically and socially so as to prevent a vigorous pursuit of the war in Algeria. Politically, the French government should be completely isolated from the Algerian people it claimed to control, and a campaign should be undertaken to ostracize it from the international community. Finally, the platform declared that the uprising should be so directed as to adhere to all the principles of international law. To this end it foresaw the creation of a nationalist government that would gain recognition in the world at large, through its scrupulous observation of international principles of war and the exercise of normal administrative procedures in the liberated zones.[21]

Other portions of this program outlined long-range objectives and incidentally gave evidence of a growing awareness of Algerian history. The most important statements dealt with the indivisibility of Algeria, her independence, the liberation of all political prisoners, and the recognition of the FLN as the only legitimate representative of the Algerian people. The rebels' insistence on the unity of Algeria was a natural reaction to a proposal of partition that found expression in certain segments of the French press. These publications argued that the Sahara province, with its wealth of untapped resources, should be removed from the jurisdiction of the government in Algiers to avoid any risk of its loss by a possible rebel victory. The Front replied by an appeal to history, claiming that it would not repeat the error of Abd-el-Quadir, who in 1837 had permitted the partition of Algeria. This reference to history was all-important as it began a definition of Algerian nationalism. A people who have a common history also have a common present and future, and probably constitute a nation state. In any case, the Soummam delegates flatly demanded the complete independence of Algeria as it currently existed, with sovereignty in every domain of government. As the sole representative of the people, the FLN would naturally take control of the newly sovereign nation. It would, for example, assume responsibility for and guarantee any armistice in the name of the Algerian population.

The platform did not lay down any conditions for a possible future armistice, although it did look forward to eventual peace negotiations. In this context it insisted again on one condition in particular: only the FLN must represent Algeria. The French government would have no right to interfere in the internal affairs of the country. Discussions would take place only on the basis of military and diplomatic independence. Finally, certain points would be stressed in the initial phase of negotiations. These specific demands called for, among other things, the recognition of Algerian frontiers as they existed in 1956, including the Sahara. The rights of the European minority would be defined. Europeans might, for example, opt for Algerian citizenship, but no one would be permitted to maintain a dual citizenship. The title to all property owned by Europeans would be carefully investigated. Procedures would be established for the eventual transfer of administrative powers from the colonial regime to the FLN. Assuming that the new Algeria would retain certain economic, social, and cultural ties with France, the platform declared that the nature of this collaboration should be outlined in the first stages of any negotiations.

Looking farther into the future, the Soummam delegates foresaw a second phase in the discussions, at which time a freely elected government would replace the Front as the representative of the country. Early in this last stage, or perhaps sooner, the FLN would cultivate Algeria's ties with Morocco and Tunisia, in order to avoid an uprising by the chauvinistic element within the national movement.[22]

With the publication of the Soummam platform, the stark contrast between the goals of the rebels and those of France was revealed more clearly than ever. The colonial administration sought to nullify the popular appeal of the nationalist movement by presenting a broad program of political and economic reforms. From 1954 on, and even more boldly in 1956, the insurgents demanded a complete break with the past and a new independent life for their nation.

In the period between the outbreak of insurgency and the Soummam Congress the moderate nationalists had continued to seek change within the framework of the colonial situation. But their proposals rarely coincided with the goals of an administration that was dominated by the *colons*. Even Ferhat Abbas, long before he decided to join the Front, wrote that no social reforms could be effected in a country whose people did not enjoy political liberty.[23] The inadequacies of the first French reaction to the insurgency and the growing pressure exerted on the populace by the nationalists combined to drive most non-Europeans into opposition to the colonial regime.

The FLN-ALN enjoyed widespread support by the fall of 1956. The Forces of Order, for their part, continued their efforts to adapt to the guerrilla war and to strike at the causes of revolution through various military, political, economic, and social measures.

11 | Some Institutions of Counterinsurgency

THE ALGERIAN INSURGENTS FORCED THE FRENCH TO FIGHT TWO kinds of war at the same time. First, as representatives of the established government, the Forces of Order had to maintain territorial control, an objective dictated by the classical concept of war according to which soldiers fought for terrain. The French needed an overwhelming numerical advantage, both to protect the civilian population from rebel terrorism and to win the military contest. They had to garrison all important settlements. As a result of this protective function, a large proportion of the Forces of Order was constantly immobilized. Second, the French soldiers attempted to control the activities and the thoughts of as many Algerians as possible. This second war committed the army to novel tasks that required organizational and institutional adaptations and, eventually, an understanding of the concepts of psychological action.[1]

172

In forcing the French to engage in an antisubversive war the FLN-ALN brought the political and military debate down to the level of the individual. It was in the realm of the peasant and his mind, not in terms of power or established law, that the nationalists challenged France. After 1956 even military activity was reduced to the level of a few individuals at a time. The key figures on the French side became the commanding officers of the Special Administrative Sections. Single terrorists or small cells of two or three guerrillas represented the rebels and, for all practical purposes, soon came to play the only active armed role.[2]

Between 1954 and 1956, while they held the initiative, the rebels attempted repeatedly to reorganize the ALN. The nationalist leaders hoped to replace the scattered and ill-equipped guerrilla bands with a more conventional military organization.[3] Characteristic guerrilla operations, they thought, could give way to more orthodox and modern forms of warfare. However, repeated failures of the ALN's attempts to liberate a portion of the national territory and the growing pressure exerted by the Forces of Order obliged the rebels to reconsider their policy.[4] By the end of 1956 ALN units within Algeria had begun to split into ever smaller fractions as the nationalists realized that they would not defeat the French in a military sense.

Theoretically, the rebels could still mount operations involving several companies simply by regrouping the splinter units, but the appearance of insurgents in such relatively large concentrations was rare. The nationalists apparently preferred to use terrorism, a tool that was cheaper in terms of manpower and material committed to action.[5] The resort to terrorism can also be seen as a reaction to the execution of the first two rebel prisoners by the French in June 1956. The rebels' strategic and tactical changes multiplied the difficulties of the Forces of Order. Instead of searching for enemy companies, the French had to contend with ten, twenty, or more fragments of former companies that could attack French military or administrative units at will or remain in the shadows and simply make their presence felt by exactions perpetrated on the unarmed local citizens. The latter were kept in fear as long as any vestige of rebel organization remained.[6]

Because the insurgents did not suffer a political defeat commensurate with their reduced military strength, the most important consideration in the struggle against subversion was rebel authority. In the early stages of the Algerian war of independence the French sought to destroy nationalist influence over the Muslim population by demolishing the local units of the ALN-FLN. It is evidence of their success in this regard that the guerrillas were forced to divide their army into very small units. Unfortunately for the colonial power, however, the enemy could not be completely eradicated, and important vestiges of the rebel organization survived the French military build-up from 80,000 to nearly 500,000 men and the consequent operational pressures. Furthermore, because of the different methods used by the French and the rebels to gain control over the masses, the disproportionate military advantage of the French was not decisive.

Each of the opposing sides realized that victory could not be attained without the establishment of firm control over the uncommitted majority of Algerians. The nationalists, with little more than a skeleton organization and the shrewd use of terrorism, could maintain their ascendancy even in areas of relatively high French military concentration.[7] Failure to obey rebel directives often brought multilation or execution to uncooperative Algerians; on the other hand, when Arabs and Berbers who engaged in nationalistic but non-military activities were captured by the French, they customarily received only a short prison term. The choice was easy. It is understandable that most Algerians refused to espouse Francophile views openly or to join any French-sponsored program as long as the slightest vestige of the FLN-ALN remained in the region.[8] As a result the rebels drove the Forces of Order, whose government had seized the initiative with respect to policy decisions, to react to the nationalists' tactical and strategic adjustments. The army had to adapt to what French scholars named revolutionary warfare, a combination of guerrilla tactics and psychological action.[9] The new situation also brought the military to reform its character and organizational structure.

By mid-1956 the French army in Algeria consisted largely of reservists and conscripts.[10] In far off Indochina all but some 175,000 of the more than 500,000 defenders had been Indochinese, and a large proportion of the imported troops were members of African corps or Foreign Legionnaires. Thus relatively few French families were directly touched by the Asian war. Algeria, however, was much closer to France. Also important was the fact that there were over a million European settlers in Algeria, while the Asian colony contained no more than 15,000 European inhabitants.[11] The effort to defend French domination in the central Maghrib was consequently much more uncompromising, and many more troops were used in this effort. There were simply not enough professional soldiers to meet Algerian manpower requirements. In addition, military leaders, partly because of the Indochinese experience, were leery of locally recruited military personnel. In any case, the ratio of European to native soldiers in Algeria was roughly the opposite to what it had been in Indochina.[12] Another source of recruits was French youth, who were drafted in large numbers and who changed the character of the army.

The problems faced by French military leaders in Algeria and in Indochina were different, and the changes were due mainly to the dissimilar character of the two expeditionary forces. In Asia officers had dealt with professional soldiers. In North Africa they led French citizen-soldiers who were more susceptible to rebel propaganda and many of whom already had firm political opinions about the Algerian situation before they crossed the Mediterranean.[13] The infusion of conscripts made mindless adjustments to the nature of subversive warfare insufficient; officers discovered that they had to use psychological action on their own men. They had to convince their men that the fight was just, they had to combat rebel propaganda, and they had to explain the difference between European France and African France.[14]

Still another difficulty arose out of the army's relationship with the population that it was trying to control. As the military institutions became steadily more involved in social experiments, as soldiers developed a social policy for Algeria, they began to change both the society and the army itself. Some of these experiments were little more than police actions. But others were truly revolutionary and involved fundamental institutional and social reforms. Better to meet the challenge of the rebels' methods, for example, the French army created a Center for the Teaching of Pacification and Counter-Guerrilla.[15] Located at Arzew in Oran province, this school began operation in March 1956. There, reserve officers called back for active duty took an arduous twelve-day program that presumably prepared them for their command positions in Algeria. Groups of 250 received this advanced training, although occasional classes were larger.

The curriculum was not rigid. At first the director of the school and his staff were mainly interested in the study of operational activities. In effect, the staff simply reacted to the Algerian military situation. The personality and background of later directors, however, led to sweeping modifications in the program. In August 1957 Colonel Bruges became director. He had been a prisoner of the Viet Minh, an experience that led him to an intense interest in psychological action, psychological war, and Marxism. Under Colonel Bruges the officers paid careful attention to the writings of

Mao Tse-tung and other theoreticians of revolution. These studies were added to the previous program, which retained its strong emphasis on military operations. Muslim and Algerian questions not direcly related to operational procedures played only a minor role in the curriculum.

Colonel Kermadec replaced Colonel Bruges in the autumn of 1959. Because of his background of long service in the Maghrib, the new director found a flaw in the classes given at the Center. This he quickly corrected by adding lectures on Islamic civilization and various aspects of Algerian life. By the end of 1959 the staff had developed the basic curriculum of the Arzew Center, a widerange program that communicated much information in twelve days. The program of study was not altered under the next director, Lieutenant-Colonel de Mareuil. In a report given in 1961 at the *Centre de Hautes Etudes Administratives sur l'Afrique et l'Asie Moderne,* he presented a detailed account of the Arzew Center.[16] This report, important because of its description of the evolution of the curriculum, sheds much light on the difficult subject of the army's adjustment to the revolutionary war in Algeria.

The earliest program of study at Arzew concentrated almost entirely on empirical data concerning the Algerian insurgency, and there was a corresponding stress on operational activities. The first important additions to the program, those ordered by Colonel Bruges, show how the lessons learned in another situation were applied to the Algerian question. The later evolution of the curriculum points to a growing awareness of the importance of the political factors in a subversive war. The officers came to understand that military considerations alone would not provide a suitable solution to the war.[17] The Center then began a careful study of Algeria and Islam; the leaders at Arzew came to understand that Algerian politics could only be truly understood in the context of Islam.

By early 1960, when de Mareuil was appointed to Arzew, the instruction at the Center concerned three general areas of interest. The first was an introduction to the whole Algerian problem. There was a statistically oriented discussion of the number of casualties on each side within specific periods of time.[18] The officers then directed their attention to the world context of the Algerian question. Lectures and discussions, often offered by guests who were academic specialists, demonstrated that the insurgency arose from internal social and political contradictions as well as from certain international forces. Among the foreign influences studied were the development of revolutionary warfare, world Communism, and other political and historical movements such as decolonization, pan-Arabism, and pan-Islam. Lecturers also discussed the chief characteristics of Algerian society, the enemy's oganization and history, and psychological action.

As presented at Arzew, psychological action concerned the officers' relations with their own men in the Forces of Order, and the Center's staff devoted little attention to the problem of influencing public opinion among the Algerian inhabitants of the regions to which the officers would be assigned.[19] Presumably, specialized units trained to work on psychological action would try to induce Arabs and Berbers to choose France and to turn their backs on the nationalists. Most French officers would have too many other duties. But in a revolutionary war, a struggle in which propaganda plays a major role, the influence of an officer upon the draftees serving under him is a supremely important consideration. Parenthetically, de Mareuil noted that most French reserve officers at Arzew were unprepared for these lessons on psychological action. Those who had thought about the topic had presumed that psychological action should only be applied to Algerians.

The officers trained at the Arzew school, de Mareuil argued, should and did receive an "objective" introduction to the situation in Algeria. The problem was that many of the soldiers of the Forces of Order, whether officers or privates, had read accounts of the Algerian Revolution and had formed opinions on the question. Many were deeply concerned about the racist aspects of the French war in North Africa. Others were disturbed about the use of torture on captured guerrillas or suspected rebels. Such doubts had to be assuaged, and the officers and men were forced to test their preconceived ideas against the fact, for example, that nearly 200,000 Algerians served with the Forces of Order.[20] That, at least, was true in 1961, although it had not been in 1956. In any case, there were many Algerians who did not want independence, and the fact was used to quiet the conscience of troubled officers. The answer to inquiries about the use of torture was also constant but perhaps less convincing. The high cadres usually replied with the time-worn argument that a brief period of suffering for one man often saved hundreds of innocent people.[21] Many military leaders may have believed this assessment to be true, or they may have failed to understand the loss of human dignity brought about by this procedure of justifying the means, presumably condemned, in terms of a desirable end. Officers at the Arzew Center might in turn be asked the same questions by men under their orders, and this is why they received training in psychological action.

Protection of the population by the Forces of Order formed the second of three main topics studied and discussed at Arzew. Officers studied tactical lessons, of course, but the most important portion of the second stage of the Arzew program was the analysis of, and debate about, the role of intelligence officers in the Algerian insurgency. Instructors described the work of these specialists, who were trained in another counterinsurgency school, at each territorial and administrative level, and in the process explained a great deal about the nature of the Algerian conflict. The students at Arzew learned about the critical importance of intelligence, lessons they would certainly find useful once they took up their future positions of command. Once on their own, they would know how to find the intelligence specialists and would understand the nature of the information they received. The understanding gained at Arzew presumably helped them to perform better their own primary duties, the protection of the population at large and the defense of the territory.

In an effort to help the Forces of Order protect the Algerian population from rebels who enjoyed sanctuary in Tunisia and in Morocco, France built two huge barriers across the frontiers. By 1960 several barbed wire fences, some of them electrified, and a complicated system of mine fields denied access into Algeria to tens of thousands of ALN soldiers stationed in the eastern and western Maghrib. Behind these border defenses the French created vast no-man's lands by clearing the areas of all inhabitants. In the desert to the south of the barriers radar and reconnaissance flights scanned the border regions for possible interlopers.[22] While at Arzew, officers training for command positions throughout Algeria visited the frontiers to observe these technical aspects of protection.

The Arzew Center also introduced students to such technical aspects of protection as aerial support,[23] the concept of "police-help" *(police-secours)*, and the theory and organization of "hunting commandos" *(commandos de chasse)*.[24] These commandos formed highly specialized units that operated independently, living much the same life as did the rebel bands. While few of the officers at Arzew would become commandos, they might well encounter these units during counterguerrilla operations. Therefore, it was essential that they understand the role of the commandos in a counter-revolutionary war. The police-help system involved the mobilization of all available local resources in case of a sudden attack on a small to medium-sized urban or rural-urban center. The officers learned that, besides the various military units available in cases of emergency, they could also call on various units of police, some of which were paramilitary, and on groups of citizens, Algerian and European, who had been organized for self-defense. Aerial support could be requested for offensive or defensive purposes, and an understanding of its nature and uses was important. Such support could, for example, be called in by ambushed units of the Forces of Order.

Lessons on "instinctive shooting" brought the second general area of study to an end. Although this technique, applied in case of ambush, was ill defined, it apparently meant the application of concentrated firepower in an area of from less than one meter up to twenty-five meters in diameter. Having learned this technique of random but organized firing of small weapons, the students now turned their attention to the third topic, a study of pacification.[25]

Basically, pacification was an attempt to persuade the Algerians to commit themselves to France. Winning the allegiance of the civilians, de Mareuil explained, was all-important; the object of the struggle was support of the people and not the conquest of terrain. This statement shows how much the French had already learned from their experiences in Indochina and Algeria. To succeed, de Mareuil continued, pacification must be carried throughout the country by soldiers who understood the local inhabitants, who could inform them, and who could gather intelligence. Such a task required careful organization even below the municipal level. Although the director did not specifically mention SAS officers, it is clear that he had them in mind. Nor would it be sufficient for an officer to account for and control the movements of all the Algerians living in his assigned area. By their presence, by their precept and example, the officers and men had to win over the Arabs or Berbers with whom they had daily contact.[26] In order to achieve this end the Forces of Order found it best to fight fire with fire, duplicating the political and military organization of the enemy for the opposite ends.[27] They faced a severe handicap, however, in their inability to use the rebels' best tool, terrorism. Since most members of the Forces of Order were Europeans, they also had to overcome the disadvantage of being representatives of an alien culture. Had this problem been a racial one, the disadvantage would probably have been even greater.

During the campaign of pacification the French military leaders developed many institutions designed to give the Forces of Order absolute control over the Algerian population. The creation of the Arzew school and other specialized training centers was evidence of the fact that military strategy changed. Simultaneously, the army attempted to alter the society in which it functioned. Late in April 1955, for example, some 160 suspected members or sympathizers of the FLN-ALN were assembled at Khenchela.[28] Acting under the authority of a law passed in March of the same year, the military had, in effect, created its first prison camp. The law in question allowed the confinement of suspects to forced residence but specifically forbade the creation of prison camps. There was neither compound nor barbed wire to be seen at Khenchela, but the prisoners could not leave and could receive visitors only rarely. According to a careful study made by Jean Durroux, a member of the Chamber of Deputies, there were more than 4,000 political prisoners in Algeria by the end of July 1955.[29]

The counterinsurgency forces quickly took the short step between a technical fiction and a full-fledged prison camp. Internment camps appeared at Aflou, M'Sila-Chellal, Guelt-es-Stil (abandoned in July 1955), Ain el Amara, Berrouaghia, and at many more sites.[30] This method of control became steadily more sophisticated; eventually there was a series of camps, graduated according to degree of security, to which prisoners were assigned according to the gravity of the charges against them.

Another aspect of the pacification campaign was the precise cataloguing of persons and houses. Officers compiled card catalogues with entries for each household in the villages of their district.[31] Each house was assigned a number, to be painted in large numerals on or near the door. The card for each house contained all the pertinent information—the number of occupants, a complete description of each, and many other useful facts. These records served as the basis for spot checks or house-by-house searches, which the troops usually made at night during curfew hours. Any unauthorized person found during these visits was presumed suspect, as were any absent members of the household.

These key methods of static control, cataloguing and imprisonment, were obviously extremely useful to the army in its attempts at pacification. However, a third and much more drastic tool was also employed. In specified areas French soldiers systematically destroyed the small villages, forcing the citizens to settle in new villages or regroupment centers. The purpose of the regroupment policy was to remove whole populations from any contact with the nationalists.[32] In some instances, it should be noted, the villagers volunteered to enter the regroupment centers after requesting protection from the French authorities against the exactions of the rebels.[33] Such protection was often extended on condition that a given community resettle closer to a military establishment. More often than not, however, coercion was used in the name of a more rational military organization of the districts.[34] Once a regroupment had been accomplished, anyone found in the abandoned settlement was presumed guilty of rebel connections and was liable to be shot on sight.[35]

Within the new centers the houses were numbered and detailed records were compiled. The barbed wire that surrounded these communities, ostensibly to keep out the nationalists, contributed to the atmosphere of a prison camp, as did the presence of a military checkpoint at the main gate to the compound. The whole village was usually dominated by one or more watch towers occupied by guards armed with machine guns.[36] There can be no question about the military value of the regroupment centers; missions against the enemy were much simpler when the ordinary citizens had been removed. Furthermore, the rebels were deprived of all contact with and support from the inhabitants of the reorganized districts. Politically, however, the pitfalls exceeded the opportunities presented by this policy. If a new village was so composed that it shortly became an economic and social unit, the French could reap the credit and the political advantages. If the new community failed to function as a social unit, as was often the case, the nationalists quickly infiltrated it and began operations under the noses of the guards.[37]

An essential factor in the success or failure of the regroupment centers was the character of the officer in charge. He was usually a member of the SAS and wielded great power over each individual within the centers. He could, for example, withhold any portion of the money orders that were commonly sent to Algerians by their relatives working in France. On the theory that excess cash would soon find its way into rebel hands, the officers permitted the families who received these checks to cash only enough to satisfy their basic needs.[38] The officer in charge of the regroupment camp determined the precise amount in each case. Individuals, it was assumed, would donate any extra capital to the Front; if not, the FLN would seize or extort it. Many people in Algeria, even the Europeans, paid the rebels for protection. The premiums represented a hedge against the future no matter what the outcome of the revolution.[39]

As a means of fighting the insurgency, then, the French authorities controlled all income within Algeria, and particularly the revenue received from abroad. The regulation was generally more severe in the case of the Algerians than of the Europeans. As a rule, the Arab and Berber population was not permitted to cash checks without permission from the proper military or municipal authorities.[40]

While the circulation of currency was closely controlled, so was that of the population. In a sense, the Algerians were placed on parole. Travel permits, usually granted by the military, were necessary for even the briefest trip away from home, and local records carried the appropriate entries. These restrictions did not apply only to that fifteen per cent of the population who lived in the regroupment centers;[41] almost every citizen was affected by the laws and decrees limiting civilian travel.[42]

The extent of this control can be illustrated by reference to an interesting memoir prepared in 1959 concerning the limitations on travel in the department of Constantine.[43] This document contained the regulatory measures taken to put obstacles in the way of rebel supply. The first administrative order stipulated the cataloguing of all animals that might be used to transport goods. These were to be registered at the central offices of the SAS sectors throughout the province. Each sector was to devise a distinctive brand and apply it to its registered beasts of burden. Other portions of the directive called for the confiscation of animals or merchandise in case of infraction of these regulations and ordered the SAS commanders to enforce the directive in its entirety.

A further order decreed the prohibition of all transport of goods without prior written permission from the military authorities. The prohibition applied to all kinds of goods, moved by truck or by animal, and to movement either within the province or across its borders. The written permission could only be granted by the commander of the military sector or subsector. Finally, both the vehicle and the cargo had to be examined at the destination stated in the written permit.

Some of the regulations were extremely specific. On July 6, 1959, for example, orders were given to stop all traffic in cereals and cereal products except within a few specified centers. Even within these centers—Collo, Djidjelli, Mila, and El Milia—bureaus for the distribution of certain goods were to be created under the direct authority of the sector's commander. If the latter could not do so, the SAS officers were to take charge. The local producers of cereals were obliged to deposit their entire crop with these new bureaus, which would in turn distribute it to the local population by the use of ration cards. Seed grain was equally severely regulated, and no farmer could keep more than 100 kilograms per hectare. Individual consumption was fixed at 80 kilograms per year per person, and barley for livestock was set at 700 kilograms. These regulations were to take effect on July 15.

According to the explanatory note that accompanied the order, the controls were not intended as repression. It fact, it was noted, the controls might well serve as a method of increasing the contact between the military authorities and the local citizens. It was admitted, however, that the measures were chiefly an instrument of economic warfare. The note also cited recently captured rebel documents to illustrate the effectiveness of this kind of regulation.[44]

Economic warfare, then, went hand in glove with the control and partial insulation of the population from rebel influences. A basic thread of military necessity also ran through each measure taken by the colonial regime. It was difficult to fight an enemy who accepted combat only on his own terms. The Forces of Order were therefore obliged to devise ways to starve the rebels of support and to deny them weapons and food. The regroupment camps, the barricaded frontiers, and the economic restrictions were all military necessities. Military factors also dictated the creation of many specialized military schools and of the no-man's lands of empty villages. Most of these policies possessed a potentially redeeming political, social, and human value. These aspects were not considered of prime importance, however, and could be brought into play only according to the wishes of the individual commanders. Some of these policies and their attendant institutions can be better understood in a study of the SAS and the regroupment theory.

Certain aspects of the regroupment policy, the creation of no-man's lands, for example, were entirely without positive value except in terms of military necessity. The nationalists were poised to exploit this negative concept, especially after the Soummam Congress. The rebels also profited by the failure of some SAS commanders to develop the economic and social possibilities that were latent in other policies. The FLN undoubtedly gained enormously from the negative aspects of the relocation policy. The threat of forced regroupment caused a great emigration to Morocco and Tunisia. These people were lost to the French cause, and were alienated from their own country as well.

On the other hand, the Forces of Order earned the respect of the enemy and of impartial observers. The French army adapted itself, although often too late, to an extremely complex and new situation. In the end they failed because their government lost the desire to hold Algeria. The army blamed the defeat in Indochina on the politicians, and blamed them also for the situation in Algeria. The Algerians, particularly the Berber minority, obviously contributed to the loss of the French will to fight by continually harping on "the 1% they did not get and forgetting the 99% they did get."[45] To this might be added the fact that a small percentage of soldiers in the French army, as in any army, destroyed the work of the majority of their companions through individual acts of reprehensible behavior.

12 | The Special Administrative Sections

THE VOTE BY WHICH THE CHAMBER OF DEPUTIES GRANTED SPE-cial powers to the colonial administration clearly marked a turning point in the war. The resident-minister used the new law almost immediately to dissolve the Algerian Assembly. The dissolution occurred on April 12, 1956, and the resident-minister ruled by decree from that time on.[1] As the chief representative of France in Algeria, he quickly ordered a territorial reorganization of France's departments south of the Mediterranean. On paper at least, these Algerian units now began to resemble their French counterparts (see chapter 8). Then, acting under a series of decrees, the army and the government, in close association, began to implement a program of political, psychological, economic, and social reforms.

The most important aspect of this program was that it led to the creation of many Special Administrative Sections (SAS) throughout Algeria.[2] Through the SAS far-reaching reforms were effected at the municipal level of administration. Also important, though perhaps less dynamic, was the establishment of what the French called the *quadrillage*.[3] Under this policy, the entire country was divided into small units, most of which were garrisoned as quickly as possible.[4] The garrisons were intended to ensure the protection of the local population and force the rebels to regroup in new districts, usually areas that had been marginal to the rebellion.[5] Associated with the *quadrillage* was the regroupment policy, which led in turn to the creation of no-man's lands.

Although static rather than dynamic, the *quadrillage* and regroupment were useful military devices. Their application enabled the French to rob the rebels of their sources of revenue and supplies. However, the establishment of the SAS, introduced in 1956 as the other phase of the counterinsurgency program, was much more important. It was the policy of the French to create as many SAS units as possible in an attempt to reestablish contact between the administration and the administered.

Because the civil service could not furnish sufficient personnel to eradicate the chronic underadministration of Algeria, Resident-Minister Lacoste turned to the military. He encouraged officers to volunteer for service in the SAS, where they would perform tasks usually undertaken by civilians. From these volunteers and from those who were arbitrarily assigned to the SAS, Lacoste expected arduous service unstintingly given. He also relied heavily on the army as a whole. "The political and psychological work which I now expect from the army," he said in April, "is as important as its purely operational activity."[6] As he indicated in a directive, the essential task of the SAS program was the winning over of the Algerian masses by persuasion, not by force. It followed, he remarked, that the laws should be enforced according to their spirit rather than their letter.

On the whole, Lacoste was optimistic about the chances of success for his counterinsurgency program. He may well have been too idealistic. Most of the 400,000 troops available to the resident-minister were quickly tied down by garrison duties in the *quadrillage*. Boredom, which became endemic as the men waited in vain for contact with the enemy, was the most common feature of military life noted by journalists who traveled in Algeria late in 1956.[7] The deployment of garrison troops in the population centers also diminished the French operational superiority over the rebels.[8] The actual fighting was often left to the elite units—the Foreign Legion, the paratroopers, and those who had volunteered for commando service. Other members of the Forces of Order played chiefly a passive or defensive role.

Within the French army specialization spawned its own problems. In order to reinforce their numerical superiority over the rebels, the operational units required the utmost mobility. The technological advantage of the helicopter helped the French to achieve this mobility despite the rugged terrain. By and large, the Forces of Order were content to use their helicopters for transport purposes. Moving to and from battle areas, the helicopters themselves were rarely armed because of their vulnerability and because the guerrillas rarely used their few antiaircraft weapons.[9] Other less vulnerable craft, such as Piper Cubs for observation and other planes for fire cover, were therefore used to protect the movements of the helicopters.[10]

The technological adaptation of the helicopters was of elementary simplicity compared to the psychological transformation required of the officers of the SAS. The fighting men were now asked to carry on the struggle with ideas instead of weapons, to resist terrorism with understanding for the people. Among those whose duties seldom involved them in any military operations were the SAS officers, their staffs, and their locally recruited auxiliary troops. The last were chiefly a defensive force although the men might serve as informants or interpreters. The gathering of intelligence was one of the principal functions of the men of the SAS, who then passed the information on to the nearest combat unit.[11] More often than not their economic means were not adequate to their task.[12] Fortunately, many SAS officers have written about their experiences and it is possible to study individual adaptations to varying situations.

The origins of the SAS system lie in a 1955 experiment in the Aurès mountains (see chapter 8). An earlier historical precedent was the *Bureaux Arabes* of the nineteenth century. Basically, each of the institutions was a method of direct military administration.[13] In the Algerian insurgency the SAS was designed to overcome a long-standing colonial deficiency, the underadministration of vast areas populated primarily by Arabs and Berbers. A second objective of equal importance was the establishment of an institutional infrastructure capable of withstanding and eventually replacing the rebels' Political Administrative Organization (OPA). In addition, the SAS was intended to be temporary, destined to survive only until Algerian civilians could take over their own local administrations. Finally, the SAS program was closely linked to various governmental reforms such as the organization of new departments and communes.

At the outbreak of revolution Algeria was divided into three departments, each of which was subdivided into 4 or 5 *arrondissements,* the realm of a subprefect. The administrative reorganization decreed by Lacoste in 1956 led to the creation of 14 departments, containing some 71 *arrondissements.* In this way positions were created for many new prefects and subprefects.[14] The new larger units contained 1,438 new communes, many of which were partially or entirely designated as Special Administrative Sections and most of which had previously been mixed communes in rural areas.[15] Within the new units volunteer and appointed SAS officers were supposed to take up the slack left by the abolition of these hybrids of the earlier colonial administration. In most of them the new staff was assigned to supervise virtually the entire local government and to assist in pacification measures where needed. These sweeping reforms, which also affected the smaller units, the *arrondissements* and *douars*, altered the entire relationship between the French government and its Algerian charges.

Politically, the first duty of an SAS officer was to supervise the nomination and election of communal delegates who were to direct the affairs of the new communes. The candidates had to be selected with care, since they were intended to further the goals of France in their communities. The ALN-FLN had terrorized the population to such an extent that in many areas it was at first almost impossible to find Algerians willing to present themselves as candidates. The SAS officers were thus obliged to take this burden upon their own shoulders, at least on a temporary basis.[16]

As temporary special delegates the officers could draw on important monetary credits extended by the government in Algiers. Thus they could begin economic reforms with political dividends in view. More immediately, they could open work projects such as the repair or construction of roads. Help was thus extended to the neediest families in the commune, and despite the efforts of the guerrillas some contact was thus established between the administration and its charges. By skillful use of the credits, the officers were able to meet the men in their section, and often their families as well. The relationship, it must be admitted, was somewhat forced since the peasants, fearful of rebel reprisal, often accepted the work only when threatened by starvation or by the military administrators themselves.[17]

The Algerians were equally hesitant to make a political commitment.[18] The power of the rebels thus severely limited the effectiveness of the credits as an economic and political weapon.

The region of Tablat provides a good example of the re-organization and its effects.[19] Originally, the mixed commune of Tablat was but a subdivision of an *arrondissement* not far from Algiers. In December 1956 it was replaced by twelve new communes. These new communes took the place of the numerous *douars* into which the old mixed commune, like all the others, had been subdivided. It was not without good reason that the reforms of 1956 put an end to the *douar* as an administrative unit. Each *douar* was headed by a native *caïd*, and by 1956 it was evident that in the *douars* around Tablat, as all over Algeria, most of the citizens had escaped the authority of the *caïds*. In order to create an effective system of administration the new reforms abolished the office of *caïd* and his realm, the *douar*. Also destroyed was the concept of the mixed commune.

There were many reasons for the decline of the *caïdat*. Not the least of these was the fact that the office did not pay wages sufficient to meet expenses. After their appointment by the governor in Algiers, the *caïds* often robbed their fellow Algerians under cover of their position as head of the *douar*.[20] These Arab or Berber officials were the natural target of rebel pressures and threats. To protect themselves the *caïds* fled to the anonymity of the cities or ceased to fulfill their duties.[21] Since the mixed communes by their very nature contained only a small European minority, the government soon lost all contact with these Algerians. During the first twenty-two months of fighting nothing was done to protect or replace the *caïds*. Then, in one stroke of reform, the government sought to re-create the whole Algerian administrative system and make it into an effective political weapon. The most obvious and widespread change was the creation of new communes all over Algeria, and the appearance of the new departments and *arrondissements*. The administration itself was unable to supply the vast number of functionaries necessary to staff these new units, and the army was asked to furnish competent cadres to serve during a transition period whose duration remained undefined. The SAS officers were those asked to serve in the pacification at the communal level.

It was unfortunately impossible to staff all the communes with SAS teams. In the Tablat area, for example, only two of the twelve new communes could be staffed in 1956. A third section was added in August 1957, but nothing more could be done during the balance of the war.[22] The three teams of SAS officers were evidently to serve as examples for the other nine communes to follow after the war. A further complication soon arose, however, even as these SAS men were trying to implement reforms in their communes, when several regroupments of the population were ordered.[23] The Tablat region was not alone in this respect. Indeed, the SAS officers and their teams were often assigned to regroupment camps rather than to established communities. As a result, many new problems were thrust at these inexperienced officials, whose original assignment encompassed difficulties of much longer standing. These soldiers found their civilian tasks virtually impossible to accomplish.

In Kabylia, for example, an area of 4,000 square kilometers, whose population exceeded 900,000, 73 sections were to provide the groundwork for communal reform.[24] If the government had placed SAS commanders in charge of the entire population, each would have administered over 12,000 people. Among the inhabitants, however, was a sizable European minority that lived in some fifteen self-governing communes and was thus not within the jurisdiction of the SAS officials. But the task assigned to the SAS was enormous in any case. The collapse of the *caïdat* and of the system of mixed communes had left a political vacuum in which the officers were to build a viable new local administration. There had been eight such mixed communes in Kabylia alone,[25] where the large population had virtually lost contact with an understaffed and chronically ineffective administration.[26]

Where possible, the team of an SAS chief included an assistant, generally a noncommissioned officer or a civilian on contract, who usually served as secretary-treasurer. A second secretary normally did double duty as interpreter. The last member of the team was the radio operator. The secretary-interpreters were, at first, especially hard to find.[27] The government succeeded in recruiting some *colons* who knew Arabic or one of the Berber languages. Some of these positions were filled by Algerian veterans of the French army or by retired noncommissioned officers. A few other Arabs or Berbers who had had some education in French schools were also available. The latter two groups, however, were very much in demand and usually occupied more lucrative positions in the government or in government-controlled industries (see chapter 8). The recruitment of radio operators was equally difficult. These men were usually lent reluctantly by their army units, whose officers complained, not without justification, that the radios of the SAS teams were unused for long periods and that the skilled operators were thus wasted when they joined the SAS teams. The recruitment of operators became progressively more difficult as the war continued.[28]

These SAS teams of four specialists, who worked often in remote and troubled regions, naturally needed protection from the rebel forces. This was provided by locally recruited *maghzens,* detachments of thirty to fifty Algerian volunteers. Although armed by the Forces of Order, these men could not always be trusted. There were many cases of desertion, both individual and collective.[29] The deserters generally took their weapons with them when they defected to the enemy ranks. Occasionally they killed their French officers before they left. Quite naturally the European community, both military and civilian, had mixed feelings about arming Algerians.[30] An opposite point of view, however, was expressed by some writers who idealized the *maghzens,* arguing that these and other Muslim units among the Forces of Order were composed of the only men truly committed to the maintenance of the French presence in Algeria.[31]

De Montalembert, who served as an officer in the SAS and wrote a short memoir of his experiences, listed several qualities required or expected of a good *maghzen.* It was essential, he said, that the recruits for these units be chosen with the utmost care. If a unit contained too many men from the same village or clan, the defection of one might well precipitate the loss of the entire group. In terms of Algerian sociology and loyalties, this rule was indeed excellent. A second consideration was to keep down the size of a new unit so that men seeking protection could join at a later date. Among these late volunteers were some who had worked for France in other capacities until their lives were directly threatened. Some *maghzen* took in deserters from the ALN and the FLN.

A carefully formed *maghzen* could be expected to fight well and to perform effectively its primary duty, the defense of the Special Administrative Section to which it was assigned. Since the SAS chiefs customarily recruited Algerian men in their own district to join a local *maghzen,* the recruitment campaign often constituted the first contact between the colonial authority and the peasants of the region. Members of the *maghzen* were also expected to provide intelligence about the local guerrillas and their activities. In the face of rebel threats the peasants employed on the work projects often needed protection, and the local *maghzen,* whose men knew the district intimately, were the perfect tool for this. In dire emergencies the SAS chief could call on the French garrison deployed in the local *quadrillage.* He might do so, for example, when his wards asked to be relocated near a military post where the garrison would protect them. In this case the officer would grant credits to enable a new village to be built as close as possible to the post. However, the new community would be left defenseless when the garrison was summoned to join military operations elsewhere.

The entire concept of the *maghzen* drew a steady barrage of criticism from certain military men, who could never condone a policy that put weapons in the hands of potential soldiers of the ALN. Most of the *maghzen* recruits were deserving of such suspicion, for many had relatives in the enemy ranks and many were defectors from the guerrillas. Still, a reliable *maghzen* was essential to the defense of its section, protecting its chief, his team, and the peasants at large, as well as providing crucial intelligence about the activities of the local rebels.[32]

The SAS team remained in its section under practically all conditions. By combining in one person the duties of half a dozen or more officials, the men in charge of the system put a crushing load on the shoulders of the chiefs. But it was precisely this combination of duties and powers which gave the best of the officers the flexibility and the means they needed to combat the insurgency most effectively. At all times it was the primary duty of these officers to reestablish contact between the people and the administration by economic and political means. In addition, they helped to protect the population by gathering intelligence for the Forces of Order. Each team provided, if possible, medical and educational services to the district. Finally, they customarily participated in local operational activities such as visiting unsecured villages at night and assuming the protection of the peasants who attended the weekly open markets.[33]

The SAS teams often took advantage of the market crowds to engage in psychological warfare. Among the merchants and their stalls they made political speeches and showed films. Occasionally they were replaced by teams of psychological specialists, who toured the country with sound trucks and other instruments of propaganda.[34] Usually, however, the local SAS teams did their own work along these lines. The propaganda routinely sought to convince the Algerians of the benefits of the French regime. It often contained comment on current events and a rebuttal of the nationalists' publicity. The effectiveness of this work may be seen in the events of May 13, 1958, when thousands of Arabs and Berbers turned out to cheer for a continuation of the association between France and Algeria.[35]

An essential factor in the success or failure of the SAS was the character, ability, and background of the various chiefs. M. Holstein, an administrator who regularly received reports from three officers in the Barika region, has provided insight into the subject. According to M. Holstein, one of the officers had served in Morocco in the *Bureau des Affaires Indigènes*. As a specialist who had considerable experience in dealing with North Africans, he was at once able to render useful service to the administration. A second chief, who had volunteered to serve in the SAS, had previously commanded an Algerian corps. With this background, he was easily able to adapt to his new duties. His task, to establish contacts with Algerians whom he was to lead, was not completely new to him. The third officer, however, had come from France against his will and never adjusted to his new position; he did not understand his wards or their culture and customs.[36]

In May 1958 a final change was made in the SAS system: to meet the demands of the war, officers and men were henceforth arbitrarily assigned to service in this experiment in counterinsurgency. Simultaneously, the political and military leaders in Algiers tried to put the entire SAS on a firmer basis by establishing direct military rule in the sectors at large. Specifically, the colonels commanding military sectors assumed the rank and duties of subprefects.[37] Thus the SAS chiefs, previously responsible to both the political and military authorities, now dealt only with their superiors in the armed forces, who represented both the civil and military powers.

These changes had been dictated by the development of the system, which had grown unwieldy. The reforms introduced a new efficiency, but resulted at the same time in a certain loss of prestige and *esprit de corps*. The concept of employing military men in administrative positions was an adaptation from the Indochinese War. In Asia, however, officers who served in this earlier version of the SAS were volunteers to a man.[38] In Algeria the new communes assigned to the SAS were manned at first by volunteers whose energy and enthusiasm contributed much to the effectiveness of their work, but, as more sections were established, these highly motivated men were increasingly replaced by officers who did not volunteer and most of whom somewhat resented their new assignment away from the fighting front.[39] The continued extension of the system necessitated the widespread appointment of lieutenants to positions that had heretofore been reserved for captains. In addition, the establishment of direct military control entailed more paper work and a narrower range of initiative for the section chiefs. In short, the SAS strategy had passed its peak by the end of 1958.

Observers have emphasized the fact that the SAS officers were first of all soldiers. But they were also temporary administrators in areas where local government had broken down. Until May 1958, owing to their double function, these officers had two sets of superiors. As soldiers they were naturally responsible to the higher ranking officers in the sector and in the department; as administrators they were subordinate to the subprefects and prefects of the department and to the local civil authorities, if any. With respect to the communal governments, where they existed, the SAS officers were advisors whose powers were vague and whose authority varied according to circumstances.

Furthermore, there existed no legal definition of their powers and duties.[40] Wherever the rebel hold was strong and the authority of the government had broken down, the chiefs could easily play the part of minor dictators, as in those sectors formed in areas of abolished mixed communes; but even here they depended on their own abilities to rally the people behind them. Wherever European settlers had a voice in the administration, however, especially in the full communes, an ineffective or uncooperative mayor or other official could easily scuttle any SAS program.[41] The chief could attend meetings of the municipal council but he had no legally defined duties within that body. His advice could be refused, and he could be denied the use of local funds for work projects designed to improve relations between the Europeans and the Algerians.[42]

The community of Gounod, a colonization village begun in the nineteenth century, provides a good example of how the SAS system and its officers could founder in the antipathy between Europeans and Algerians. The region of Gounod was not a full commune, although the settlers had a voice in the local government. Within the village itself were a few European families and several hundred Algerian families. In late 1956 Captain Laurent was assigned to create an SAS unit in the village.[43] He began his work by studying the local situation and by consulting with the chief administrator of the former mixed commune of Oued Cherf, half of which became the Gounod SAS. He met with all the civilian authorities such as subprefect, health officials, and the chief of police. Laurent had familiarized himself with the situation and taken every precaution against irritating the established authorities. He then began to prepare the budget for the section; since there were no budetary guidelines, the approach might vary from one area to another. Nonetheless, Laurent pressed on. He was obliged to contact the commander of the sector before the material for the new section could be ordered. Delivery of these supplies had to be assured. All this took time. Although the Gounod SAS was established in late 1956, it did not begin operation until early 1957.[44]

As soon as possible, work projects were begun on which Algerians were employed. The workers were paid from municipal unemployment funds. Captain Laurent's attention was increasingly occupied, he reports, by paper work, the composing of military and administrative reports, and the settlement of petty disputes. Despite these distractions Laurent and his team directed many projects that reestablished contact with the people. For example, 120 houses were built on municipal lands near Gounod. In a larger perspective, the region contained in the second Gounod SAS was reorganized into five communes, four of which had been *douars.* The fifth was the colonization center itself. Rebel activity declined continually, in part because of these SAS initiatives, and normal municipal governments were established.[45]

After the departure of Captain Laurent, however, the mayor of Gounod began to charge rent for the 120 houses. In spite of efforts to give titles of ownership to the tenants, as originally intended by the SAS officer who advised the building program, nothing was done. The Gounod section therefore serves as an example of how one oversight on the part of European officials undermined a project which would have given some Algerians a stake in the status quo and which would have attracted other Arabs and Berbers to support the French presence in their country. Laurent concluded his report with a tone of understandable bitterness.[46] And yet, the Gounod SAS was essentially a successful experiment. It was only with the resumption of normal municipal administration that the failure came.

In other former mixed communes, the SAS experiment was usually quite successful. When three SAS units were established around Aumale, for example, the old administrative system had died. *Caïds* still met regularly with the chief administrator of the commune, but they had lost control of the situation and only met to request that they be sent on vacation to France. As a result, the three SAS chiefs were not hin-

dered by the petty interventions of ineffective civilian administrators. Once they had established themselves in their own
sections, these officers were able to gain the support of the
population and to resist the efforts of the rebels. They also
gathered invaluable intelligence on the struggle between the
Mouvement National Algérien (MNA) and the FLN. Above
all, the personnel of the SAS gained some popularity because
they were always present at weekly markets and thus protected both the merchants and their customers. Ironically, the
only notable failure of the SAS around Aumale involved
purely military considerations. The SAS units did not have
an effective fighting potential; as a result, they were discredited in the eyes of the French army.[47]

One of the best available accounts of the operation of an
SAS unit is J. Y. Alquier's book, *Nous avons pacifié Tazalt*.
The author, a reserve officer in a paratroop unit, was sent to
the Tazalt region in the fall of 1956. In the course of his service
there he was exceptionally successful in drawing the local
population, previously cowed by rebel terror tactics, toward
cooperation with the French regime.[48] Alquier's experience
may be taken as typical of the best of the early SAS units.
Temporarily at least, his team was an effective tool of counterinsurgency. His account of this social experiment, however,
also illustrates a weakness inherent in the entire pacification
effort.

Alquier's assignment was to reactivate the SAS section at
Tazalt, which the French had earlier been forced to abandon.
Their retreat had left some 20,000 people at the mercy of the
rebels for three months. Alquier and the others in his unit
reestablished the French presence and reconstituted the SAS
with all its projects and services. Alquier himself voluntarily
extended his tour of duty at Tazalt by six months, after which
he left to return to civilian life.[49] There was no assurance,
however, that his successor would be nearly so effective.
Those Algerians who had defected from the rebel camp to

join Alquier in his work had done so because of their loyalty to and esteem for Alquier as an individual. The notion of the French cause was a vague abstraction to these peasants, but personalities were immediate and important. Their pledges of support, while couched in the language of politics, were seen in much simpler terms by the villagers. Under these circumstances, then, it fell upon the succeeding officer in his turn to earn the respect of the Berber tribesmen in his charge. Alquier and his team accomplished this task during their tour in Tazalt, but their very success serves to illustrate a fundamental weakness of the pacification program. Although the SAS was an effective tool in the hands of officers such as Alquier, success could not be assured for less capable leaders in other units or indeed for Alquier's replacement. Also, and as the doctor in this same unit observed, the winning of the villagers of Tazalt did not mean that the French were defeating the enemy in Algiers. The doctor, in fact, thought Algeria lost at the very time when his immediate battle had been won.[50]

Alquier, for his part, saw some reason for optimism.[51] This SAS chief describes in some detail the work of his unit in Tazalt. The preceding officer had run the risk of being shot each time he left his offices. The new team under Alquier, however, boldly visited hostile villages at night and gradually forced out the representatives of the ALN and the FLN. Several villages were thus induced to free themselves of rebel control. At first, these night patrols and their Algerian auxiliaries found the villages deserted upon their arrival. The guerrillas maintained a comprehensive network of guards, who watched the Frenchmen's every move. These lookouts warned the peasants of impending official visits and ordered them to desert their homes. Eventually, however, Alquier's team managed to surprise a few families in their homes. The chief officer gradually compiled a census list, warning those he found at home not to flee the French in the future, under penalty of being assumed rebels who were liable to be shot on sight. With this combination of persuasion and coercion, Alquier's unit induced a growing number of Algerians to visit him in his office, to bring their sick to the team's doctor, and to submit themselves increasingly to French influence and authority.

It was a laborious struggle to break down the fear of the French among the people of Tazalt. Their apprehension and suspicion had been implanted and sustained by rebel propaganda and threat of reprisal. In the effort to overcome this attitude the Europeans relied to a great extent on a wide range of programs to help the Algerians. The SAS unit created a medical dispensary, for example. At first, the chief and his men forced the Algerians to come for needed treatment; gradually, as the influence and power of the ALN-FLN ebbed, the people came freely. When the schools were reopened and an SAS man began to teach, the parents at first refused to send their children. Again attendance became compulsory, and, while the French simultaneously gained for the people relative freedom from the exactions of the rebels, the enrollment at the school grew slowly.[52]

The men stationed at Tazalt found their task complicated by the insufficiency of the economic and military means available to them. They enjoyed a certain success, however, despite the drawbacks. The Algerians' confidence in them grew steadily, and the local administration commenced once more to function. For the first time in months the inhabitants of some liberated villages could freely collect veterans' pay, family allowances, and supplements for the poor, and could accept employment on the government's work projects.

Around Tazalt not every village was openly committed to the French when Alquier, one of the best SAS officers, left. Still, the rebels were on the run when he departed. While bending every effort to gain general popular support, the SAS teams were particularly interested in finding rebel sympathizers who would work against the ALN-FLN. These reformed nationalists were usually required to prove their sincerity by taking positions of leadership within their community. Depending on local conditions, they might, instead, be asked to gather intelligence from the enemy. The SAS would accept as proof of loyalty only information communicated before the event.

Once it became clear that a village was firmly committed to the government, it also became necessary to defend that community against the inevitable guerrilla retaliations. Those officers who believed most firmly in the feasibility of a continued French Algeria worked to establish *auto-défense* (self-defense) villages in their areas. The results of the program were uneven. Generally, the SAS officers devised methods of arming the peasants themselves. When a village was ready for self-defense status, weapons were furnished not from the regular army stocks but from supplies of hunting rifles and obsolete equipment.[53] The government also donated barbed wire and other material needed to set up a defense perimeter.[54] While thus demonstrating its faith in these Algerian supporters, the administration also hedged its bet by distributing only outdated weapons that would be of limited value should they fall into the rebels' hands.

The distribution of arms served as an occasion for festivities, in which French and Algerian customs were blended. Typically there would be a flag raising and the ceremonial sacrifice of a ram. This would be followed by a *mechoui*, when the slain animal was cooked on an open fire and there was feasting for all. According to Berber and Arab customs, this feast served to seal their oath of loyalty. The entire ceremony was dictated by ancient and hallowed ritual, familiar to every tribesman, and the most minute variation from the prescribed forms rendered the entire function meaningless and false. Even though the villagers had pledged their allegiance previously, only a valid ceremony could make the pledge binding.

Jean Servier, a leading French ethnologist who specializes

in Berber activities, was invited to observe the arming of a village and the subsequent festivities.[55] He noticed that the village smith, a man in whose veins Negroid blood obviously flowed, was parading with the *jama'ah,* or village council.[56] As Servier knew, a smith was a lowly person whose position was close to that of a medieval serf and thus he would never be a member of the *jama'ah.* Carefully questioning some elders, Servier ascertained the true membership of the *jama'ah;* the real council then met to speak for the village. Consternation turned to delight as the peasants realized that here was a Frenchman who *knew.*[57] They had not been able to deceive him as they had the local SAS officer. Once the trick had been exposed, the time came to make the sacrifice. An old man informed the authorities that some soldiers had already slaughtered the sacrificial ram. Once again Servier interfered, knowing that the dead animal was worthless as a peace offering. In addition, the soldiers who had cut its throat were referred to as "butchers," an insulting term in Kabyle parlance. The polite phrase would have been "people of the meat."

Now the smith was called upon to perform his rightful duties. It was he who slaughtered the oxen for the harvest ceremonies each fall and who now slit the ram's throat with the ceremonial knife that had been handed down within the tribe. The sacrifice thus proceeded as tradition dictated.[58] The village now considered itself bound; the members would not break the oath. But they had attempted to deceive the SAS men with a false ritual, and only the accidental presence of an expert observer assured the authorities of peace in this village. This community, nevertheless, could thereafter be armed and be expected to defend itself against the rebels and to fight for the preservation of the French presence.

It is impossible to overemphasize the importance of an understanding of Algerian customs. In its crudest form pacification often meant that the peasants were simply and un-

knowingly tied to the colonial regime by a handshake between some French officials and the village elders.[59] In other
instances, as in the case cited by Servier, a pacification agreement could be discredited because of intentional flaws in the
accompanying ceremony. For the Algerians, lasting peace
must be based on more solid rock than that of fear or coercion.

The following serves as a further illustration of the importance of a familiarity with Muslim customs. The Arabs,
and the Kabyles as well, traditionally hold the written word in
high esteem, particularly Arabic script, in which the *Qur'an*
is written. Typically, if a man finds a scrap of paper with
Arabic written on it, he will pick it up and put it in a safe
place; to walk on the script is to defile it. It is thus almost
incredible that the French should repeatedly have painted
election slogans on the streets. Young Algerians stamped on
the painted phrases, happily expressing their contempt for
the administration.[60] The slogans were a disastrous mistake
and the Forces of Order should have been advised to paint
them on walls, where they would have been at least less liable
to arouse open contempt. Alquier, working in the Tazalt region, knew better. He made night visits to hostile villages
and plastered slogans on the doors.[61] As a result, the Algerians
were forced to notice the French proximity to their homes and
the propaganda, but they had no opportunity to defile the
words of a French officer.

Knowledge of the milieu, then, was all-important. In the
army's psychological action units, however, very few men
had adequate training in the ways of Algerian society. Knowledge of half a dozen phrases in Arabic or Kabyle might qualify
a man for this type of service.[62] Mistakes were inevitable.
Even though specialized schools existed to train soldiers in
psychological warfare, many of the instructors, who supposedly were propaganda experts with special knowledge of
Algeria, were themselves badly trained.

Moreover, the Algerian society was in a state of flux. Many

families were fleeing their rural homes in an attempt to find work and freedom from nationalist terror in the anonymity of the cities.[63] Between January 1955 and the end of 1957, for example, some 125,000 refugees flooded into Algiers.[64] This sudden influx resulted in the mushrooming *bidonvilles* which surrounded the capital. These were slums of the worst kind, in which thousands of wretchedly poor peasants slowly starved.[65] The men found neither employment nor relief from rebel exactions; despair soon replaced their dreams. In these filthy and teeming hovels, the guerrillas ruled supreme. The task of helping these people and rooting out the rebels was assigned to the SAS and its urban equivalent, the SAU (Urban Administrative Sections).

Cité Mahieddine, near Algiers, was the scene of a typical experiment in urban pacification. From the point of view of the leaders of the program, this *bidonville* was at its worst when the paratroopers first moved in. The first order of business was to identify the hovels and their occupants. Simultaneously, enemy cadres were sought out and imprisoned. The gradual reestablishment of security was followed in due course by the resumption of aid to the indigents. Within a few weeks jobs were created for 200 of the 12,000 inhabitants of Mahieddine. A majority of families, now that the rebel tax collectors had been eliminated, were able to collect the government's allowance of 2,400 francs per child per year, the equivalent of about $50.[66] The ALN-FLN for several long months had forced the citizens of Mahieddine to refuse this customary family allowance and every other form of aid.

After the French regained control, a Franco-Muslim school began operation in Mahieddine, and 1,800 children attended almost immediately. In addition to this institution, the SAU unit also started a vocational school for teenagers. It was not possible to reinstate all the colonial institutions, however, and there was necessarily a certain amount of improvisation by the officer of the SAU and others. The SAU officer, for example, served as justice of the peace. Here and in other similar situations, however, the officers ran their courts more in accordance with the spirit than the letter of the law, emphasizing reform and wherever possible handing down only light sentences for the crimes of the ignorant and the poor.[67]

Decent and solidly built housing replaced the hovels. Only then did the owner of the land on which the slum stood become alarmed. The landlord, a usurer, sued for his rents in order to stop the "illegal" activity of the SAU unit at Mahieddine.[68] The SAU officer was furious to see his pacification program brought to a standstill by this usurer. Some of his colleagues in other regions, even in rural areas, had similar difficulties. Not all the selfish landlords were individuals; in some cases the communes themselves owned the land on which the SAS units built new housing. In some of these the European mayors insisted on charging rent for the new units.[69]

The assumption by the army of complete control over much of rural Algeria did not bring a quick solution of *l'affaire algérienne.* While there was a renewal of confidence between the population at large and the administration, many Algerians were dissatisfied with many aspects of the military government. Of necessity many SAS teams were assigned to the relocation or regroupment villages. Even the best of these communities enjoyed only a relative success.[70] Not only was there the usual friction between the civil and military authorities, but every mistake committed by the SAS and SAU officers was amplified by a barrage of rebel propaganda. Thus exposed and exaggerated, the most minor errors often proved diastrous in terms of lost Algerian confidence.

Ignorance of indigenous customs contributed to many of these mistakes. The pacification ceremony described by Servier is only one example. The SAS committed a similar blunder in the hasty administrative reorganization of Bou Nour, where an SAS unit was charged with the running of the commune of Beni-Kouffi. Unfortunately, the Beni-Kouffi and the Bou Nour tribes were hereditary enemies.[71] Their union in one administrative unit was hence a serious mistake that led to many setbacks and problems.

In the full communes the SAS experiment was by and large a failure. There the chiefs and their projects could be challenged by the more or less selfish representatives of *colon* and other European interests. At Bir Rabalon, for example, an officer of the local SAS unit was reassigned to another area soon after he became involved in a disagreement with the local mayor. The two had argued about the use of unemployment credits, and the SAS chief, having no legally defined powers, had lost.[72] Other competent officers found that petty considerations led local officials to block all their efforts.[73] Many settlers were unwilling to make any concessions to the Algerian population. These *colons* and their elected representatives resisted the French army officers who occasionally espoused the cause of the natives. Nor were the officers of the SAS the only proponents of a more liberal attitude in the face of *colon* resistance to reform. While some SAS officers reacted bitterly to *colon* interference on the local levels, the administration tried to improve the lot of Algerians from above.[74] The passing of laws that facilitated the appointment of Arabs and Berbers to positions of importance in the government and in industry is only one example of the colonial government's efforts.[75]

In spite of all its limitations the SAS experiment was often a successful counterinsurgency institution. There were, however, many weaknesses in the system. The legal authority of the SAS officers was never clearly defined. Success or failure was too dependent on the personal qualities and abilities of the officers, who at their best were benevolent dictators. If they operated in areas inhabited by strong European minorities, they had to be expert diplomats as well. Above all else, they were French soldiers who, in a nonmilitary capacity, had to convince Algerians that France was not the enemy. Moreover, although it was one of the most effective components in the overall French effort of counterinsurgency, the SAS could not solve all the problems inherent in the colonial situation. Finally, after 1958, when the regroupment program and the SAS system were more tightly centralized and placed under the absolute control of the French army, and when assigned officers replaced volunteers, the SAS was lost.

13 | *The Resettlement Policy and the Refugee Problem*

THE ALGERIAN REVOLUTION CREATED ITS SHARE OF REFUGEES. As in any war, the population fled the battle areas. Those who left their homes included many who were simply fleeing the exactions of the terrorists or repressive French measures against those villages which had aided the nationalists. In addition there were many refugees who favored independence or who were suspected of rebel sympathies. Many of those who fled for political reasons resettled in other Maghribi or Arab countries, but mainly in Morocco and Tunisia. The minority of Francophile Algerians often tried to reach France or at least move to urban centers within Algeria where the Forces of Order could better protect them. Finally, thousands of basically indifferent Algerians and their families joined the flood and tried to start a new life in the large cities of coastal Algeria.[1]

Many refugees moved of their own free will, but they were quickly joined by an equal number who were forced to desert their homes because of the regroupment policy. Under this strategy new villages were built, usually by the refugees themselves, near French military posts. There the refugees, assisted by SAS officers, tried to pick up the threads of their broken lives. Despite various attempts to aid them in this readjustment, most of the resettled peasants remained sunk in apathy; they had been uprooted from the land—unyielding and hostile though it might be—to which they felt closely bound.[2] While all refugees throughout Algeria faced the same insoluble problems, those confined to the relocation camps were generally the most wretched.

The policy of resettlement was born of purely military considerations, although other factors later played a part in its development. The objective was to deny the rebels the aid and comfort that they undoubtedly received from much of the population.[3] In this war, as in earlier wars of national liberation, the terrorists relied on guerrilla fighters who blended into the masses as "fish in the water."[4] By forcing small and scattered communities to regroup under military protection into larger and more compact units, the "water" would in effect be drained away and the "fish" would be left exposed in the empty lakes. The rebels would lose the essential support of the peasants, and the deserted villages would be destroyed. Within the designated no-man's lands any Algerian would be suspect and fair game for the Forces of Order.

It cannot be claimed that regroupment was the cause of the entire refugee problem. Nevertheless, it has been estimated that roughly half of the three million people who in 1960 did not live in the same home as in 1954 were displaced because of this policy.[5] The remaining half were chiefly part of a generalized movement from rural to urban areas that, having begun before 1954, was greatly accelerated by the conflict between the FLN-ALN and the French. Included in both groups were tens of thousands who sought temporary refuge abroad, mainly in Morocco and Tunisia. By the end of the war more than one million people, most of whom were women, children and old men, had passed through the relocation centers. The figure represents between fifteen and twenty-five per cent of the rural population of Algeria.[6]

The first regroupments were organized in the Aurès region in November 1954.[7] In 1956 the system was applied to three new regions—Dahra, Kabylia, and the Bône area. Then in 1957 the first "forbidden zones" were created. The creation of each zone necessitated the resettlement of thousands of refugees. In the fall of 1958 the French High Command admitted the existence of 535,000 regrouped people. A month later the official figure stood at 740,000. By mid-April 1959 a team of investigators sent by the French government concluded that over one million people, some of them in illegal regroupment centers, were affected.[8] Since the Assembly had not passed a law dealing with the policy of regroupment, forced relocation was illegal except in those areas where the government specifically decreed it to be the official strategy.

From the first days of the revolution the leaders of the Forces of Order foresaw that it would be very difficult to pursue the rebels in certain mountainous areas. There the enemy would be favored by the terrain, which he knew intimately, and by the people, his own. In addition the French army had too few men to control all the trouble spots. Thus the colonial military command almost from the outset declared the most difficult mountain regions to be forbidden zones. The inhabitants were ordered to evacuate their homes, but unfortunately the military had no plans for the resettlement of the people affected, nor were there available the means to assist these Algerians to relocate.[9]

During 1955 and most of 1956 the administrative and military authorities did nothing to solve the refugee problem. The

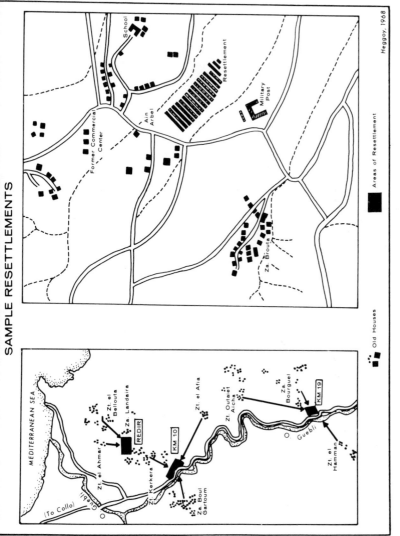

SAMPLE RESETTLEMENTS

Heggoy, 1968

MAP 6

 Areas of Resettlement

Old Houses

inhabitants of the forbidden zones were generally left to choose among three perilous courses. Most displaced persons preferred to stay close to their homes. To remain in their homes despite the military decree was the most dangerous course, but, because the army carried on only superficial searches of these empty villages, it was a simple matter to hide until the soldiers had returned to their bases. A second possibility was to resettle as close as possible to the illegal zone, build temporary dwellings, and await the end of the war. Even while the fighting continued, those who chose this course might still creep stealthily into their lands to cultivate their abandoned gardens and to use their pastures. Needless to say, this was not a prudent choice, but it enabled some peasants to be near their ancestral lands. Finally, these displaced peasants might resettle at the nearest rural center, or, if they had the resources for the journey, in an Algerian city, in France, or in a neighboring Arab nation. Nearby towns and villages, however, probably attracted most of the refugees.[10] Some villages of 500 inhabitants gained 1,500 or more almost overnight in areas close to the forbidden zones.[11] In addition many joined the flood to the cities. Between 1954 and 1960 towns in the old department of Algiers saw a population increase of 67.5 per cent. Urban growth in the Constantine and Oran regions was 63 per cent and 48 per cent respectively.[12] There is a correlation between these increases and the intensity of rebel activity in the countryside, especially in the rugged interior. The Oran region had a smaller influx than the areas of Constantine or Algiers where the rebels were much more active for a longer period of time.

In rural centers, towns, or cities the refugees from the forbidden zones created insoluble housing shortages. They were soon forced to build shantytowns similar to Cité Mahieddine near Algiers (see chapter 12). Because they were now landless and thus deprived of their only source of income, the newcomers were wretchedly poor. Where the colonial administration was still in control, they became public wards, abject indigents. The fugitives quite naturally blamed the French army for their reduced circumstances, thus providing the rebels with fertile ground for their nationalist theories.[13] By their strategy of relocation, the French had, in effect, helped their enemies.

Those refugees who resettled as close as possible to their former homes also proved ready to accept the propaganda of the ALN-FLN. Like their fellow transients elsewhere, they hated the French for forcing them from their lands. These peasants built new homes when their old houses were usually only partially destroyed. As a result, the rebels gained even more potential supporters and more sanctuaries.[14] Among those who refused to move from their homes, many were probably active nationalists. Some, however, may well have been apolitical individualists who preferred to suffer rather than abandon their land. In any case, the French army had apparently failed because it had not completely cleared out the forbidden zones and because it had not foreseen the bitter reaction of those forced to flee their homes.

Those who were forced to resettle faced enormous social and economic difficulties, for which they received no assistance. There were, for example, no established supply routes to serve those who remained in the vicinity of the forbidden zones.[15] The peasants did not have title to the land on which their new dwellings stood. They were usually thrown into direct contact with other tribes in their new areas, sometimes with enemy tribes. These contacts also affected those who relocated in villages and urban centers. The net effect was to upset the established social patterns. Indeed, the whole fabric of tribal society was threatened. Yet the military and civil authorities were slow to react, and the Algerians' hatred for the French and their impersonal military strategies grew.[16]

The first official solutions emerged at the time when the SAS system was becoming firmly established. Since the SAS presented direct military administration, a military solution to the refugee problem suggested itself. Instead of abandoning the displaced persons to their own initiative and thus creating new problems for the villages and towns where they resettled, the army would direct the homeless to new villages. These would be built by the refugees themselves and would be protected by the army. An added advantage would be that the rebels would find it more difficult to exploit the unhappiness of the fugitives. The resettlement policy gradually emerged in late 1956 and early 1957.[17] It was closely connected to military exigencies, to political reforms effected during the same period, and to the SAS system that combined both the military and adminstrative aspects of counterinsurgency. There were to be rural as well as urban relocation centers.

In urban areas the building of resettlement housing was almost invariably linked to the suppression of the shantytowns created or magnified by the inflow of refugees from all over Algeria. Cité Mahieddine, already mentioned, is an example, as is the slum of Sidi Salem, a section of Bône. The Sidi Salem experiment fits into a generalized building program that affected the whole colony. In Algiers alone, for example, some 8,000 dwellings were built in a five-year period ending in 1959. Housing was thereby provided for 60,000 people in a relocation project that far surpassed similar efforts even in Paris. Most of the new buildings were so-called HLM (Habitations de Loyé Moyen), or apartment complexes with rents fixed low enough to be within the reach of most regularly employed men, even unskilled workers. But the effort was insufficient to meet existing needs. An official estimate showed that at least 80,000 new units were needed in 1954 to meet Muslim needs alone. The same report claimed that 522,000 urban and 165,000 rural apartments or houses would have to be built to meet the demands of the entire colony by 1966.[18]

In the suburbs of Bône, which is near the Tunisian border and was therefore one of the most unstable regions of the country, 11,000 to 12,000 people had been unable to find adequate housing. As a result a shantytown grew up in a marshy area just east of the city. Conditions were crowded and unhealthy. The refugees lived in shelters made of discarded wood, cardboard, tin cans, and bamboo slivers. Some 3,000 women and 5,000 children, but hardly any able-bodied men, made their home there. The shacks were so crowded together that motor vehicles could not circulate. The whole area was unsafe for Europeans, and officials had given up attempts to control the residents. The nationalists, of course, circulated at will. They had made the shantytown a refuge for rebels responsible for attacks against the authorities in other quarters of the city and throughout the whole region.[19]

From a military and political point of view, it became absolutely necessary to correct the situation. In December 1955 the problem of the shantytowns around Bône was tackled. The first priority was to build new and decent housing with adequate space and usable streets provided. Direction of the project was given to the local SAS officer, who simply added this to his other numerous duties.[20] Even before new construction had begun to replace the shanties the responsible officer of the Urban Administrative Sections (SAU) had begun a propaganda compaign. He sought, with considerable success, to induce the shanty dwellers to move to a new location. Available credits for new buildings were still far too modest. So the original move from the unhealthy marshes to a new location necessitated a transfer of the shanties. These were simply torn down and rebuilt, with a little extra material made available for repairs, at the site of the future Sidi Salem. The military authorities supplied some labor for the tearing down and rebuilding of houses, as well as trucks for transportation and tents for temporary shelter during the transfer operations. By the end of March 1957, or three months after the first move was made, the entire slum had been transplanted. The new village was cleaner, healthier, and had access to new water and electrical services.[21] The time had come to open new credits and to plan the construction of better houses.

While the move from one location to another was in progress, a representative of the SAU was assigned to the future Sidi Salem village to direct the entire project. This official collected information about all the newcomers and established official documents of all kinds for his new wards. He adjudicated conflicting claims, solved differences of opinion, and saw to it that the people got their share of semolina and other foodstuffs. He also ordered work projects to be commenced. Three hundred men at first and eventually almost 800 were put to work. They fabricated such things as windows and doors, made bricks, and prepared other component parts for the permanent housing project.[22]

Solid brick or stone houses were gradually built. Most were very modest indeed. These were typically composed of one room 3.45 by 3.70 meters (about 11 by 12 feet) and of a courtyard 3.25 by 4.85 meters (about 11 feet by 16 feet). A second room, covered but completely open on the court side, might be added. A compound was surrounded by a high wall, a concession to Algerian custom designed to protect women from the eyes of men outside their immediate families. Important to the officials was the fact that these dwellings proved to be much less expensive than had been expected. The basic units had been put up for an average of 70,000 francs (about $145) instead of the projected 350,000 francs. The bigger units had cost 180,000 francs rather than 550,000 francs. By the end of 1958 shanties had been replaced by new units.[23]

The new village paid handsome political dividends. Better town planning permitted the authorities to control the inhabitants, something they had been unable to do in the old shantytown. In addition, the better housing attracted new refugees, as did the possibility of finding employment in the new urban center. By the end of 1958 the original population of 11,500 had swollen to approximately 17,000. Meanwhile, official buildings of various kinds were also erected. The SAS had its own station, as did the police department. A post office, a bus terminal for service to Bône, a school, a social and cultural center, an infirmary, and several technical shops where young people might learn trades were also provided. At least 1,300 children began attending classes where they learned, among other things, the French language.[24] The frequency of medical consultations, usually free of charge, rose just as dramatically.

The French of course wanted to profit from this experience. They attempted to apply what had been learned in Sidi Salem to many other shantytowns throughout Algeria, as well as to some other centers of Arab or Berber population. The effectiveness of the type of resettlement carried on at Sidi Salem was quickly proven. Acts of terrorism, for example, dropped from 186 incidents in 1956 to 48 in 1958. In the same region there were 236 victims in 1956 and only 80 victims in 1958. Progress was evident although not all problems were solved. Many of the inhabitants of Sidi Salem were not able to find work, and constant unexpected checks at their homes undoubtedly irritated some. Because of the card catalogue filled with information at the time of the move to Sidi Salem, it was practically impossible for the inhabitants of the new village to give refuge to the rebels. The army, with this information at hand, could check the community at any time of the day or night and arrest anyone not accounted for. Also, there were more men in the Forces of Order in 1958 than there had been in 1956. But the emptying of the original shantytown also contributed much toward desired ends.[25]

There were other centers just as successful as Sidi Salem.[26] Nevertheless there were many more poorly conceived and executed, where people were forced to live in abject misery. Failures could occasionally be blamed on an officer who was not devoted to duty or to the betterment of his wards' lives.

More often, however, the fault lay elsewhere. There were rarely sufficient credits available to generate a program of building and of social services needed to correct social ills and to counter rebel propaganda. Also, the policy of resettling whole villages or of concentrating the population of several villages in one new village was often applied too quickly and too haphazardly.[27] Excesses eventually led to a parliamentary investigation and, in 1958, to an official admission that there were well over 1,000,000 people in resettlement centers, some of which were illegal.[28]

The most unfortunate aspect of the resettlement policy was that the refugees within new population centers had been forced to leave behind the land which gave them sustenance. They usually managed to bring their livestock with them, but the difficult access to pasture lands, provided these were available, led to a quick diminution of the small flocks. When the relocated families became too hungry, they ate their animals. In this way goats and, with them, milk for the children disappeared. The people who had owned these animals sank deeper and deeper into squalid poverty as their source of food disappeared. They became hungry beggars who were forced to depend completely on meager official handouts.[29]

It became quite evident that the resettlements were often created with inadequate preparation and that many natives were forced to move before substitute housing could be provided. Often the new center was not self-supporting. Orders to relocate the inhabitants of particular hamlets and villages had obviously been issued because of military considerations. Little care had been taken to help the affected populations make the necessary transition. Finally, the authorities were rather slow to react to conditions created by the application of relocation orders. It was not until 1957 that official guidelines were finally issued on the question of resettlement.[30]

Beginning in November 1957, directives from Algiers explained the resettlement policy. One of the first official orders created a distinction between two kinds of relocation centers.[31] Some new villages, built in poor locations from the standpoint of economic and social realities, were to be temporary institutions. The refugees were to be permitted to return to their original homes as soon as political considerations would permit. Very little capital was to be used for this type of population concentration. A second category of resettlement, it was hoped, would become permanent rural villages or suburban centers. These centers were to be very carefully planned to serve in the future some necessary economic, social, or political purpose. At least three types of permanent resettlement were recognized almost immediately.[32] A center might become, for example, the county seat of a new commune; thus a completely new village would be created. Second, villages destroyed because of the war might be rebuilt; the occasion would be seized to suggest or impose better town planning. Finally, a permanent resettlement might be conceived as a workers' suburb on the outskirts of an existing city, as were Sidi Salem and Cité Mahieddine.

Whichever of the three types a particular center might be, it was usually granted sufficient credits to assure it a chance to become a permanent settlement. This had not always been the case before 1957. In addition, specialists met to plan in advance for all the economic and physical aspects of a permanent settlement. Experience might lead to revisions in the plan, but there was always some direction. There was a framework that permitted planners to avoid past mistakes and to suggest improvements. The SAS officer at Sidi Salem, for example, was able to build individual units for far less than had been anticipated. Since so many new refugees came freely, the houses he built were obviously attractive.[33] In reaction to the resettlement program adopted by the French, nationalists accused France of imitating the Nazi concentration camps.[34] The French, on the other hand, developed a somewhat idealistic attitude that they expressed in their resettlement policy.[35] Gradually a purely military policy became something much more important. Here was a truly concentrated effort to help at least some Algerians to jump into the twentieth century.

In its origins, the resettlement policy was military. But by 1958 at the latest it was generally agreed that the policy could be morally acceptable only if it led to an amelioration of the lives of the people. Achieving better control of certain areas was not sufficient justification; poor conditions within a relocation center would drive the people into the nationalist camps.[36] There were, unfortunately, too many experiments that did not take into account such considerations. A rule of thumb was that if a regroupment had 1,000 inhabitants, one child died every two days.[37] There were, however, usually many more people concentrated in typical regroupments. It was common to see pot-bellied children, young Algerians with rickets, and many others obviously close to starvation. On one occasion, for example, the Red Cross distributed 50 pints of oil to 2,774 people in a camp where no fatty food had been distributed for over a year.[38] This example becomes meaningful when one considers the fact that most Algerians get over 90 per cent of the fat in their diet from olive oil, probably their most important staple after cereal and dried figs or dates. In another camp an SAS officer complained that he distributed only 10 liters of milk a day for children, but he needed 300 liters to meet the basic needs of his wards.[39]

The effect of regroupment was thus often tragic. When it affected certain special categories, such as the nomadic population, the results were cataclysmic in their destructive consequences. When nomads were forced to resettle in permanent sites, their whole way of life was destroyed. In the semi-arid fringes of the Sahara these people survived only because of their sheep and goats, which they moved constantly in search of pasture. When men and animals were forced to stop wandering, the food supply around the resettlement camp was quickly consumed. The herds were decimated; animals died, people began to starve, and the remaining sheep and goats were slaughtered and eaten. The nomads thereby lost their only wealth in addition to their supply of milk, meat, and wool. As a result, they faced a harsh winter without food, blankets, or clothing. The military who had forced the no-mads to become sedentary had presumably done so to con-trol them better or to protect them from the rebels. The same officers, however, had not taken steps to feed their "impris-oned" nomads.[40]

Still another set of problems arose when interdicted zones were created near the Tunisian and Moroccan frontiers. Most of the displaced inhabitants there were not resettled but escaped French control by crossing the borders. In western Algeria, for example, a large no-man's land was decreed in 1956 and 1957 all along the Moroccan border.[41] The French hoped to avoid expected trouble from the newly independent realm of Mohammed V, but as a method of counterinsurgency the search and clear operations near the border were poorly directed and conceived. Instead of beginning with their backs to the Moroccan frontier, the French army units moved from east to west, pushing the people ahead of them so that they were forced into Morocco as refugees. Thus the inhabitants became displaced persons in Morocco instead of being forced to resettle elsewhere in Algeria.[42] It might also be noted that most of the 40,000 to 50,000 who fled were sedentary people who temporarily took up nomadism in Morocco, where they usually lived in tents.

As was typical of many Algerian refugees, those who went to Morocco resettled as close as possible to their original homes.[43] The rebels blamed the colonialist hordes for the exodus, claiming that the refugees were faced with the choice of flight or massacre, but there was actually little bloodshed associated with the search and clear operations along the bor-der.[44] The rebels, of course, suffered from the depopulation of

MAP 7

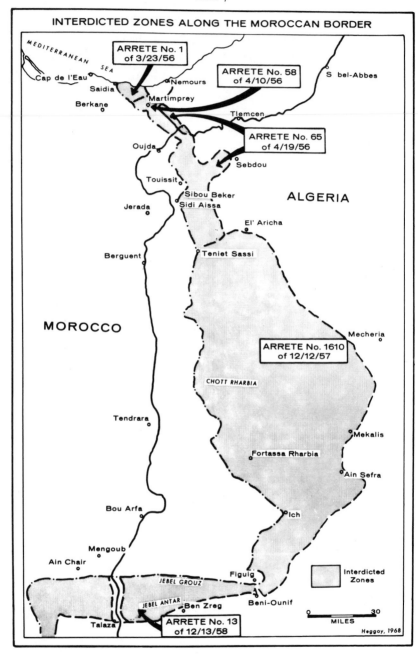

INTERDICTED ZONES ALONG THE MOROCCAN BORDER

MEDITERRANEAN SEA

Cap de l'Eau

ARRETE No. 1
of 3/23/56

Nemours

Saidia

Berkane

Martimprey

ARRETE No. 58
of 4/10/56

S bel-Abbes

Tlemcen

ARRETE No. 65
of 4/19/56

Oujda

Sebdou

Touissit

Sibou Beker

ALGERIA

Sidi Aissa

Jerada

El' Aricha

Berguent

Teniet Sassi

MOROCCO

Mecheria

ARRETE No. 1610
of 12/12/57

CHOTT RHARBIA

Tendrara

Mekalis

Fortassa Rharbia

Ain Sefra

Bou Arfa

Ich

Mengoub

Ain Chair

JEBEL GROUZ

Figuig

Interdicted
Zones

JEBEL ANTAR

Ben Zreg

Beni-Ounif

0   30
MILES

Talaza

ARRETE No. 13
of 12/13/58

Heggoy, 1968

vast zones that they wished to use for transit of weapons and ammunition procured abroad. A study that appeared in *El Moudjahid* late in 1957 claimed that the FLN gave orders to Algerians not to leave their national soil.[45] They needed people in the deserted regions to carry on their guerrilla warfare. The French suspected everyone who remained in the area, however, and the airmen who flew over interdicted zones strafed anything that moved.[46]

Even after the Forces of Order built barriers of mine fields and electrified barbed wire, Algerian refugees continued to cross the borders from time to time. Many apparently did so in defiance of the rebels' orders.[47] They resettled as much to get away from rebel pressure as to escape French control.[48] In time the barrier was perfected and became nearly impassable; yet the number of Algerians reported in eastern Morocco continued to grow.[49] Many explanations have been offered. It is probable that the Moroccan government simply took advantage of the situation to get the United Nations and other agencies to feed some of its own hungry people. Well over 131,000 people received food and other supplies meant for Algerian refugees even though only 85,000 repatriates were expected to return to Algeria from Morocco in April 1962.[50] Just as the Algerians in Morocco had not really been conscious of the fact that they were foreigners or refugees—after all, they were Muslims in a Muslim state—many Moroccans did not mind being called Algerians if they coud get food for doing so. All parties profited. The host government and the Algerian nationalists found a common cause on which they could cooperate, but the FLN undoubtedly profited most. They found in the refugee question an inexhaustible source of useful information to be used in their propaganda and in debates in the UN.

When the French created no-man's lands along the borders of Algeria, their primary objective was to take in hand rather large segments of the Algerian population that were presum-

MAP 8

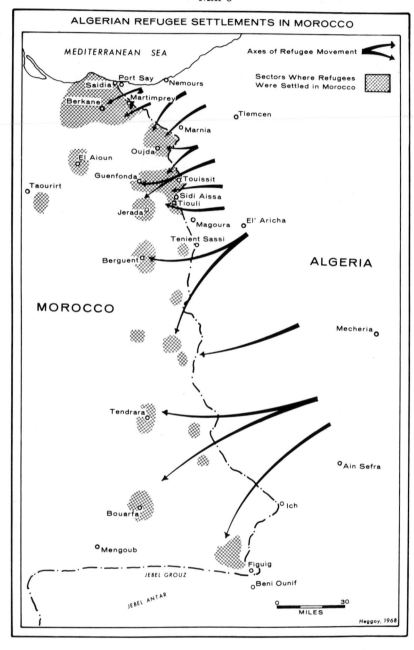

ALGERIAN REFUGEE SETTLEMENTS IN MOROCCO

Axes of Refugee Movement

Sectors Where Refugees
Were Settled in Morocco

MEDITERRANEAN SEA

Port Say
Saidia   Nemours
Berkane Martimprey
                           Tlemcen
                    Marnia
          Oujda
El Aioun
          Guenfonda   Touissit
Taourirt   Sidi Aissa
                        Tiouli
          Jerada
                   Magoura   El' Aricha
           Tenient Sassi
    Berguent   ALGERIA

MOROCCO
                                      Mecheria

         Tendrara

                                      Ain Sefra

    Bouarfa   Ich

      Mengoub   Figuig
                    JEBEL GROUZ   Beni Ounif
                                        0   30
         JEBEL ANTAR   MILES

                                    Heggoy, 1968

ably helping the rebels in their guerrilla war. They failed to achieve their objective when so many inhabitants of the affected regions went to Morocco or Tunisia. The refugees outside of Algeria, like their counterparts in resettlement camps throughout the colony, came quickly to blame their plight on France.[51] Hence the rebels were easily able to win most of these people over to their cause. Indeed the ALN drafted a rather large number of young Algerians from among the refugees in Morocco and Tunisia.[52]

The FLN leaders were able to use the refugee problem to focus international attention on the Algerian situation. As a result, the technical and military advantages gained by the French in their resettlement policy were largely lost because of the propaganda edge gained by the nationalists. The building of great barriers of electrified fences and mine fields along the Moroccan and Tunisian borders gave the French some technical advantages, but this too gave the rebels arguments with which to counter the French claim that the Algerian question was an internal French problem.

Together with other counterinsurgency measures, such as the *quadrillage* and the SAS, regroupment did give France the upper hand in her military conflict with Algeria.[53] The internal forces of the rebellion had been nearly choked. The ALN, although quite strong in Morocco and in Tunisia, had been forced within Algeria to splinter into small units that were extremely difficult to supply. But the true strength of the nationalists lay elsewhere. The nationalists had seized on the failures and the undesirable aspects of the French counterinsurgency and had turned the war into one in which propaganda truths were often more important than military facts. In the end politicians, not soldiers, were to decide the outcome of the Algerian question. By 1958 military considerations had become secondary.

14 | The Battle of Algiers and the Use of Torture

THE FIRST TWENTY-TWO MONTHS OF REVOLUTION BROUGHT NO solution to the basic problems that had led the CRUA to declare war on France. By the end of 1956 the nationalists had survived a long period of organization, of trial and error, and of gathering momentum. While the FLN had not managed to resolve the disunity within its own house, it had managed to put off divisive questions. These would presumably be decided after independence had been achieved. The survival of the MNA as a political party not affiliated with the Front was an outstanding exception, although Messali's group was very weak.[1] The FLN, whose members led the rebellion against French authority, had built up a much more solid organization and now had a better chance to survive. By the time they met in the Soummam Valley, its members had made the necessary

the delegates of the UN and to prove that the FLN was the only representative of the majority of Algerians, the nationalists also turned to urban terrorism, a tool of revolutionary warfare to which the Communists had already drawn the FLN's attention (see chapter 15).[6] A bitter test of strength and will developed as a result. Beginning in the fall of 1956, the essential theater of operations was the colonial capital itself. The struggle was to last almost nine months.

The Battle of Algiers had its origin, first of all, in the rebels' reaction to their loss of military initiative. The FLN-ALN also felt obliged to take notice of the first execution of nationalist prisoners, which occurred in June 1956. Furthermore, French counterterrorists had exploded bombs in the Casbah, the old Algerian quarter of the city. The Rue de Thèbes incident was especially significant. European terrorists discovered the address of a nationalist who had been killed while trying to assassinate some Europeans. They took revenge for this attempted murder by blowing up the building in which the would-be assassin had lived. Several presumably innocent people died, and many more Algerians were left homeless.[7] The rebel leaders, aware that inaction on their part would reduce their influence, felt obliged to take revenge—both for the prisoners' executions and for the victims of the Rue de Thèbes incident. On September 31, 1956, the nationalists exploded a bomb of their own.[8] Both sides were to repeat this kind of performance with terrible frequency and gruesome, indiscriminate effect. To the murder of selected individuals was added that of unknown people whose only sin was to be caught at a bus stop or in a cafe by the terrorists' bombs or grenades, which were often hurled from passing cars. Meanwhile, a propaganda struggle developed. While the French authorities quickly blamed the Communists for the explosion on September 31, the FLN insisted that it was responsible and should receive the credit or the blame.[9] The arrest of Ben Bella in October 1956 added fuel to the fire. The Algerian Revolution now entered a phase characterized by urban terrorism.

For the French government the issue was clear. Could the rebels, who had created their own clandestine administration in sections of the colonial capital, maintain themselves and their institutions? If France was to stay in Algeria, the answer had to be negative. The rebels, for their part, perceived the need for some spectacular success to help nationalist morale, which had been badly shaken by increasing military pressures and lack of weapons. The nationalists also wished to remind the people who lived near SAS centers, in *quadrillage* towns, or in resettlement camps that the ALN was still very much alive and active. Finally, nationalist diplomats, who were all members of the exterior FLN group, needed cards to play in foreign capitals and in the UN. Terrorism in the colonial capital was expected to impress foreign governments as well as to weaken the French administration in Algeria.

The single most important official reaction to the development of urban terrorism in Algiers was revealed in the decree of January 7, 1957. By this act Resident-Minister Lacoste handed to General Jacques Massu and his 10th Parachute Division all police powers and all responsibility for the maintenance of peace in the capital.[10] The Battle of Algiers immediately entered its most violent phase. In the next several weeks the two opponents appeared at their worst. The Forces of Order tortured the guilty and the innocent indiscriminately in an attempt to uncover all the nationalist leaders. The rebels reacted to the execution of captured friends and to the use of torture by resorting to blind urban terrorism. Massu and Lacoste, of course, tried to excuse the brutality of the Forces of Order on the grounds of expediency.[11] Although a few innocent people suffered, they claimed, the use of torture permitted soldiers to root out the terrorists and thereby to protect many more innocent people. The nationalists, in turn, justified their violence on two grounds. First, they were not strong enough to fight the French in the open. Second, they felt that without some conspicuous successes they would be deprived of their popular following.[12]

Those Algerians who had generally reacted strongly against the first instances of urban terrorism in 1955 gradually came to approve of the extreme measures taken by the nationalists. The Rue de Thèbes incident appears to have been a turning point in this respect.[13] A complete change in public attitudes among Arabs and Berbers occurred in the next few months as they reacted to the tactics employed by Massu's men. Indeed, the extreme measures taken by the French to eradicate the terrorist cells in Algiers led to some unexpected results. Most of the FLN leaders and their specialists in urban terrorism were captured or killed, and the rebel cells in the capital were nearly eradicated, but Massu's methods led nevertheless to a tightening of the rebels' hold on the Algerian population.

As the Muslim sectors of Algiers were completely sealed off from the city at large, most Algerians found themselves moved by a new sense of solidarity, by Francophobe and pro-nationalist opinions.[14] To leave or to enter the Casbah, for example, its inhabitants had to show their identification papers at police check points manned by soldiers. Within the cordoned sectors patrols were constantly on the move both before and after curfew hours. These patrols represented an immediate danger to nationalists who might not be able to justify their presence when stopped for questioning or for verification of required identification papers.[15] But the citizens at large were constantly annoyed because the soldiers kept them from going about their own business.

The Forces of Order acted upon every scrap of information with the utmost speed, meting out rough treatment to all those, guilty and innocent alike, about whom they had the slightest suspicion. Virtually all of their victims were Algerians. Some who had given rebels refuge were undoubtedly guilty of collaboration with the nationalists, but not all were involved. Arabs and Berbers almost inevitably identified with the victims and, since most of the latter were rebels, with the nationalists.[16] The French, for their part, thought the struggle was based on the collection and rapid exploitation of intelligence. The battle would be lost if leniency to protect the innocent was allowed to slow down the processes set in motion by Massu.[17]

The Battle of Algiers was a tactical victory for the Forces of Order. The terrorist cells were dismantled and most of the members were arrested or killed. The strategic victory, however, belonged to the nationalists, who reaped immense political gains from the high-handed military tactics of Massu. The Forces of Order created isolated Algerian ghettos whose occupants grew increasingly united in their hatred for France and their support for the FLN.[18] The difference between Algerians and Europeans living in Algeria became markedly clearer; only the Algerians were set apart by Massu's *cordons sanitaires*. This development, together with the growth of *colon* counterterrorism, forced the two communities to drift further and further apart.[19] The nationalists capitalized on the social fault thus created and undertook the leadership of the Algerian population as a whole. During the Battle of Algiers Arab and Berber children cheered as victims of FLN terrorism were carried away in ambulances. Even the prisoners of the Forces of Order cheered each new horror whenever they learned of such events.[20] Nor were the nationalists peculiar in this respect; Europeans applauded their own counterterrorists, who were often more murderous. A whole range of attitudes was unleashed during the Battle of Algiers. Horror and glee, joy and despair, and any number of other emotions were apparent after each new crime.[21]

Typical of the military reaction to criticism about the use of torture were General Massu's instructions concerning the interrogation of prisoners. These orders, which referred to "close interrogation," stated that there should be, at each level of the interrogation system, well-trained personnel and sharp interrogation teams.[22] Such orders quickly led to the wide-spread use of torture as a normal means of obtaining intelligence. When questioned about this delicate subject, officers routinely answered that they had not asked for the job of policing Algiers, but the task had nevertheless been given to the army with instructions to rid the capital of terrorism and to use any means necessary. Civilians should therefore keep out of army business and let the paratroopers clear out the city as they themselves thought fit. Resident-Minister Lacoste, who had abdicated civil control by handing all police powers to General Massu, was also very blunt in response to embarrassing questions. Thus a journalist was brusquely told to "Let us do our work. I ask only one thing of you . . . foreign correspondents: it is to please not come and bother us."[23]

Unfortunately, the French activists who worked with Lacoste pulled the innocent off the streets along with some guilty nationalists. When the prisoners of the paratroopers were released, they told terrible stories. Many accused specific officers of having used inhuman methods to force information or confessions from suspects.[24] Torture on a wide scale was obviously being used in Algeria. Official attempts to minimize or to ignore the problem were thus put in doubt. Moreover, the use of torture was not new in Algeria. The text of the Wiullaume Report of March 2, 1955, should convince even the most doubtful readers.[25] During the Battle of Algiers its use became widespread. Massu's orders of March 19, 1957 read, in part: "A *sine qua non* of our action in Algeria is that we should accept those methods heart and soul as necessary and morally justifiable."[26] Father Delarue, a French army chaplain, took it upon himself to quiet Massu's conscience:

Faced with a choice between two evils, either to cause temporary suffering to a bandit taken in the act who in any case may deserve to die, or leave numbers of innocent people to be massacred by this criminal's gang, when it could be destroyed as a result of his information, there can be no hesitation in choosing the lesser of the two evils, in an effective but not sadistic interrogation.[27]

Massu himself, at his own request, had already been sub-jected to torture by use of electrical shocks. Pleased by the effects of his own experiment, he thanked the chaplain for the justification.[28] He was not, however, able to control the types of torture used, nor was he able to keep innocent people from suffering with the guilty.[29] Finally, he was unable to check excesses that often led to the death of the prisoners. One particular casualty was Maurice Audin, a European who was an Assistant Professor of Science at the University of Algiers. He was also a member of the PCA (Algerian Communist Party) and had collaborated with the nationalists. The news of his death in strange circumstances could not be quashed.[30]

Henri Alleg, another important Communist and the editor of his party's newspaper in Algiers, suffered through a series of tortures but lived to write about the activities of some mem-bers of Massu's 10th Parachute Division.[31] The revelation that these two Europeans, Audin and Alleg, had been tortured at the hands of the French army shook the conscience of France. Alleg's book and other reports of the kind were quickly sup-pressed by the government.[32] But the battle was under way, and Algerian claims could no longer be discounted. Nation-alists were given a tool for political subversion that would soon shake French resolve in both Algeria and France. In-deed, an important phase of the battle was waged in France. According to an author who praised the activities of the Forces of Order during the Battle of Algiers, the essential struggle had shifted from Algiers to the banks of the Seine before the end of February 1957.[33] The army in Algiers would henceforth be bothered by more frequent visits of parliamentary com-missioners and by more embarrassing questions than ever before.[34]

What the paratroopers discovered and destroyed in the Battle of Algiers was a typical clandestine organization. Its members had divided the capital into sectors *(quartiers)*, each of which was administered by a chief and several assistants. Among the latter were a political commissioner, a transmission agent responsible for communications with the ALN at the next higher level, and an undetermined number of men collectively known as the protection committee. Political and action teams reported to the chiefs and received their orders from them. The political group was in charge of collecting funds and disseminating nationalist propaganda. The action group was the more complex in its organization. It usually contained several cells, one for fabricating bombs and another for putting the bombs to use. A third cell was staffed by specialists in arson. Finally, there were cells whose only task concerned sabotage and others whose work was to kill people who, in the opinion of the rebel leaders, were dangerous to the cause or undesirable for any number of reasons.[35]

By tracing the owner of a coat used to conceal a bomb that exploded at a soccer match on February 10, 1937, the Forces of Order were able to discover and dismantle an organization such as the one just described. One arrest, together with the use of torture and further intelligence, usually led to others. The network of conspiracy was thereby destroyed. By March 21 Lacoste could claim that 182 killers, 160 cell chiefs, and 232 collectors of funds had been arrested.[36]

Massu's methods were obviously effective. His interrogators also extracted information about the rebel organization above the level of the *quartier* chiefs. Acting through a liaison officer, the ALN's specialized committees gave orders to the political and action cells. There were four important committees in charge of finances, justice, intervention or military affairs, and intellectual affairs. The last named body apparently passed on doctrine, set up important propaganda guidelines, and ordered boycotts or strikes at specific times during the Battle of Algiers.[37]

The elaborate nationalist organization of Algiers was matched by French determination to surround the city completely and to divide it into four compartments. In this way the French sought to protect and clear up the colonial capital.[38] French troops eventually captured Saadi Yacef, the supreme rebel commander of the autonomous region of Algiers. Yacef's chief assistant, Ali la Pointe, the bandit who became a nationalist hero, was killed in a street fight with paratroopers.[39] The editors of the nationalist organ *El Moudjahid* lost their equipment and were forced to begin anew on foreign soil.[40] The internal leadership of the nationalist movement was compelled to leave Algeria and to take up the life of political émigrés.[41] This group, known as the CCE (Executive and Coordinating Committee), was quickly forced to compromise with the external leaders, whom they had belittled and replaced at the time of the Soummam Congress.

The outside delegation joined the exiled CCE in Tunis.[42] Thus Massu's pressure on the internal leaders and disagreements between the other revolutionary Algerians and the Egyptian government led the FLN to adopt a new base of operations. Tunis was closer to the theater of operations than Cairo. Difficulties between the FLN and Cairo were paralleled by struggles for influence within the nationalist ranks. Soon after the move, which was announced on April 17, 1957, the fight between the external delegation and the now exiled internal leaders reached a high point. Tempers were quickly cooled, however, and a compromise emerged from a congress held in Cairo on August 25. Although the meeting took place in Cairo, the CCE retained its base in Tunis.

Ramdane Abbane, the Kabyle who had seized supreme command at the Soummam meeting, was eased out of his position. The CNRA was enlarged by the appointment of twenty new members so that this body was henceforth composed of fifty-four delegates. The CCE itself functioned as a virtual government in every respect except in name; its nine members divided their work along lines from which emerged ministries. The new CCE drew one-third of its membership from the old CCE and one-third from external delegations; the remaining third were *wilaya* commanders. Ferhat Abbas, the old leader of the relatively moderate UDMA, was the leading member of the new government. His presence, probably the most notable aspect of the FLN's reorganization, indicated the revolutionary leadership's willingness to compromise with bourgeois elements.

The choice of Tunis as the base of operations for the nationalist leaders was an indirect effect of the Battle of Algiers. This development led more and more Frenchmen to realize the war could probably not be won by military means.[43] Tunis protected Algerian rebel soldiers and screened from the French the revolutionary government led by Ferhat Abbas. Massu's success, then, was hollow because the enemy could not be physically destroyed unless the French decided to violate Tunisia's pro-FLN neutrality.[44]

The French had nearly completed a barrier of electrified wires and mine fields to prevent rebel units and supplies from entering Algeria. But the same barrier kept the French from pursuing these enemy units and striking at rebel supply bases in Tunisia. Eventually, French officers tried to force their government to extend the war to Tunisia, to violate a self-imposed limitation. They wanted the right to use the principle of "hot pursuit." The result was the Sidi-Sakiet incident.[45] The French bombed a Tunisian village in which Algerian soldiers were training and from which the same nationalists had attacked French units in Algeria.

Despite a certain amount of despair about the possibility of ever crushing the insurgency, the Forces of Order continued to fight the rebels within Algeria. They continued to relocate or regroup whole villages, to assign thousands upon thousands of Algerians to house arrest, and to imprison many more. In the Battle of Algiers alone, 3,024 of more than 24,000 persons arrested disappeared while in the hands of Massu's paratroopers.[46] This figure was ascertained by an official count in June 1957 before the battle was over. Rebels who suffered personally showed little bitterness toward the French, but they would later insist that no one could know how many Algerians were actually arrested. The nationalists guessed that between 4,000 and 5,000 prisoners disappeared. Most of those who were lost died in torture chambers or were shot "while fleeing."[47]

Nor were the rebels and other Algerians who happened to live in the colonial capital the only people to suffer during the Battle of Algiers. The French effort to destroy the nationalists' terror organization in the capital was surely one of the most violent phases of the country-wide struggle against the FLN-ALN. The rebels committed their own atrocities and employed terror tactics. Most of the nationalists who took part in the Battle of Algiers were *fida'iyin,* people sworn to die for the cause, who usually volunteered for desperate missions. These volunteers were often seeking admittance into the ALN, which now accepted only those who were already completely compromised because of their terrorist activities. *Fida'iyin* were soldiers in civilian dress, indistinguishable from the "peaceful" Algerians among whom they lived or worked. They were like the political leaders of the rebel shadow administration (OPA) who lived in secrecy throughout the country. As a result, the French fight against urban terrorism was also a simple extension of the attempt to eradicate the OPA cells throughout Algeria (see chapter 5).[48]

The Battle of Algiers can be seen as simply the most violent facet of what some authors have called the second phase of the Algerian Revolution.[49] In the first phase the Forces of Order had tried with indifferent results to adapt to the type of war forced on France by the insurgents. The second phase began in 1956 when the French army seized the initiative. By January 1957 and the beginning of the Battle of Algiers, the Forces of Order were, by and large, in control. They were implementing the government's grand plan for political, administrative, and civic action that would, it was hoped, swing the balance of public opinion in favor of a continued French presence. The struggle in the colonial capital was the first phase of the program without which the positive aspects of reform could not be carried out. Before schools and infirmaries could reopen, before administrative services could function normally, the local OPA cells that terrorized the population had to be eliminated.

To keep rebel administrative units on the run, Massu used a special category of Algerian informants, for the most part former members of the FLN or ALN. These "Blue Caps," so named because of their uniforms, were ordered to take charge of specific groups of houses or apartment buildings.[50] They were held responsible for any illegal activity that might occur within the human or territorial unit to which they were assigned. Usually their very lives depended on the good behavior of the people on whom they were forced to inform. Since most were former members of the FLN or ALN, the pressures on them were evident.

The Blue Caps were only the lowest officials in a highly organized system designed to repress and regiment the Algerians in Algiers. General Massu and such aides as Lieutenant-Colonel Roger Trinquier, a member of Massu's brain trust, proved during the Battle of Algiers that torture could be organized.[51] Acting on this premise, they built a police state. Similar repressions were attempted in Oran and in Constantine, but, since all the specialists were with Massu and his paratroopers in the capital, the provincial measures were not very successful.[52] In Algiers the Blue Caps reported to the "Offensive Intelligence" section of the Algiers-Sahel sector, headed by Lieutenant-Colonel Trinquier. The real chief, in fact, was Colonel Godard, a master of anti-subversive warfare. Trinquier's representatives in the various subsectors used torture on persons arrested, often on the basis of the reports of informants.[53] The object was to elicit further intelligence.

Persons who were imprisoned by members of the 10th Parachute Division brought many complaints into the courts of justice. Specific cases of people who suffered atrocities in jails provided a detailed record of the key actors and the methods most often used to torture prisoners. Lieutenant André Charbonnier, for example, was named in numerous cases as a specialist in the art of applied torture, as were Captain Devis, Lieutenant Philippe Erulin, and any number of other officers.[54] Henri Alleg has also described the activities of Devis and Erulin.[55] Colonel Trinquier and an immediate assistant, Captain Faulques, offered advice and technical assistance when necessary.

In July 1957 Massu's 10th Parachute Division and, more particularly, its intelligence section were reorganized and named the CCI (Interservice Coordinating Center) and the DOP (*Dispositif Opérationel de Protection* or Operational Security Organization). The CCI-DOP could not, of course, operate in an administrative vacuum. It was supported by a local institution, the DPU (*Dispositif de Protection Urbaine* or Urban Security Service), whose creation was announced by Lacoste in March 1957. The new organization was a supplementary police force whose members were all Europeans and whose object was to help regiment the city. Somehow only Algerians came to be the objects of the constant surveillance. This new body also coordinated its work with the Blue Caps. Counterterrorism thereby became the official policy of France because officers, whether legally or not, applied it. Even Dr. Kovacs, a counterterrorist who was arrested in January 1957 in connection with the bazooka attempt on General Salan's life, was appointed to a position of leadership in the DPU by the Algiers-Sahel general staff, which took orders from General Salan.[56] The attempt on Salan's life had been made because extremists thought him too moderate. Such doubts were displaced by Salan's part in bringing Massu to Algiers.[57]

In retrospect it is hardly surprising to find that Salan and many of his staff later joined the OAS (Secret Army Organization). Beginning in early January 1957, they had in fact directed the creation of a political situation that can hardly be distinguished from a fascist state with very definite racial overtones. The victims of this system, the Algerian population of Algiers and, to a lesser extent, of Oran, Constantine, and other urban centers, reacted as might be expected. The Algerians came to hate their oppressors with more bitterness than before and, because the latter were representatives of republican France, turned against France.

Because of the excesses used in achieving their legitimate objective of counterinsurgency, the French clearly vitiated any immediate positive result of the suppression and eradication of the rebel organization in Algiers. In the end rebel excesses were largely forgotten. Saadi Yacef's *"crise de conscience,"* which was so clearly revealed during an interview about the use of indiscriminate terrorism, and particularly about the use of bombs wherever crowds gathered, was likewise not important in the long run.[58] But the hatred created by arbitrary arrests and the widespread use of torture against the rebels and suspected sympathizers was a determining factor. The question became a political issue that gravely weakened the Fourth Republic in France and definitely divided the Algerian population into two groups. The racist characteristics attributed to the colonial system were proven in the Battle of Algiers. Algerians swung to support the FLN-ALN, which at least tried to avenge them. A final note of bitterness for the French psychological and propaganda sections also remained. Their efforts to show that the rebels were in fact Communists —or at least closely allied to the Communists—failed.

15 | Communism, the UN, and the Algerian Revolution

THE USE OF TORTURE BY ELEMENTS OF MASSU'S 10TH PARA-
cute Division quickly became the central issue of debate in
the Battle of Algiers. There were, however, several other
critical questions raised by this struggle. The nationalists, for
example, opened the most violent phase of the conflict by
decreeing a general insurrectional strike that was to last from
January 18 to February 4, 1957, in order to impress the delegates at the United Nations. The rebels also wanted to
convince world opinion that the FLN-ALN was the true representative of the Algerian people.[1] If enough Muslims followed the decree, the point would be made.

French leaders, as they had done earlier but now with more
vigor, tried to discredit their enemies by accusing the insurgents of complicity with world Communism. The counterrevolutionary campaign in Algeria, France argued, was in fact

but one battle in the world-wide struggle against Communist expansion directed from Moscow.[2] The FLN denied this claim.

There was truth in each side's thesis. In its origins, for example, the Algerian nationalist movement was deeply indebted to the French Communist Party, which had financed the creation of the North African Star (ENA).[3] As the first institutional expression of Algerian nationalism, the ENA was born in Paris and developed but slowly in the colony itself. Yet the ENA was exported to Algeria, where by the 1950's it had become the MTLD, one of three important parties completely dedicated to the interests of the Muslim population.

Messali Hadj, leader of the ENA, then of the MTLD, had been quick to break with the Communists.[4] He retained the lessons he had learned from his early benefactors, however, and kept the party organized along Marxist lines. Then, in 1948 or 1949, over Messali's objections, some young hawks in the MTLD created the Secret Organization (OS),[5] clearly a Bolshevik type of institution completely dedicated to insurrection, to preparation for revolution. Practically all of the personnel of the CRUA, which started the revolution in November 1954, were former members of the OS. The CRUA in turn became the FLN.

It was easy to trace Algerian nationalism back to its Communist origins. Simplistic theses based on such considerations stated that Moscow was responsible for the Algerian insurrection and that the rebel leaders were basically Bolsheviks. Such conclusions, however, overlooked several facts. Most of the originators of the revolution, for example, were moved by a strong distrust of Communists. The rebels also objected to Marxist atheism and were jealous of the press coverage enjoyed by the PCA and the PCF. All of this did not mean that the FLN-ALN would not accept aid from the Communists; they would, and did, but on their own terms. A better analysis of the relationship between the nationalists and Communists in Algeria has been offered by Ch.-A. Julien, a leading French scholar of North Africa. According to Julien the revolution was not a Communist movement, but that did not mean that the Communists might not profit from the tragic situation.[6]

If most revolutionary leaders in the FLN distrusted Communists in general, they were particularly wary of the PCA.[7] The Algerian Communist Party was created in the 1930's as a branch of the PCF soon after it became evident that the latter had lost all influence over the ENA. Once launched, the PCA tried to win popular support among Muslims in the trans-Mediterranean departments of France. But this party could hardly compete with the MTLD for Algerian votes; the MTLD, created by ENA leaders, was just as proletarian as the PCA and clearly a North African institution. To the Muslims the Communist Party seemed to be a foreign import. Because of their traditional distrust of things from abroad, particularly European ideas, few Algerians joined the PCA. As a result, this party had a European membership, and the members kept their leaders from following an outright nationalist program.[8] Mutual trust and cooperation between the nationalists and the Communists thus came only slowly.

The first concerted effort at cooperation between the PCA and parties that were devoted specifically to Muslim interests developed in 1951. In August of that year the Algerian Front for the Defense and Respect of Liberty was formed. In addition to the MTLD, the UDMA, and the PCA, this Front also included the Ulama Association. The coalition had limited objectives, however, and could not, or in any case did not, lead its members to work collectively on essentially anticolonial programs.[9]

This rather weak alliance broke up, then was rebuilt during the spring of 1953 to support the nationalists, or at least the opponents of the colonial administration, in various elections. In the past such efforts had generally failed because Algerian votes had been split among UDMA, MTLD, and PCA candidates. In 1953 a temporary success was achieved when a few nationalist candidates were elected. The coalition, however, could not be kept alive. Control of events was slipping out the hands of the established political leaders in the anti-colonial camp. The MTLD was splitting at the seams in an internal struggle that led to the emergence of three factions. One faction, the Centralists, rejected the leadership of Messali Hadj; a second group, while in congress at Hornu in Belgium, declared itself faithful to the old leader; the third splinter organization was the underground CRUA, which was committed to unity through violent action and quickly took up arms against France.[10] The CRUA precipitated the events of November 1954 and the founding of the FLN. The PCA and Communists in general were caught by surprise. They had not believed the time ripe for action and they had no one representing them on the revolutionary "general staff."

The Communists reacted rather slowly after events had passed them by. Somehow, they hoped, they might infiltrate the camp of the insurgent nationalists. Above all, they wanted to retain their own party identity. The PCA, because of its ties to the PCF, was in a strange position. As long as the latter had thought it could share power within the French government, it had favored integration as a policy for Algeria. The PCA followed suit. By the early 1950's, when it became apparent that the PCF would not gain or even share power in France, there followed a change of party policy that brought immediate repercussions in Algeria. More Muslims were put into positions of leadership in the PCA and efforts were made to coordinate activities with the nationalists.[11]

As late as October 31, 1954, Communist leaders in the colony and abroad promised assistance to the rebels. From satellite countries propaganda programs in Arabic were immediately beamed toward North Africa. In Algeria the PCA collected clothing and other supplies for the insurgents. The Communists also fought repression through the press and in the courts after the beginning of revolution and as long as the government allowed them to persist. But the PCA continued to maintain its own fighting units and refused, at first, to join the FLN.

Important attitudes and issues divided the PCA and the FLN. The difference of opinion stemmed from the continued existence of the Communist Party as an entity not integrated into the Front. The CRUA had earlier been antagonized by the PCA's announced desire to cooperate with the MNA.[12] The nationalist leaders distrusted the Communists' motives. Perhaps the Communists intended to follow patterns of action outlined in the *Manifesto*. They would initially join the FLN (and, according to their own announcements, the MNA) in action, then denounce their allies, seize power, and create a democratic republic on the Soviet model.[13] The Algerian nationalists in control of the insurrection were wary. They insisted that the Communists agree to a dissolution of the PCA so that members of that party might join the Front as individuals.[14] The PCA found this proviso extremely difficult to accept. The party leaders answered the rebels' demands with the complaint that they could not disband and so renounce the glorious struggles of the past.

Privately the PCA had more pressing reasons for refusing the FLN's terms. Acceptance of the conditions demanded by the rebels would not allow the PCA to maintain an organization with which to seize power, hence to profit from the insecure political situation that would certainly follow a long war against France. The PCA leaders hesitated. They tried to support the rebels while at the same time maintaining a parallel armed rebellion of their own. An Algerian version of the Chinese situation during World War II developed. The nationalists of the central Maghrib, however, were more willing to work with the PCA, which they did not trust, than Chiang Kai-shek had been to cooperate with Mao Tse-tung. Another difference was that the Algerian Communist Party, because it was for so long a branch of the PCF, was relatively much weaker than its Asian counterpart had been.

Negotiations between the FLN and the PCA continued until the summer of 1956. Finally, the PCA was forced to accept the nationalists' terms. The Algerian Communist Party had been officially dissolved by order of the French government on September 13, 1955,[15] however, and life had become more difficult for the Communists. Meanwhile, French officials had not relented in their campaign to prove complicity between the rebels and the Communists. This in turn led the FLN to comment somewhat bitterly about their ally in the platform of the Soummam Congress:

> The Algerian Communist Party, even though it has become illegal and the colonialist press has gratified it with noisy publicity in order to prove its imaginary collusion with the Algerian Resistance, has not managed to play a role which deserved to be pointed out.
> The Communist leadership, which is bureaucratic and has no contact with the people, has not been capable of analyzing correctly the revolutionary situation. The PCA has disappeared as a serious organization.[16]

Algerian nationalists objected to, and probably envied, the notoriety that the PCA had received. The rebels felt they had left the Communists far behind; nevertheless, FLN leaders felt compelled to criticize their new ally. Although the FLN thought the PCA had "disappeared as a serious organization," the latter still had some possibilities of success. After all, the nationalists themselves had been seduced by totalitarian methods. Also important was the fact that the Communists did help the rebels, and individual members of the PCA or of the PCF did get into the FLN-ALN.[17]

The Maillot incident was one of the most spectacular events pointing to collusion between the nationalists and the Communists. Maillot and a friend, Laban, both members of the PCF, gave the ALN 135 submachine guns and a stock of ammunition when they deserted their unit in the Forces of Order to join the insurgents. Having given the ALN this important material aid, which they had stolen from French supplies, they stayed on to fight against France until they were killed by French troops on June 5, 1956. On the first day of the following month the PCA issued a handbill advising members of the Communist Liberation Commandos to join the ALN with all their equipment and to recognize the authority of the FLN.[18] The Communists had finally bowed to the conditions imposed by the nationalist leadership.

The PCA decision to disband and the death of Maillot were probably connected. Communist units had suffered bad reverses on their own, but it was the death of these particular party members, who had joined the ALN, that forced a decision. Long before July 1, 1956, armed elements responsible to the PCA were actively participating in the insurrection against French authority in Algeria. The Communist Commandos had naturally coordinated their activities with local or neighboring nationalist units, but they had steadfastly refused to accept FLN control.[19] Until July of 1956 the PCA maintained its own units. Some Communists and ex-Communists had of course fought with the ALN almost from the beginning,[20] but the PCA willingly freed members from party direction only when forced to do so by events. The Communists had apparently counted heavily on men such as Maillot and Laban to influence the FLN-ALN from within. When such men died, the PCA leaders were forced to remold their thinking. Time had also forced change. The insurrection, which the Communists thought premature in the fall of 1954, had lasted into the summer of 1956.

Changes in the thinking of PCA and PCF leaders can be clearly seen by comparing the directive of July 1956 with an analysis of the Algerian insurgency that appeared on November 2, 1954, in *L'Humanité,* a party organ published in Paris. The tone on this second day of revolution was cautious. The editors wrote that terror could not be a solution; it could be legitimate only if it led to the realization of liberty for the Algerian people.[21] In Algeria the Communist newspaper *Alger Républicain* began attacking repression while the top echelons of the PCA tried to decide what to do. According to J. Soustelle, who served as governor-general in Algeria during the critical period in rebel-Communist relations, the PCA leader Mohamed Guerrouf failed to persuade his party to help the nationalists without reservations. The Communists did lend a hand with propaganda, and they furnished legal aid to captured nationalists, but they were slow to commit themselves. Not until July and August 1955 did it become evident that the PCA and FLN were working together.[22]

The Communists later tried to gather glory. They claimed that it took the Marxist revolution and the birth of the PCF to establish the right of colonized people to rule themselves.[23] They continued to play on this theme until the Algerians had won their independence. Yet as late as March 2, 1956, the PCF, and by implication the PCA as well, declared itself a partisan of permanent political, economic, and cultural ties between Algeria and France.[24] It is difficult to resist the temptation to ask what this would have meant had the PCF been in power in France. In 1959 Bachir Hadj Ali, an Algerian Communist, wrote a history of Algeria to fit his party's idea of the continuing struggle against the colonial power. He thanked the PCF for its support and gave the PCA a lion's share of the credit for the Algerian Revolution.[25] Jacques Couland, a French writer, argued in much the same way in a similar book.[26]

Many opponents of the FLN blamed the PCA, the PCF, and Moscow for the Algerian Revolution. A typical argument claimed that the Communists had precipitated the events on November 1, 1954. The nationalist organization was so rich and so complex that it could not have been the work of the Algerian Muslims; all of it had come from the Kremlin.[27] If the racist implications of this thesis are overlooked, the argument fits nicely into the proposition that just as independence in the Middle East had opened the way for international Communism, the liberation of Algeria would mean the substitution of French control for direction from Moscow. In the end the Marxists would take Europe by flanking it in Africa.[28] Such specious arguments about collaboration between the Communists and Algerian rebels do, however, give a clue that might explain the failure of the PCA. This party *was* too much involved in consideration of world politics. The revolution directed by the FLN was much more localized. The Algerian nationalists did not trust the Communists because the latter were not concerned solely with winning Algeria's freedom and because they obviously took orders from outsiders. This attitude did not imply an unwillingness on the part of the FLN to accept aid from the Communists in Algeria or from Marxist governments anywhere. Both Arab and Communist nations cooperated with the FLN, and all three groups presented a unified propaganda campaign against French colonial authority in Algeria.[29]

The Algerian nationalists needed all the help they could get. They were particularly willing to accept help that would affect France, help that would, for example, put pressure on the French through debates in the UN. The Battle of Algiers, which cemented the FLN-PCA agreement revealed in the summer of 1956, was fought largely to influence an expected debate on the Algerian question in the UN. The "grave situation" in Algeria was first brought to the attention of the Security Council on January 5, 1955.[30] Strangely enough, the conservative government of Saudi Arabia was the first to point to this question. Also concerned were the twenty-nine states that participated in the Bandung Conference. The campaign was largely conducted by Arab friends of the FLN and strongly supported by the Afro-Asian bloc.[31] Although cautious at the beginning, the Communist bloc also joined the effort in the

UN and in international diplomacy.[32] Thus the assault on the French position in Algeria quickly became an anticolonial struggle.

In the UN a decisive step was taken on July 29, 1955. In a letter to the Secretary-General fourteen governments requested that the Algerian question be inscribed on the agenda of the 10th session. All the signatory governments represented Arab and Asian nations, most of them containing important Muslim elements. The matter was referred to the General Committee, which, after difficult deliberations, recommended that the question not be considered by the 10th session of the General Assembly. In the Committee itself the negative recommendation was adopted by a vote of eight to five with two abstentions. In the Assembly, however, many delegates were unhappy with this decision. A procedural debate on the issue began on September 29, 1955. Supporters of the FLN tried to reverse the decision that excluded the question from the agenda of the 10th session.

France and others who opposed debate on the Algerian question argued that it was a domestic issue, hence the UN had no jurisdiction. The French constitution stipulated that Algeria was an integral part of the nation. The rights of France were based on the right of conquest, and Algeria was in no way different from other conquered provinces such as Flanders or Burgundy. The insurrection was fomented by foreign powers, and the government in Paris had every right to defend itself from such attacks on its integrity. Moreover, the problem was being settled and there was consequently no threat to international peace and security.[33]

The Afro-Asian group, joined by the USSR, argued that the UN should at least investigate to determine whether this was really a domestic issue. Going a step further, those who supported the FLN claimed that the situation was a threat to international peace and security, as clearly indicated by the fears expressed by Saudi Arabia in January 1955 and by the participants in the Bandung Conference a little later. In any case, there was a war on, and it was the UN's duty to end wars. Contesting each French argument, the allies of the Algerian nationalists claimed that the right of conquest was not applicable in Algeria. To support this point they referred to the 1830 treaty that marked the end of Turkish domination. Furthermore, human rights and the right to self-determination should be taken into consideration.[34]

The debate was resolved on September 30. By a majority of only one vote (twenty-seven to twenty-eight with five abstentions) the General Assembly refused to accept the General Committee's recommendation to keep the Algerian question off the agenda. The next step, to agree to a discussion of the question during the 10th session, came easily. The French delegation reacted violently, walking out of the Assembly on October 1, 1955. It did not return until November 25, when the debate on Algeria was postponed. The FLN's allies in the UN had discovered differences of opinion among themselves; perhaps they also wished to give France time to react. Above all, no one wanted the French government to leave the Assembly indefinitely.[35]

When the Algerian question again came up for consideration, during the 11th session of the General Assembly, France again argued that the UN had no jurisdiction. But this time the French delegates did not walk out of the meetings. Not wishing to be absent when the Suez affair was discussed, they stayed to present their side of the Algerian question.[36] France explained the pacification program but refused to participate in the debate about the actual phrasing of a resolution that was finally passed.

Although France did not grant her consent to the UN consideration of the Algerian question, the Assembly debate did influence French decisions on the subject. Pressure was exerted, paralleling and supporting that of ALN operations in Algeria itself. Premier Guy Mollet's declaration of January

1956 announced that France would "recognize and respect the Algerian personality."[37] Although the connection between this pronouncement and the UN resolution cannot be proven, it appears that there was one. The FLN was not satisfied with this vague phrase, nor did the Algerian nationalists like the Assembly's resolution of February 15, 1957. The resolution was innocuous, simply expressing the hope that a "peaceful, just and democratic solution" might be found.[38] This kind of declaration was certainly not what the rebels had in mind when they launched the insurrectional strike early in February 1955. By forcing the strike the FLN had undoubtedly wanted to prove that France, with over 400,000 men in Algeria, could not check the activities of a small nationalist battalion of between 200 and 300 men.[39] The Battle of Algiers was fought because the FLN wanted to prove that it controlled a large portion of the population. Perhaps they wanted to prove to themselves, as well as to others, that they really represented the Muslim population.[40]

By the end of 1957, partly because they lost the Battle of Algiers, and partly because of the French *quadrillage* and the frontier barriers that had now become effective, the ALN was unable to maintain its strength within Algeria. There was, as a result, a marked decrease in the number of rebel military operations.[41] The battle in the UN continued, but the FLN was again disappointed by the resolution of December 10, 1957, which they thought too mild. This time the Assembly simply took note of offers of good offices made by the governments of Morocco and Tunisia, and expressed the hope that talks might soon be held between the opponents with a view toward a solution of the Algerian war. Again, France did not vote, but in spite of FLN dissatisfaction, pressure had been exerted on the French government. The *loi cadre,* introduced in the French National Assembly on September 17, 1957, was adopted on January 31, 1958. The preamble to the September proposal for the *loi cadre* read, in part: "For several months, the government of the Republic has sought to find the basis for a peaceful, democratic and just solution to the Algerian problem." The words "peaceful, democratic and just solution" were the words of the UN resolution of February 15, 1957.[42]

While France suffered the pressures created by debates in the UN, Morocco and Tunisia were also affected by events in North Africa. The two nations had recently won their independence from France, and almost inevitably their governments became spokesmen for the FLN in the UN. In 1957 the Moroccan and Tunisian representatives, Ahmed Balafrej and Mongi Slim, worked for a resolution that would strongly condemn France. They failed. The Assembly accepted a mild proposal for mediation that had been suggested by Mohammed V. By the end of the year there was therefore a possibility of a Tunisian-Moroccan mediation between the FLN and France.[43] Although the French government refused until much later to accept the suggestion that a third party be allowed to interfere in the Algerian question, two independent North African nations had offered their good offices.[44]

As a Muslim, Mohammed V felt sympathy for the Algerian nationalists, but he also had ties with the former protector of his realm. The Moroccan monarch needed French technical assistance. He thus was attempting to overcome the tense diplomatic situation that had been created by the kidnapping of Ben Bella from a Moroccan plane by French military elements in Algeria. President Bourguiba's position was even more precarious. He was impelled to help the FLN because of his sympathy for the nationalists who had been backed to the wall by the pacification program. He also acted because the ALN's power outside Algeria, particularly in Tunisia, had grown tremendously. Some regions of Tunisia were virtually occupied by Algerian nationalists,[45] and Bourguiba did not have the military power of his own to resist them.

France, meanwhile, continued its attempts to deny the UN

the right to discuss the Algerian problem. Nevertheless, the French helped bring the question before international opinion. That the French government wanted the Algerian problem to remain a domestic issue was amply demonstrated by the departure of the French delegation from the General Assembly in October 1955. In 1958 the representatives of France withdrew from the Political Committee. In 1958 and 1959 the French fought hard and successfully to keep the UN from adopting a resolution on the Algerian question.[46] To a certain degree France defeated herself by bringing up the question of military aid to the rebels furnished by Egypt.[47] The Security Council, asked to consider this question in October 1956, took no action as French, British, and Israeli troops invaded Egypt a few days later.

When Egypt's enemies withdrew from their positions near the Suez Canal, Nasser's prestige was given a boost, as was that of his ally in Algeria, the FLN-ALN. Then in February 1958 French airplanes bombed Sidi-Sakiet-Youssef, a Tunisian village previously used by ALN units as a base for attacks on French positions in Algeria. It was Tunisia's turn to complain in the UN, thus drawing attention once more to the threat to international peace and security represented by the Algerian question.[48] The effect of the incident was to draw international attention to the FLN's struggle for independence. This was exactly what the French should have avoided. Now the allies of France, including the United States and Great Britain, intervened by offering their good offices.[49] Although the opponents of the French did not secure all they desired from the UN, they did achieve their essential purpose: Assembly resolutions were adopted in 1956 and again in 1957, though not in 1958 and 1959. But even in these last two years, the Algerian question was discussed in the UN. The French helped by committing such errors as the capture of the *Athos* in international waters, the kidnapping of Ben Bella, the sending of an expeditionary force to Suez, and the bombing of Sidi-Sakiet-Youssef.

Militarily, the French had beaten the ALN by early 1958. When ALN units in battalion strength tried to cross the frontier barrier from Tunisia, they were decimated. The same French soldiers who had won the Battle of Algiers in 1957 defeated the ALN on the frontiers in 1958. According to the French General Staff, 12,641 rebels were killed and 2,508 were captured during the first four months of 1958.[50] Although the French could probably never hope to eliminate the ALN completely, the rebels were definitely forced into a period of operational stagnation. Large nationalist units were replaced by smaller armed groups of a dozen or fewer men.

As the FLN-ALN abandoned hope of a decisive military victory, the exterior delegation of the nationalist camp took up the relay. The war would henceforth be fought by diplomats in the UN and elsewhere. While the ALN struggled to survive on a small scale within Algeria, the essential battles were fought in the press, particularly in the French press. Gradually, France lost her will to win in Algeria. The important decisions were political decisions reached after 1958 and imposed by Charles de Gaulle. Soldiers who had fought to keep Algeria French felt betrayed. Many could not understand that the struggle was no longer a military conflict, that the war had become a psychological war that the French army could not win.[51] Soldiers could hardly fight effectively in the UN or in the international press, especially since their government was no longer willing to continue the struggle. The political goal of the counterinsurgency government had been changed by the protracted character of the war and by international pressures that could not be ignored.[52]

16 | Conclusion

BY THE END OF 1957, AND CERTAINLY BY THE MIDDLE OF 1958, the nationalists had all but lost the military conflict within Algeria. Armed attacks against French authorities in the colony continued, but on a dramatically reduced scale. Instead of progressing from partisan struggle to the more classical forms of warfare, the ALN had reverted to the very basic form of guerrilla action. Small groups of three or four men continued to throw bombs, strafe crowded cafes or beaches, and engage in other spectacular acts of insurrection. The larger nationalist units, however, found their movements cramped by the French military presence; since France had effectively closed the frontiers of Algeria, the rebels could rarely supply their own soldiers adequately. Not all Algerians were nationalists. There had been an important shift of public opinion toward the FLN in 1956, but there were still some

171,000 Algerian soldiers in various French auxiliary units as late as January 1960.[1]

And yet, the French victory was hollow. Poised in neighboring Morocco and Tunisia, the ALN maintained a sizable army of well-trained men equipped with modern weapons. Although it could probably not have defeated the Forces of Order, this external army was possibly more powerful than anything the French had ever confronted in Algeria itself. Nevertheless, the French could not eliminate this new regular army because it was sheltered in sanctuaries beyond their control. The consequent frustration of the French military leaders was compounded by the fact that even within Algeria complete order could not be restored. An army of well over half a million men could not control an Algerian population of nine million who shielded several thousand intractable nationalists. In spite of the obvious good will of many of its men, the French army could not gain the confidence of enough Algerians to counteract the efforts of the elusive terrorists.

Facile comparisons between the Algerian insurgency and other similar insurrectional crises naturally suggest themselves. In Southeast Asia, for example, the Viet Cong enjoy sanctuary in North Vietnam as well as material and moral support from North Vietnam, China, and Russia. The ALN-FLN could count on safe bases, supplies, and diplomatic and ideological assistance from Tunisia, Morocco, and Egypt, the Arab world in general, and other sympathetic governments. The Algerians could not, however, count on recruits from their allies. Furthermore, the Algerian insurgents were not afforded the same topographical protection in the admittedly rugged North African terrain as were their counterparts in the jungles of Southeast Asia, in other parts of Africa (Kenya, for example), or in Latin America. Hence, in the central Maghrib the French counterinsurgency forces were able to build effective border defenses of barbed wire, mine fields, and no-man's lands through which Algerian rebels in Tunisia and Morocco rarely passed.

The French themselves tried to apply their own Indochinese experience to Algeria. The SAS, whose officers performed both administrative and political functions, was an institution inspired by a similar organization developed during the French period of the Vietnamese conflict. The adaptation, however, involved changes. Only officers of the rank of captain or above, all volunteers, had served the Indochinese organization. In Algeria the numbers required to fill the administrative need necessitated a broadening of qualifications so that lieutenants, many of them assigned to duties they did not desire, were the rule rather than the exception in SAS positions.

Also important, in Algeria as well as in Southeast Asia, were racial and cultural factors. The revolutionary Asians and their Algerian counterparts stood in sharp contrast to the military and administrative personnel of the counterinsurgency forces. Although Algerians served in French auxiliary forces and South Vietnamese contingents fought with the French military units, in both revolutionary wars the protectors of dying colonial systems were clearly foreigners.

The Algerians who served France in a military capacity were not integrated into French units. Algerian career soldiers in the French army rarely saw action in their native land after 1954; instead, they were assigned to garrison duties in France, Germany, and elsewhere. Discrimination against Algerians in the French army was not new, but the war in Algeria made the inequities based on racial considerations more obvious. Thus, as a result of the prejudice on the part of many officers in the Forces of Order, even those Algerians who showed their devotion to France by serving in her armed forces were never treated as the equals of their European peers. The traditional nomenclature used to refer to Algerian officers in the French army is a clear index of the insidious discrimination: these leaders were at one time or another called autochthonous, native, Franco-Muslim of native statute, and Muslim officers.[2] This reality created a *"crise de conscience"* for many Algerian officers in the French army; some deserted to join the FLN, while others never solved their personal problems but nevertheless ran afoul of military administration.

As soon as the insurrection became widespread, the military made a sustained effort to meet the many problems of civil administration. They developed the *quadrillage* to protect the people and the authorities. A further step was the creation of the SAS system, under which soldiers were assigned to fulfill administrative duties that would normally have been performed by civilians. These men served as teachers, nurses, doctors, and performed any number of nonmilitary tasks. This same army, however, never overcame its distrust of the Algerians within its own ranks. Rather than integrate them fully, it created the *harkas* and *maghzen,* auxiliary forces of Algerians commanded by French officers.[3] After the outbreak of revolution this policy may have been wise, a means of avoiding infiltration of military institutions by the enemy, but the policy was chiefly a historical legacy. This was the way the natives had been dealt with in the past. As a result, even the best officers of the SAS seemed to be hypocritical in their attitudes toward the Algerians in their charge. While keeping the Muslim soldiers in separate units, they simultaneously urged all Arabs and Berbers to rally to the French flag. This appeal for unity in the face of the nationalist threat rang hollow to those who knew the treachery with which some French officers had treated many Algerian prisoners.

While the nationalists made full use of this racial animosity in their propaganda, the officers of the SAS and the Forces of Order blamed their own government for France's failure in Algeria. The administration and the Chamber of Deputies had failed to meet the social and economic problems of Algeria, had lost contact with its people, and had never given the army all that it required to suppress the revolution.[4] After 1954, however, the administration attempted not only to help the Algerians both economically and socially but also to eliminate the more blatantly discriminatory aspects of the colonial situation. Through legislation and decrees it lowered the sales tax on essential commodities and made policy-making positions more accessible to Algerians. But these efforts came so late that they appeared to many as bribes for popular support and as concessions designed to counteract the rising violence that was sweeping the country. Even though these changes did not grow entirely from selfish considerations, their very nature and timing made them dangerously vulnerable to the propaganda of the enemy.

In spite of these obvious difficulties, the French counterrevolutionary effort was remarkably effective on the whole. On an international scale, however, and in France itself, pressures mounted that could not long be ignored or resisted. Public opinion in the mother country showed a steady decline in support for the Algerian war.[5] In Morocco and Tunisia the ALN continued to maintain strong forces that could not be destroyed without a drastic widening of the Algerian conflict. To win militarily, the government would have had to convince a large majority of Frenchmen that Algeria was worth the tremendous sacrifices that would be required to defeat the FLN. To assure a political victory, France would have had to defeat the GPRA *(Gouvernement Provisoire de la République Algérienne)* by propaganda and diplomacy; this she could not or would not do. After the demise of the Fourth Republic the government was no longer willing to continue the conflict at any cost. Frantz Fanon was essentially correct when he wrote, in 1959, that the revolutionaries had already won.[6] It was only a matter of time, time to find the appropriate formulas by which Algeria could emerge from her colonial past and assume all the prerogatives of an independent nation.

The most difficult question in insurgency and counterinsurgency warfare was and remains that of the use of torture and other excesses of violence. France stands condemned for deeds that do not differ in degree or number from excesses perpetrated by the nationalists against the Algerian population caught between two armed camps. Yet the rebels somehow get the benefit of the doubt and tend to be forgiven for inhuman treatment. Insurgents, then, can use torture and terrorism to further their own aims. Because they are or can claim to be the underdogs, they are usually forgiven their crimes by a weary national and international public opinion. The counterinsurgency forces do not fare so well because they represent perhaps another race, certainly another people and culture. Without going into the moral issues raised, for example, by the rebels' indiscriminate bombing of public places, as in the Battle of Algiers, or the counterinsurgency forces' use of air power in rural areas or against Algerian villages, the different reactions to essentially the same excesses reveal one of the problems which counterinsurgency forces must solve. In a way, they must appear to be angels while fighting a dirty war. Some SAS officers in Algeria managed this role. But the local population preferred to remember the greedy officers who took advantage of their powerful military and political positions, who used their authority rashly, or who were incompetent. In contrast, ineffective or ruthless leaders on the insurgents' side were, on the whole, forgiven and regarded as heroes for challenging a superior authority, for daring to attack an established government. Counterinsurgency forces in formerly colonial areas will probably always be foreigners who are blamed for offenses that are more quickly forgiven when perpetrated by insurgents who are racially and culturally the same as the victims.

There are lessons to be drawn from the Algerian war. To defeat insurgent nationalists is an extremely difficult task. When beaten in organized groups of company size, for example, the insurgents tend to break up into smaller and often suicidal units of three or four men. The terrorism such splinter groups can perpetrate is frightening, and the problem of controlling and eliminating them is probably insoluble. On the other hand, counterinsurgency forces are strictly limited in their ability to exploit their numerical and technological advantages. It is easy to deploy planes and bombs to destroy a village used as a cover by insurgents, but the political effect of such application of power is disastrous. It tends to turn the whole village against the defenders of the colonial regime. To defeat the insurgents it is probably essential to meet them on their own terms. A unit of insurgents using the local population for cover must be met by armed men, volunteers who, while risking their own lives, can distinguish between the guilty armed insurgents and the bystanders whose only sin is to be in the wrong place at the wrong time.

Proper methods for controlling the movements and political activities of Algerians who might otherwise contribute to the rebel effort, including internal passports, card catalogues for every dwelling unit, border barriers, permits for the movement of goods, particularly food staples, and checks on these goods at the point of origin and at the end of the transfer—all of these control devices are useful. When applied in conjunction with programs for the social and economic betterment of local populations, such static policies might enable the counterinsurgency forces to isolate and starve their opponents into submission. Promising preliminary results of the counterinsurgency effort were achieved too late, however, in isolated situations in Algeria. After 1956 Algerian public opinion had swung to the nationalist cause.

Glossary

French words used by nationalists are identified by (F).

adjudant (F): company sergeant-major
aspirant (F): officer candidate
Bey: title of Tunisian ruler
cadi: judge
caïd: native administrative officer
caidat: French system of native administrators
chechia: woolen caps
cheikh: chief
çoff: federation, political party
colon (F): European settler
Dey: title of Turkish ruler of Algiers
douar: village
élite (F): elite, usually political or educational
fellagha: outlaws

fida'iyin: urban terrorists (combatants of the faith)

fraction (F): part of a tribe or of a village

groupe (F): squad

hadj (hodjadj): one who has made a pilgrimmage to Mecca

Jama'ah: village assembly, assembly of elders

Maghrib: Arab Northwest Africa

maghzen: usually, tribes allied to the ruler; also, French native auxiliary troops in the SAS

moudjahid: combatant

mousseblin: militiamen

quadrillage (F): system of static control

quartier (F): sector

Qur'anic: of or pertaining to the Qur'an

razzia: foray, coup

section (F): platoon

sergent-chef (F): lowest-ranked sergeant

Bibliography

UNPUBLISHED DOCUMENTS

While it would be impossible to enumerate all the relevant documents available at the Centre de Hautes Etudes Administratives sur l'Afrique et l'Asie Modern (CHEAM), some effort should be made. The list that follows includes only the typed reports and mimeographed memoirs mentioned in the notes. Since first names were often not given, only names as listed on the documents can be reproduced in this partial citation.

Ancel. "L'Administration à l'échelon de l'arrondissement en Algérie." Memoir. CHEAM–2973. Paris, 1959.

Bastide, H. de la. "Le FLN et les membres de l'actuel gouvernement." Memoir. CHEAM–3716. Paris, 1962.

Bennamour, Ahmed. "L'Accession des Musulmans à la fonction publique." Memoir. CHEAM–3033. Paris, n.d. [1958?].

Bernhardt, J. "La pacification dans un quartier d'Alger: 1957–1959." Memoir. CHEAM–3077 [1959].

Berard, Cdt. "La Rébellion algérienne vue à travers ses chefs." Memoir. CHEAM–3228. Paris, 1959.

Betbeder, Lt. Col. "Le Nationalisme Algérien." Memoir. CHEAM—1219. Paris, 1947.

Bogros, Capt. "Quelques aspects du contrôle des nomades en guerre subversive." Report. CHEAM—3474. Paris, 1961.

Boissenot. "Les conditions de l'émancipation de la femme musulmane." Memoir. CHEAM—3061. Paris, 1959.

Borja, Capt. "Sidi Salem: cité nouvelle de l'Algérie nouvelle." Memoir. CHEAM—2842. Paris, 1958.

Boutin, Jacques. "De certains aspects de la guerre de pacification en Algérie." Memoir. CHEAM—3089. Paris, 1959.

Candelier. "Information et propagande radiophonic en pays arabes." Memoir. CHEAM—3737. Paris, 1959.

Comité Central de Hautes Etudes Administratives sur l'Afrique et l'Asie Moderne. "Mémoire sur la machination par les gouvernements des Etats Arabes pour déloger la France de ses positions en Afrique du Nord." Memoir. CHEAM—50.018. Paris, n.d.

Depis, Paul. "Notes sur le problème des réfugiés algériens du Maroc oriental." Memoir. CHEAM—3597. Paris, 1962.

Dubarry, Maurice. "Rôle de l'officier, chef de S.A.S. dans la réforme communale en Kabylie." Memoir. CHEAM—2888. Paris, 1957.

Eoche-Duval, R. "Aspects locaux et perspectives de la rénovation rurale en Algérie." Memoir. CHEAM—3631. Paris, 1961.

Espeisse, Capt. "Les regroupements de populations dans l'arrondissement de Tlemcen." Memoir. CHEAM—2888. Paris, 1959.

Faivre, C. "Une révolution administrative en Algérie: La réforme communale." Memoir. CHEAM—3740. Paris, 1959.

Florentin, Cdt. "Origines et raisons de regroupement des populations algériennes." Memoir. CHEAM—3374. Paris, 1962.

"Francs propos d'un Africain." Memoir. CHEAM—3491. Paris, 1955.

Groupe d'Etudes. "Les Centres de regroupement en Algérie." Memoir. CHEAM—3277. Paris, 1960.

Guvan, G. "Etudes de quelques motivations et comportements du nationalisme musulman d'Algérie." Memoir. CHEAM—3614. Paris, 1961.

Haegeli, P. "L'Attentisme des classes bourgeoises musulmanes de l'Est Constantinois." Memior. CHEAM—3584. Paris, 1962.

Haut-Comité-Méditerranéen. "Les grands courants d'opinions dans l'Islam Nord-Africains." Memoir. CHEAM—23. Paris, 1937.

Hocquet, Y. "Un aspect de la guerre d'Indochine: Les Bureaux de liaison pour la pacification." Memoir. CHEAM—2896. Paris, 1958.

Holstein, R. "La fin d'une commune-mixte algérienne." Memoir. CHEAM—2909. Paris, 1957.

Jammes, R. "Les Ecoles Réformistes Oulamas d'Algérie." Memoir. CHEAM—1328. Paris, 1948.

Laburthe, Jean. "L'Evolution de la djemaa kabyle dans la commune mixte de Fort National." Typed memoir prepared for CHEAM, 1947.

Lafage, L. "Un important chapitre de l'histoire politique de l'Algérie: Ferhat Abbas et l'Union Démocratique du Manifeste Algérien." Memoir. CHEAM—3934. Paris, 1964.

Laurent, Claude. "Implantation d'une S.A.S. en zone d'insécurité." Memoir. CHEAM—3655. Paris, 1962.

———. "La naissance d'une commune musulmane." Memoir. CHEAM—3524. Paris, 1961.

Le Tourneau, Roger. "La Vie politique musulmane en Algérie jusqu'ua 1er Novembre 1954." Memoir. CHEAM—3358. Paris, 1960.

Manière, P. "Un essai de suppression des bidonvilles: Création Cité de Sidi-Salem à Bône." Memoir. CHEAM—3005 bis. Paris, 1959.

Mareuil, Lt.-Col. de. "Le Centre d'Instruction de Pacification et de Contre-Guerilla d'Arzew." Memoir. CHEAM—3383. Paris, 1961.

Marmey, Pierre. "L'Electeur Musulman." Memoir. CHEAM—2910. Paris, 1957.

———. "Le droit de vote de la femme musulmane algérienne." Memoir. CHEAM—2909. Paris, 1958.

Martin, Doctor George. "Centres de regroupement et mille villages en Algérie." Memoir. CHEAM—3526. Paris, 1959.

Merlet. "Evolution de l'organisation administrative de l'Algérie." Memoir. CHEAM—2911. Paris, 1957.

"Mesures règlementaires prises dans le Constantinois en vue de mettre obstacle au ravitaillement des rebelles." CHEAM—50660. Paris, 1959.

Miette, Roland. "Le destin algérien." Memoir. CHEAM—2515. Paris, 1956.

Montalembert, M. de. "Action des S.A.S. en Algérie." Memoir. CHEAM—3264. Paris, 1959.

Naudy. "L'affaire algérienne à l'O.N.U." Memoir. CHEAM—3572. Paris, 1956.

Petitjean, R. "Les opérations de regroupement et la création de nouveaux villages dans l'arrondissement de Tablat." Memoir. CHEAM—3613. Paris, 1962.

Rager. "L'Emigration des musulmans algériens en France." Memoir. CHEAM—2691. Paris, 1957.

Rohard, Capt. P. "L'Evolution sociale et politique dans le Guerrouma (arrondissement de Palestro)." Memoir. CHEAM—3334. Paris, 1960.

Trézel, Gén. "Observations sur le projet d'ordonnance créant les troupes indigènes en Afrique, 12 juin 1839." H226 (Algérie,

272 *Bibliography*

Mémoires Diverses). Archives du Ministère de la Guerre, Section Moderne, Chateau de Vincennes, Paris.

Vieillot, Jacques. "Monographie de la S.A.S. d'Ain Boucif." Memoir. CHEAM—2870. Paris, 1958.

Vincent, Lt. Guy. "Monographie de la commune de Guelt-et-Beida." Memoir. CHEAM—3548. Paris, 1961.

Zebert, Georges. "Etude d'un projet d'aménagement pouvant permettre dans un laps de temps relativement bref l'accession rapide des musulmans aux divers postes qu'ils soient d'éxecution ou de maîtrise." Memoir. CHEAM—3075. Paris, 1959.

Un Africain. "Le nationalisme extremiste en Algérie: ses forces, ses faiblesses. Comment les [sic] combattre." Memoir. CHEAM—50.113. Paris, 1957.

Books

This list includes only items actually cited.

Abbas, Ferhat. *Guerre et révolution d'Algérie.* Vol. I: *La Nuit Coloniale.* Paris: Julliard, 1962.

Ageron, Charles Robert. *Histoire de l'Algérie contemporaine.* Paris: Presses Universitaires de France, 1964.

Ait Ahmed, Hocine. *La guerre et l'après-guerre.* Paris: Editions de Minuit, 1964.

Algeria, Cabinet du Ministre Résident. *L'Algérie, 1956.* Algiers: Baconnier, 1956.

Algeria, Gouvernement Général. *Essential Notions about Algeria.* Paris: Imprimerie Georges Lang, 1959.

Algeria, Ministère de l'Algérie. *Guide de l'officier des Affaires Algériennes.* Paris: Imprimerie Georges Lang, 1957.

Algeria, Ministry of Information of the Algerian Republic (GPRA). *Genocide in Algeria: The Resettlement Camps.* 1960.

Algeria, Service de l'Information du Cabinet du Ministre Résident en Algérie. *Programme et action du gouvernement en Algérie: Mesures de pacification et réformes.* August, 1956.

Algerian Red Crescent. *The Resettlement Camps.* Rabat and Tunis, n.d. [1960?].

Ali, Bachir Hadj. *Aspects actuels de la guerre de libération en Algérie.* Ed. by *La Nouvelle Revue Internationale.* Paris: Richard, n.d. [1959?].

———. *Notre peuple vaincra.* Geneva: Du Fennec, 1960.

Alleg, Henri. *The Question.* Trans. by John Calder. New York: George Braziller, Inc., 1958 .

Alquier, Jean Yves, et al. *Ceux d'Algérie: Lettres de rappelés prece-dées d'un debat.* Paris: Plon, 1957.

Alquier, Jean Yves. *Nous avons pacifié Tazalt: Journal de marche d'un officier parachutiste.* Paris: Laffont, 1957.

Alwan, Mohamed. *Algeria Before the United Nations.* New York: Robert Speller and Sons, 1959.

Ambler, John Steward. *Soldiers Against the State: The French Army in Politics.* New York: Doubleday and Co., 1968.

Andrews, William G. *French Politics and Algeria.* New York: Appleton-Century-Crofts, 1962.

Arab, Bessaoud Mohamed. *Heureux les martyres qui n'ont rien vu.* Colombe (Seine), France: Imprimerie Cary, 1963.

Aron, Robert, et al. *Les Origines de la guerre d'Algérie.* Paris: Fayard, 1962.

Barbour, Nevill, ed. *A Survey of North-West Africa. The Maghrib.* New York: Oxford University Press, 1959.

Bedjaoui, Mohammed. *Law and the Algerian Revolution.* Brussels: International Asociation of Democratic Lawyers, 1961.

Behr, Edward. *The Algerian Problem.* New York: Norton and Co., 1962.

———. *Dramatique Algérie.* Trans. from the English by Michel Deutsch. Paris: Stock, 1962.

Beloff, Max. *The Foreign Policy of Soviet Russia: 1929–1941.* London: Oxford University Press, 1947.

Benabdallah, A.; Oussedik, M.; Vergès, J.; and Zavrian, M. *Défense politique.* Paris: Maspero, 1961.

Benzine, Abdelhamid. *Le Camp.* Paris: Editions Sociales, 1962.

Bernard, Stephane. *Le Conflit franco-marocain, 1943–1956.* 3 vols. Brussels: Imprimerie Vedeco, 1963.

Bert, Paul. *Lettre de Kabylie.* Paris: A. Lemerre, 1885.

Beuchard, Georges. *L'Equivoque algérienne.* Paris: Nouvelles Editions Debresse, 1959.

Boisard, Michel. *La Guerre d'Algérie à travers la litterature: 1954–1961.* Thesis, Institut d'Etudes Politiques of the University of Paris, 1962.

Bonnet, Gabriel. *Les guerres insurrectionnelles et révolutionnaires de l'antiquité à nos jours.* Paris: Payot, 1958.

Boudiaf, Mohamed. *Où va l'Algérie!* Paris: Editions Librairie de l'Etoile, 1964.

Bourdieu, Pierre. *The Algerians.* Trans. by Alan C. M. Ross. Boston: Beacon Press, 1961.

Brace, Richard, and Brace, Jane. *Ordeal in Algeria.* Princeton, N.J.: D. Van Nostrand Co., 1960.

Bromberger, Merry, and Bromberger, Serge. *Les 13 complots du 13 mai.* Paris: Fayard, 1958.

Bourguiba, Habib. *La Tunisie et la France*. Paris: Julliard, 1954.

Buron, Robert. *Carnets politiques de la guerre d'Algérie*. Paris: Plon, 1965.

Camus, Albert. *Actuelles III: Chronique algérienne: 1939–1958*. Paris: Gallimard, 1958.

Chaliand, Gérard. *L'Algérie est-elle socialiste?* Paris: Maspero, 1964.

Chamski, Thadée. *La Harka*. Paris: Robert Laffont, 1961.

Charby, Jacques. *L'Algérie en prison*. Paris: Editions de Minuit, 1961.

Clark, Michael K. *Algeria in Turmoil*. New York: Praeger, 1959.

Colton, Joel. *Leon Blum: Humanist in Politics*. New York: Alfred A. Knopf, 1966.

Condit, D. M., and Cooper, Bert H., Jr. et al. *Challenge and Response in Internal Conflict*. Washington: Center for Research in Social Systems, 1968.

Confer, Vincent. *France and Algeria: The Problem of Civil and Political Reform, 1870–1920*. Syracuse: Syracuse University Press, 1966.

Couland, Jacques. *L'Eveil du Monde Arabe*. Paris: Editions Sociales, 1963.

Cross, James Eliot. *Conflict in the Shadows: The Nature and Policies of Guerilla War*. New York: Doubleday and Co., 1963.

Delegation of the National Liberation Front. *Genocide in Algeria*. Cairo, 1957.

Delmas, Claude. *La guerre révolutionnaire*. Paris: Presses Universitaires de France, 1959.

Denoyer, François. *Quatre ans de guerre en Algérie*. Paris: Flammarion, 1962.

Déon, Michel. *L'Armée d'Algérie et la pacification*. Paris: Plon, 1959.

Deschamps, Hubert, and Chauvet, Paul, eds. *Galliéni pacificateur: Ecrits coloniaux de Galliéni*. Paris: Presses Universitaires de France, 1949.

Descloitres, Robert et al. *L'Algérie des bidonvilles: Le tier monde dans la cité*. Paris: Mouton and Co., 1961.

Driff, Zohra. *La Mort de mes frères*. Paris: Maspero, 1961.

Dronne, Raymond. *La Révolution d'Alger*. Paris: Editions France-Empire, 1958.

Duchemin, Jacques C. *Histoire du F.L.N.* Paris: La Table Ronde, 1962.

Dufresnoy, Claude. *Des officiers parlent*. Paris: Julliard, 1961.

Du Manifest à la République Algérienne. Alger: Editions "Liberation," 1948.

Esquer, Gabriel. *Histoire de l'Algérie (1830–1960)*. Paris: Presses Universitaires de France, 1960.

Estier, Claude. *Pour l'Algérie*. Paris: Maspero, 1964.

Fabre-Luce, Alfred. *Demain en Algérie*. Paris: Plon, 1958.

Fanon, Frantz. *A Dying Colonialism*. Trans. by H. Chevalier. New York: Grove Press, 1967.

Faucher, Jean-André. *L'Algérie rebelle*. Paris: Editions du Grand Damier, 1957.

Favrod, Charles-Henri. *Le F.L.N. et l'Algérie*. Paris: Plon, 1962.

Ferraoun, Mouloud. *Journal: 1955–1962*. Paris: Seuil, 1962.

Folliet, Joseph. *Guerre et paix en Algérie: Réflexions d'un homme libre*. Lyons: Imprimerie du Sud-Est, 1958.

Fontaine, Pierre. *Dossier secret de l'Afrique du Nord*. Paris: Les Sept Couleurs, 1957.

Fournier, Christiane. *Nous avons encore des héros*. Paris: Plon, 1957.

France, Cabinet du Ministre de l'Algérie. *Algérie: 1957*.

France, Ministère des Affaires Etrangères. *Discours prononcé par M. Christian Pineau, Ministre des Affaires Etrangères, Le 4 fevrier 1957 devant la Commission Politique de l'Assemblée Générale des Nations Unis*. Paris: La Documentation Française, 1957.

G. . . , Mustapha. *Barberousse*.

Galula, David. *Counter-Insurgency Warfare: Theory and Practice*. New York: Praeger, 1964.

Gann, L. H., and Duignan, P. *White Settlers in Tropical Africa*. Baltimore: Penguin Books, 1962.

Gillespie, Joan. *Algeria: Rebellion and Revolution*. New York: Praeger, 1960.

Girardet, Raoul. *La crise militaire française: 1945–1962*. Paris: Armand Colin, 1964.

———. *Victoires et servitudes des capitaines*. Paris: Imprimerie de "Combat" et Presse de France, 1960.

Hahn, Lorna. *North Africa: Nationalism to Nationhood*. Washington: Public Affairs Press, 1960.

Halstead, John P. *Rebirth of a Nation: The Origins and Rise of Moroccan Nationalism, 1912–1944*. Cambridge: Harvard University Press, 1967.

Heduy, Philippe. *Au Lieutenant des Taglaïts*. Paris: La Table Ronde, 1960.

Heilbrunn, Otto. *Warfare in the Enemy's Rear*. New York: Praeger, 1963.

Henissart, Paul. *Wolves in the City: The Death of French Algeria*. New York: Simon and Schuster, 1970.

Julien, Charles-André. *L'Afrique du Nord en marche*. Paris: Julliard, 1952.

Kabaili, Si Mohamed ou Ramdan. *La Grande Kabylie: Introduction à l'étude de la Kabylie d'aujourd'hui*. Publication du Centre d'Etudes regionales de Kabylie. Memoires et travaux, T. III. Algiers: Imprimerie Fontana, 1959.

Kelly, George Armstrong. *Lost Soldiers: The French Army and Empire in Crisis.* Cambridge: M.I.T. Press, 1965.

Kessel, Patrick, and Pirelli, Giovanni. *Le Peuple algérien et la guerre: Lettres et témoignages, 1954–1962.* Paris: Maspero, 1962.

Kraft, Joseph. *The Struggle for Algeria.* New York: Doubleday and Co., 1961.

Kuntz, François. *L'officier français dans la nation.* Paris: Charles Lavauzelle et Cie., 1960.

Labin, Suzanne. *Vie ou mort du monde libre.* Paris: La Table Ronde, 1961.

Latour, Pierre Boyer de. *De l'Indochine à l'Algérie: Le Martyre de l'Armée Française.* Paris: Les Presses du Mail, 1962.

Legum, Colin. *Pan-Africanism.* New York: Praeger, 1962.

Le Prevost, Jacques. *La bataille d'Alger: Janvier–Février 1957.* Algiers: Baconnier, 1957.

Le Tourneau, Roger. *Evolution politique de l'Afrique du Nord musulmane: 1920–1961.* Paris: Armand Colin, 1962.

Leuliette, Pierre. *St. Michael and the Dragon: Memoirs of a Paratrooper.* Trans. by John Edmonds. Boston: Houghton Mifflin Co., 1964.

Liebesny, Herbert. *The Government of French North Africa.* Philadelphia: University of Pennsylvania Press, 1943.

Ling, Dwight. *Tunisia: From Protectorate to Republic.* Bloomington: Indiana University Press, 1967.

Lombard, Pierre. *La Crise Algérienne Vue d'Alger.* Alger: Editions F. Fontana, 1958.

Lyautey, Louis Herbert. *Lettres du Tonkin et de Madagascar: 1894–1899.* Paris: Colin, 1946.

Mandouze, André. *La Révolution algérienne par les textes.* Paris: Maspero, 1962.

Martin, Alexis. *Technique de la guerre occulte.* Paris: Flammarion, 1963.

Martin, Claude. *Histoire de l'Algérie française.* Paris: Editions des Quatre Fils Aymon, 1963.

Megret, Maurice. *L'action psychologique.* Paris: Fayard, 1958.

Meningaud, Jean. *La France à l'heure algériene.* Paris: Paris-Livres, 1956.

Merad, Ali. *Le Réformisme Musulman en Algérie de 1925 à 1940.* Paris and the Hague: Mouton and Co., 1967.

Merle, Robert. *Ahmed Ben Bella.* Trans. by Camilla Sykes. New York: Walker and Co., 1967.

Miege, J.-L. *Le Maroc.* Paris: Presses Universitaires de France, 1962.

Ministry of Information of the Algerian Republic. *Genocide in Algeria: The Resettlement Camps,* 1960.

Moore, Clement H. *Tunisia Since Independence.* Berkeley and Los Angeles: University of California Press, 1965.

Morice, André. *Les Fellagha dans la cité.* Nantes, France: Imprimerie Générale, n.d. [1959?].

Naroun, Amar. *Ferhat Abbas où les chemins de la souveraineté.* Paris: Denoël, 1961.

Nora, Pierre. *Le Français d'Algérie.* Paris: Julliard, 1961.

Noureddine, Meziane. *Un Algérien reconte.* Paris: Seuil, 1960.

Nouschi, André. *La naissance du nationalisme algérien: 1914–1954.* Paris: Editions de Minuit, 1962.

Oppermann, Thomas. *Le probleme algérien.* Trans. from the German by J. Lecerf. Paris: Maspero, 1961.

Ouzegane, Amar. *Le Meilleur Combat.* Paris: Julliard, 1962.

Paillat, Claude. *Le Deuxième dossier secret de l'Algérie.* Paris: Presses de la Cité, 1962.

Periot, Gérard. *Deuxième classe en Algérie.* Paris: Flammarion, 1962.

Planhol, Xavier de. *Nouveux villages algérois.* Paris: Presses Universitaires de France, 1961.

Prenant, A. *L'Algérie: passé et présent.* Paris: Edition Sociales, 1960.

Pustay, John S. *Counter-Insurgency Warfare.* New York: The Free Press, 1965.

Rahmani, Abdelkader. *L'Affaires des officiers algériens.* Paris: Editions du Seuil, 1959.

Raymond, André. *La Tunisie.* Paris: Presses Universitaires de France, 1961.

Richard, Charles. *Du gouverneur arabe et de l'institution qui doit l'exercer.* Algiers: Bastide, 1848.

Roy, Jules. *La guerre d'Algérie.* Paris: Julliard, 1960.

Ruedy, John. *Land Policy in Colonial Algeria.* Berkeley and Los Angeles: University of California Press, 1967.

Saadia-et-Lakhdar. *L'Aliénation colonialiste et la résistance de la famille algérienne.* Lausanne, Switzerland: La Cité-Editeur, 1961.

Sarrazin, P. E. [Pseudonym of Emile Jeniès]. *La Crise Algérienne.* Paris: Edition du Cerf, 1949.

Sas, Pierre, and Romanetti, Yves. *Vie d'un peuple mort: clefs pour la Kabylie.* Paris: Editions du Scorpion, 1961.

Sauge, Georges. *L'Armée face à la guerre psychologique.* Paris: Centre d'Etudes Politiques et Civiques, 1959.

Servan-Schreiber, Jean-Jacques. *Lieutenant in Algeria.* Trans. by Ronald Matthews. New York: Alfred A. Knopf, 1957.

Servier, Jean. *Adieu Djebels.* Paris: France-Empire, 1958.

———. *Dans l'Aurès sur les pas des rebelles.* Paris: France-Empire, 1955.

———. *Demain en Algérie.* Paris: Laffont, 1959.

Soustelle, Jacques. *Aimée et souffrante Algérie*. Paris: Plon, 1956.
Tillion, Germaine. *Algeria: The Realities*. Trans. by Ronald Mat-
    thews. New York: Alfred A. Knopf, 1958.
————. *France and Algeria*. Trans. by R. Howard. New York: Alfred
    A. Knopf, 1961.
Tournoux, Jean Raymond. *Secret d'Etat*. Paris: Union Générale
    d'Editions, 1960.
Tous Algériens. Pamphlet, n.p., n.d. [1962?].
Vidal-Naquet, Pierre. *Torture: Cancer of Democracy*. Trans. by Barry
    Richard. Baltimore: Penguin Books, 1963.
Werth, Alexander. *The Strange Case of Pierre Mendès-France and
    the Great Conflict Over French North Africa*. London: Barrie
    Books, Ltd., 1957.
Yacef, Saadi. *Souvenirs de la bataille d'Alger*. Paris: Julliard, 1962.
Zenati, R. *Le Problème algérien vu par un indigène*. Paris: Comité de
    l'Afrique Française, 1938.
Ziadeh, A. *Origins of Nationalism in Tunisia*. Beirut: American Uni-
    versity of Beirut, 1962.

NEWSPAPERS

El Moudjahid (Algiers, then Rabat and Tunis)
France-Soir (Paris)
Journal Officiel (Paris)
Le Monde (Paris)
The New York Times (New York)
La Semaine en Algérie (Algiers)

ARTICLES

Again, only articles actually cited are listed below.

Ageron. Charles-Robert. "Une Politique algérienne libérale sous la
    Troisième République." *Revue d'histoire moderne et contem-
    poraine* VI (April–June 1959).
Albertini, Georges. "La Guerre que nous devons faire." *Revue Mili-
    taire Générale*, March 1961, pp. 373–81.
"L'Algérie c'est d'abord l'Algérie." *Cahiers du Témoignage Chrétien*
    XXXVII (1956).
Allard, G. J. "O.T.A.N. et A.L.N." *Revue de Défense Nationale*, June
    1958, p. 14.
Barrat, Robert. "Un journalist français ches les 'hors-la-loi' algériens."
    France-Observateur, no. 279 (1955).
Benoit, Jean-Paul. "Chronologie de la guerre en Algérie." *La Nef* XII–
    XIII (October 1962–January 1963).

Bruhat, Jean. "Nation algérienne et opinion française." *La Pensée: revue du rationalisme moderne,* New Series, XCV (January–February 1961).

Carpentier, Paul. "L'armée après six ans de guerre." *Perspectives Socialistes* XXXIX–XL (August–September 1960).

Carret, Jacques. "L'association des Oulamas Reformistes d'Algérie." *L'Afrique et l'Asie* XLIII (3rd trimester 1958).

Cherriere, Gén. "Les Débuts de l'Insurrection Algérienne." *Revue de Défense Nationale* CCLXXX (December 1956).

"Consequences tragiques de la guerre: La situation des réfugiés algériens." *El Moudjahid,* November 15, 1957.

"Courbes théoriques et réeles de la puissance militaire et de l'action térroriste." *La Semaine en Algérie* XXXVI (April 6–12, 1959).

"De la guerre d'extermination au triomphe de la révolution." *El Moudjahid* IX (August 20, 1957).

Delisle, René. "Les Origines du F.L.N." *La Nef* XII–XIII (October 1962–January 1963).

Delmas, Claude. "Les Evénements d'Afrique du Nord." *Revue Militaire d'Information* CCXC (January 1958).

Duquesne. "Septs ans de politique algérienne." *Revue d'Action Populaire* CLVI (March 1962).

Etcheverry, Chef de Bataillon. "Réflexions sur la guerre subversive d'Algérie." *Revue des forces terrestres* XVII (July 1959).

"La France poursuit ses crimes en Algérie." *El Moudjahid* IX (August 20, 1957).

Frisson, R. "La Réforme territoriale de l'Algérie." *L'Afrique et l'Asie* XXXVI (4th trimester 1956).

Gauthier, R. M. "L'Algérie en 1954." *Cahiers Maghrebins* I (1955).

Glories, Jean. "Quelques observations sur la révolution algérienne et le communisme." *L'Afrique et l'Asie* XLI (1st trimester 1958).

Heggoy, Alf Andrew. "The Origins of Algerian Nationalism in the Colony and in France." *The Muslim World* LVIII:2 (1968).

Hofstetter, Pierre. "Quel jeu joue la Suisse." *Défense de l'Occident* IX (November 1960).

Hourani, Albert. "Le Nationalisme révolutionnaire." *Preuves* CXVI (October 1960).

Lacheraf, Mostefa. "Constantes politiques et militaires dans les guerres Coloniales d'Algérie." *Les Tempes Modernes* CCLXXVII (January 1961).

Monnerot, Jules. "La guerre subversive." *Défense de l'Occident* X–XI (January–February 1961).

Morice, A. "Algérie ou les occasions perdues." *Revue Politiques Idées Inst.* XLIII (March 1959).

"Où en est l'Algérie?" *L'Afrique et l'Asie* (1st trimester 1948).

Philippe, G. "Que disait le colonel d'Alger?" *Défense de l'Occident* X–XI (January–February 1961).

———. "Témoignages et documents: Témoignages pour l'Algérie française." *Défense de l'Occident* X–XI (January–February 1961).

Poirier, Lucien. "Un Instrument de guerre subversive: Le F.L.N. (suite et fin)." *Revue Militaire d'Information* CCXC (January 1958).

"La Politique Française en Algérie." *Revue Militaire d'Information* CCLXXXIII (May 1957).

"Les Regroupements sont mal connus." *Témoignages et Documents* XII (May 1959).

Rocher, Léon. "Perspectives d'évolution politique en Afrique du Nord." *L'Afrique et l'Asie* XII (4th trimester 1950).

"Le Rôle des Sections Administratives Spécialisées." *Perspectives* II (March 1957).

Saadallah, Belkacem. "The Rise of the Algerian Elite, 1900–14." *The Journal of Modern African Studies* V:1 (1967).

Souyris, Capt. "L'action psychologique dans les Forces Armées." *Revue Militaire et Information* CCXCVIII (October 1958).

Talbo, Jean-Ph. "Qu-est-ce que la résistance?" *Partisans* VI (September–October 1962).

Thibaud, Paul. "Ce qu'est le F.L.N." *Perspectives Socialistes* XXXIX–XL (August–September 1960).

Tillion, Germaine. "Démocratie et colonialisme: II. L'Algérie malade de l'injustice." *Preuves* CXIII (July 1960).

Notes

1. THE ORIGINS AND EARLY DEVELOPMENT
OF TWENTIETH-CENTURY ALGERIAN NATIONALISM

1. Three essential books on the origins and development of Algerian nationalism are Charles-André Julien, *L'Afrique du Nord en marche*, 2nd ed. (Paris: Julliard, 1953); André Nouschi, *La naissance du nationalisme algérien: 1914–1954* (Paris: Les Editions de Minuit, 1962); and Roger Le Tourneau, *Evolution politique de l'Afrique du Nord musulmane: 1920–1961* (Paris: Colin, 1962). The first two lean left and are biased interpretations. The third is a more scholarly study although it reflects an official French point of view.

2. The best recent interpretations of the French phase of Algerian history are Claude Martin, *Histoire de l'Algérie française* (Paris: Editions des Quatre Fils Aymon, 1963) and the briefer Gabriel Esquer, *L'Histoire de l'Algérie: 1830–1960* (Paris: Presses Universitaires de France, 1960), in the "Que sais-je?" series. The latter was apparently thought to be too colonialist and was replaced by Ch. Robert Ageron, *Histoire de l'Algérie contemporaine* (Paris: Presses Universitaires de France, 1964).

3. Good treatments in English of the origins and development of Tunisian nationalism include Dwight L. Ling, *Tunisia: From Protectorate to Republic* (Bloomington: Indiana University Press, 1967); Clement H. Moore, *Tunisia Since Independence* (Berkeley and Los Angeles: University of California Press, 1965); and Nicola A. Ziadeh, *Origins of Nationalism in Tunisia* (Beirut: American University of Beirut, 1962).

4. A recent American view of the origins and history of Moroccan nationalism is John P. Halstead, *Rebirth of a Nation: The Origins and Rise of Moroccan Nationalism, 1912–1944* (Cambridge: Harvard University Press, 1967), in the Harvard Middle Eastern Monograph Series.

5. Belkacem Saadallah, "The Rise of the Algerian Elite, 1900–14," *The Journal of Modern African Studies* V, no. 1 (1967): 69–77.

6. M. Rager, "L'Emigration des musulmans algériens en France," CHEAM—2691 (1957), p. 2. For a more detailed discussion of the origins of Algerian nationalism before and during World War I, see Alf Andrew Heggoy, "The Origins of Algerian Nationalism in the Colony and in France," *The Muslim World* LVIII, no. 2 (1968): 128–140.

7. "L'Algérie c'est d'abord l'Algérie," *Cahiers du Témoignage Chrétien*, XXXVII (1956).

8. A good study of the *colons* and their role in Algeria before independence is Pierre Nora, *Les Français d'Algérie* (Paris: Julliard, 1961).

9. The best description in English of the administrative system of French Africa is still Herbert J. Liebesny, *The Government of French North Africa* (Philadelphia: University of Pennsylvania Press, 1943). Two recent interpretations about how that system worked are Vincent Confer, *France and Algeria: The Problem of Civil and Political Reform: 1870–1920* (Syracuse: Syracuse University Press, 1966) and John Ruedy, *Land Policy in Colonial Algeria* (Berkeley and Los Angeles: University of California Press, 1967). The latter, though brief, is excellent.

10. Confer, *France and Algeria*, p. 99.

11. Haut-Comité Mediterranéen, "Les Grands courants d'opinions dans l'Islam Nord-Africain," CHEAM—23 (1937), p. 45.

12. Ch-A. Julien, *L'Afrique du Nord en marche*, p. 31. See also Confer, *France and Algeria*, p. 114. Here Confer quotes figures from Charles-Robert Ageron, "Une Politique Algérienne libérale sous la Troisième République," *Revue d'histoire moderne et contemporaine* VI (April–June 1959): 148. According to Ageron, there were only 359

applications for naturalization between 1919 and 1924; 27 of these were rejected.

13. Jean Glories, "Quelques observations sur la révolution algérienne et le communisme," *L'Afrique et l'Asie*, XLI (1st trimester 1958): 18.

14. Le Tourneau, *Evolution politique*, p. 326.

15. Ibid., pp. 318 ff. For more detail see R. Jammes, "Les Ecoles Réformistes Oulamas d'Algérie," CHEAM—1328 (1948). There is an excellent article on the origins and developments of the Association of Reformist Ulama in Jacques Carret, "L'Association des Oulama Réformistes d'Algérie," *L'Afrique et l'Asie*, XLIII (3rd trimester, 1958): 23–44. Much more thorough is Ali Merad, *La Réformisme Musulman en Algérie de 1925 à 1940* (Paris and the Hague: Mouton and Co., 1967).

16. The policy was announced in the *Circulaire Michel*. See Le Tourneau, *Evolution politique*, p. 320.

17. Quoted in ibid., p. 321.

18. Esquer, *Histoire de l'Algérie*, p. 62.

19. The best source of information on the Federations of Elected Muslims is probably Ferhat Abbas, *La Nuit coloniale* (Paris: Julliard, 1962). The books by Ageron, Esquer, Martin, and Le Tourneau all contain interesting information and interpretations.

20. Ferhat Abbas in *L'Entente* (February 23, 1936) as quoted by Le Tourneau in *Evolution politique*, p. 134. The translation is my own.

21. R. Zenati, *Le problème algérien vu par un indigène* (Paris: Comité de l'Afrique Française, 1938), p. 31. Also quoted in Le Tourneau, *Evolution politique*, p. 315.

22. Ben Badis in *Ech-Chihab* (April 1936) as quoted by Le Tourneau in *Evolution politique*, p. 319.

23. Glories, "Quelques observations sur la révolution algérienne et le communisme," pp. 18–19.

24. Le Tourneau, *Evolution politique*, p. 326.

25. Ibid., p. 329.

26. In retrospect, the failure of this Blum-Viollette project was very important indeed and goes a long way toward explaining the revolutionary trend of Algerian politics from 1936 on. Most European historians ignore this project or give it little attention. See Joel Colton, *Léon Blum: Humanist in Politics* (New York: Alfred A. Knopf, 1966), p. 162.

27. Le Tourneau, *Evolution politique*, p. 330.

2. From Political Participation
to Revolutionary Nationalism

1. Ling, *Tunisia,* p. 121. Mr. Ling makes the point by quoting from Habib Bourguiba, *La Tunisie et la France* (Paris: Julliard, 1954), p. 162. See also Felix Garas, *Bourguiba et la naissance d'une nation* (Paris: Julliard, 1956), pp. 103–120; and Le Tourneau, *Evolution politique,* p. 88.

2. Lorna Hahn, *North Africa: Nationalism to Nationhood* (Washington: Public Affairs Press, 1960), p. 258. Miss Hahn, unfortunately, commits factual errors. She states, for example, that Messali took control of the ENA in 1921, years before the ENA had been created.

3. Charles-Henri Favrod, *Le F.L.N. et l'Algérie* (Paris: Plon, 1962), p. 89.

4. R. M. Gauthier, "L'Algérie en 1954," *Cahiers Maghrébins* I (1955): 18, 30.

5. Lt. Col. Betbeder, "Le nationalisme algérien," CHEAM–1219 (1947), p. 2.

6. Favrod, *Le F.L.N. et l'Algérie,* pp. 89–90; Jacques C. Duchemin, *Histoire du F.L.N.* (Paris: La Table Ronde, 1962), p. 334. Duchemin writes that Messali went to the Comintern Congress; the 5th Comintern Congress met in 1928 and the 6th was held in 1935. Favrod has Messali at the Congress of the International, but the only meetings held in 1930 were the 11th Party Congress and the Profintern meetings. See Max Beloff, *The Foreign Policy of Soviet Russia: 1929–1941,* I (London: Oxford University Press, 1947), p. 60.

7. Le Tourneau, *Evolution politique,* p. 334.

8. Ibid., pp. 347–354; Julien, *L'Afrique du Nord en marche,* p. 303.

9. Thomas Oppermann, *Le problème algérien,* trans. from German by J. Lecerf (Paris: Maspéro, 1961), p. 80; Nouschi, *La naissance du nationalisme algérien,* pp. 138 ff.

10. P. E. Sarrazin (pseudonym of Emile Jeniès), *La crise algérienne* (Paris: Editions du Cerf, 1949), p. 136. This is probably one of the most honest appraisals ever written of the Algerian question up to 1949. The author was a government official who undoubtedly had access to much information not generally available.

11. Jean Glories, "Quelques observations sur la révolution algérienne et le communisme," *L'Afrique et l'Asie,* XLI (1st trimester 1958): 19.

12. On Moroccan nationalism see Halstead, *Rebirth of a Nation* (Cambridge: Harvard University Press, 1967).

13. Ling, *Tunisia*, pp. 116, 138–139, 144; Moore, *Tunisia Since Independence*, p. 18.

14. Betbeder, CHEAM–1219, p. 19; R. Le Tourneau, "La vie politique musulmane en Algérie jusqu'au 1er Novembre 1954," CHEAM–3358 (1960), p. 14.

15. Betbeder, CHEAM–1219, p. 23.

16. Si Mohamed ou Ramdan Kebaili, *La Grande Kabylie: Introduction à l'étude de la Kabylie d'aujourd'hui,* Publication du Centre d'Etudes Régionales de Kabylie, Mémoires et travaux, T. III (Algiers: Imprimarie Fontana, 1959), Introduction.

17. Betbeder, CHEAM–1219, pp. 21–22.

18. Léon Rocher, "Perspectives d'évolution politique en Afrique du Nord," in *L'Afrique et l'Asie* XII (4th trimester 1950): 5–36.

19. Martin, *Histoire de l'Algérie française*, p. 348.

20. Michael K. Clark, *Algeria in Turmoil* (New York: Praeger, 1959), p. 51. This excellent study argues the case of the European settlers.

21. Julien, *L'Afrique du Nord en marche*, pp. 302 ff.

22. Duchemin, *Histoire du F.L.N.*, p. 32.

23. Un Africain, "Le Nationalisme extremiste en Algérie: ses forces, ses faiblesses. Comment les [sic] combattre," CHEAM–50.113 (1957), p. 5.

24. Favrod, *Le F.L.N. et l'Algérie*, pp. 116–117.

25. Ibid., p. 116, f.n. 1.

26. This argument had been used earlier. See *Du Manifeste à la République Algérienne* (Alger: Editions "Libération," 1948), p. 69.

27. Quoted in Favrod, *Le F.L.N. et l'Algérie*, p. 117.

28. Un Africain, CHEAM–50.113, passim.

29. Le Tourneau, *Evolution politique*, p. 374.

30. Ibid., f.n. 1.

31. Julien, *L'Afrique du Nord en marche*, pp. 135–136.

32. Ibid., p. 303.

33. Clark, *Algeria in Turmoil*, p. 70.

34. Ibid., p. 71.

35. Ibid., pp. 71–72.

36. The attitude is clearly expressed by Ben Bella as quoted in Robert Merle, *Ahmed Ben Bella,* trans. by Camilla Sykes (New York: Walker and Company, 1967), pp. 80–84.

37. Duchemin, *Histoire du F.L.N.*, p. 35; Favrod, *Le F.L.N. et l'Algérie*, p. 123.

38. Favrod, *Le F.L.N. et l'Algérie*, p. 124.

39. Ibid., p. 126.
40. Le Tourneau, CHEAM–3358, pp. 18–19.
41. Favrod, *Le F.L.N. et l'Algérie,* p. 124.

3. CRUA LEADERS AND REVOLUTIONARY PLANNING

1. Edward Behr, *The Algerian Problem* (New York: Norton and Co., 1962), p. 61. Mr. Behr is not specific about the founding of the C.R.U.A. He simply writes that it was organized in March. Clark in *Algeria in Turmoil,* pp. 89–90, 343, agrees, but he is too vague.

2. Hahn, *North Africa,* pp. 257–258; Behr, *Dramatique Algérie,* trans. from the English by Michel Deutsch (Paris: Stock, 1962), unnumbered pages in front of the title page. The original English version does not include the biographical sketches, hereafter referred to as "Notes Biographiques."

3. Hocine Ait Ahmed, *La guerre et l'après-guerre* (Paris: Presses Universitaires de France, 1964).

4. Behr, "Notes Biographiques"; Hahn, *North Africa,* pp. 257–258.

5. Also relevant is the fact that one of his brothers ran a watch repair shop shortly after independence in 1962. Owning such a business indicates some technical training and a fair investment.

6. The rank was a French one, *caporal chef,* to be exact. There is no exact equivalent in English for this French rank.

7. About Mohamedi Said see Duchemin, *Histoire du F.L.N.,* p. 108. Bitat and Boudiaf were definitely drafted, and some of the other members of the CRUA may have been drafted. With respect to more advanced military training, only those who moved up in grade offer particular interest, notably Ben Bella, Krim, and other leaders not in the original group of nine.

8. The best biography of Ben Bella to date, a preliminary account based on taped interview, is Merle, *Ahmed Ben Bella.*

9. When asked how many children he has, a typical Algerian will often answer with only the number of boys he has fathered. Further questioning is needed to discover the total number of children.

10. On election frauds see G. Tillion, "Démocratie et colonialisme: II," *Preuves* CXIII (July 1960): 16–17; Amar Naroun, *Ferhat Abbas où les chemins de la souveraineté* (Paris: Denoël, 1961), p. 118; Favrod, *Le F.L.N. et l'Algérie,* p. 110.

11. Claude Estier, *Pour l'Algérie* (Paris: Maspéro, 1964), pp. 96–97; Merle, *Ahmed Ben Bella,* pp. 86 ff.

12. Behr, "Notes Biographiques"; Favrod, *Le F.L.N. et l'Algérie*, p. 117.

13. Duchemin, *Histoire du F.L.N.*, p. 32.

14. Jean-André Faucher, *L'Algérie rebelle* (Paris: Editions du Grand Damier, 1957), p. 104.

15. Biographical notice on the jacket of Mohamed Boudiaf, *Où va L'Algérie?* (Paris: Editions Librairie de l'Etoile, 1964).

16. Patrick Kessel and Giovanni Pirelli, *Le Peuple algérien et la guerre: lettres et témoignages, 1954–1962* (Paris: Maspéro, 1962), p. 33.

17. Ibid., p. 34.

18. Ibid., p. 32.

19. Hahn, *North Africa*, p. 258.

20. See, for example, Bessaoud Mohamed el Arab, *Heureux les martyres qui n'ont rien vu* (Colombe [Seine], France: Imprimerie Cary, 1963), passim.

21. Robert Buron, *Carnets politiques de la guerre d'Algérie* (Paris: Plon, 1965), p. 196.

22. Ling, *Tunisia*, p. 171.

23. Stephane Bernard, *Le conflit franco-marocain, 1943–1956*, III (Brussels: Imprimerie Vedeco, 1963), 259 ff.

24. René Delisle, "Les Origines du F.L.N.," *La Nef*, XII–XIII (October 1962–January 1963): 30.

25. Favrod, *Le F.L.N. et l'Algérie*, p. 91.

26. Delisle, "Les Origines du F.L.N.," pp. 30–31.

27. Le Tourneau, *Evolution politique*, pp. 115, 176–177.

28. Duchemin, *Histoire du F.L.N.*, p. 40.

29. Le Tourneau, *Evolution politique*, pp. 220 and 225.

30. Jacques Soustelle, *Aimée et souffrante Algérie* (Paris: Plon, 1956), p. 17.

31. Faucher, *L'Algérie rebelle*, p. 77.

32. Soustelle, *Aimée et souffrante Algérie*, p. 19.

33. Ibid., p. 20; Duchemin, *Histoire du F.L.N.*, p. 41.

34. Favrod, *Le F.L.N. et l'Algérie*, p. 126.

35. Faucher, *L'Algérie rebelle*, p. 79.

36. Favrod, *Le F.L.N. et l'Algérie*, pp. 125–126.

4. November 1 and the First French Reactions

1. Robert Aron, et al., *Les Origines de la guerre d'Algérie* (Paris: Fayard, 1962), p. 319.

2. Le Tourneau, *Evolution politique,* p. 385.

3. Clark, *Algeria in Turmoil* (New York: Praeger, 1959), p. 4. Mr. Clark is using the account of Brahim Halimi, the bus driver, as quoted in the *Journal d'Alger,* November 5, 1964.

4. Jean Servier, *Dans l'Aurès sur les pas des rebelles* (Paris: Editions France-Empire, 1955), p. 14.

5. Ibid., chapter 1.

6. Ibid.

7. Clark, *Algeria in Turmoil,* p. 3.

8. Le Tourneau, "L'Evolution politique de l'Algérie," CHEAM—3768, p. 26.

9. Nouschi, *La naissance du nationalisme algérien,* p. 151.

10. Martin, *Histoire de l'Algérie française,* p. 365.

11. *Fédération 1954,* p. 421.

12. Duchemin, *Histoire du F.L.N.,* p. 50.

13. Clark, *Algeria in Turmoil,* p. 100.

14. Faucher, *L'Algérie rebelle,* p. 75.

15. Ageron, *Histoire de l'Algérie contemporaine,* p. 100.

16. Jean-Paul Benoit, "Chronologie de la guerre en Algérie," *La Nef* XII–XIII (October 1962–January 1963): 6.

17. Claude Delmas, *La Guerre révolutionnaire* (Paris: Presses Universitaires de France, 1959), pp. 51, 66–67; André Raymond, *La Tunisie* (Paris: Presses Universitaires de France, 1961), pp. 75–83.

18. J.-L. Miège, *Le Maroc* (Paris: Presses Universitaires de France, 1962), pp. 46–47.

19. Duchemin, *Histoire du F.L.N.,* p. 60.

20. Clark, *Algeria in Turmoil,* p. 106.

21. Le Tourneau, *Evolution politique,* p. 391.

22. Clark, *Algeria in Turmoil,* p. 107.

23. Raoul Girardet, *La Crise militaire française: 1945–1962* (Paris: Armand Colin, 1964), p. 187.

24. Favrod, *Le F.L.N. et l'Algérie,* p. 128.

25. Germaine Tillion, *Algeria: The Realities,* trans. by Ronald Matthews (New York: Alfred A. Knopf, 1958), p. 187.

26. Favrod, *Le F.L.N. et l'Algérie,* p. 128; Duchemin, *Histoire du F.L.N.,* p. 59.

27. Clark, *Algeria in Turmoil,* p. 123; Richard Brace and Jean Brace, *Ordeal in Algeria* (Princeton, N.J.: D. Van Nostrand Co., 1960), p. 95.

28. Le Tourneau, *Evolution politique,* p. 390.

29. Benoit, "Chronologie de la guerre en Algérie," p. 6.

30. Brace and Brace, *Ordeal in Algeria*, p. 133.

31. G. Philippe, "Témoignages et documents: Témoignages pour l'Algérie française," *Défense de l'Occident* X–XI (January–February 1961): 40.

32. William G. Andrews, *French Politics and Algeria* (New York: Appleton-Century-Crofts, 1962), p. 36.

33. Ibid.

34. Kessel and Pirelli, *Le Peuple algérien et la guerre*, pp. 1–2; Henri Alleg, *The Question*, trans. by John Calder (New York: George Braziller, Inc., 1958), passim. See also chapter 14 of the present study.

35. There is some disagreement about exactly when the FLN was founded. A. Mandouze, *La révolution algérienne par les textes* (Paris: Maspéro, 1961), p. 157, suggests the vague date of May 1955. Clark, *Algeria in Turmoil*, p. 112, writes that the organization appeared on November 1, 1954, the same day the ALN appeared. Behr, *The Algerian Problem*, pp. 70–73, avoids dating the first appearance of the FLN but strongly suggests November 1, 1954, which day he unequivocally chooses as the day on which the ALN was born.

36. Duchemin, *Histoire du F.L.N.*, p. 60.

37. See n. 35 above; Nevill Barbour, ed., *A Survey of North West Africa: The Maghrib* (New York: Oxford University Press, 1959), p. 230.

5. THE SPREAD OF REVOLUTIONARY NATIONALISM

1. Joan Gillespie, *Algeria: Rebellion and Revolution* (New York: Praeger, 1960), p. 95.

2. Faucher, *L'Algérie rebelle*, p. 80.

3. Joseph Kraft, *The Struggle for Algeria* (New York: Doubleday and Co., 1961), p. 69.

4. Soustelle, *Aimée et souffrante Algérie*, p. 21.

5. Georges Beuchard, *L'Equivoque algérienne* (Paris: Nouvelles Editions Debresse, 1949), p. 34.

6. Ferhat Abbas, *Guerre et révolution d'Algérie, La Nuit coloniale*, I (Paris: Julliard, 1962), p. 196.

7. Chaliand, *L'Algérie est-elle socialiste?* (Paris: Maspéro, 1964), pp. 34–35.

8. Kraft, *The Struggle for Algeria*, p. 69. According to Ben Bella, the insurrectionists at the start had no more than 350 to 400 weapons, mainly Italian rifles from Libya. See Merle, *Ahmed Ben Bella*, p. 95. A footnote in Merle's book notices that Jacques Chevallier and Gen-

eral Cherrière spoke of several thousand military weapons and refers to Claude Paillat, *Le Deuxième Dossier secret de l'Algérie* (Paris: Presses de la Cité, 1962), p. 56.

9. Paillat, ibid.

10. Clark, *Algeria in Turmoil*, p. 125. See also Raymond Dronne, *La Révolution d'Alger* (Paris: Editions France-Empire, 1958), p. 32.

11. Faucher, *L'Algérie rebelle*, pp. 119–120.

12. Clark, *Algeria in Turmoil*, p. 126.

13. Pierre Leuliette, *St. Michael and the Dragon: Memoirs of a Paratrooper*, trans. by John Edmonds (Boston: Houghton Mifflin Co., 1964), pp. 35–39, passim.

14. Clark, *Algeria in Turmoil*, p. 126.

15. Chef de Bataillon Etcheverry, "Réflexions sur la guerre subversive d'Algérie," *Revue des forces terrestres*, XVII (July 1959): 41–48. Although the author of this article is not specifically interested in the situation in 1954, he defines rather clearly the problem faced by the French army at that time.

16. Girardet, *La Crise militaire française: 1954–1962*, pp. 186–187.

17. Nevill Barbour, ed., *A Survey of North West Africa*, pp. 220–223. See also chapter one of the present study.

18. Ibid., p. 225. See also the more detailed description of the origins and development of the SAS in chapter 12 of the present study.

19. Kessel and Pirelli, *Le Peuple algérien et la guerre*, p. 10, note one.

20. Clark, *Algeria in Turmoil*, p. 132.

21. Kessel and Pirelli, *Le Peuple algérien et la guerre*, pp. 1–11.

22. A. Benabdallah, M. Oussedik, J. Verges, and M. Zavrian, *Défense politique* (Paris: Maspéro, 1961), passim.

23. R. Frisson, "La Réforme territoriale de l'Algérie," *L'Afrique et l'Asie*, XXXVI (4th trimester 1956): 29.

24. Pierre Bourdieu, *The Algerians*, trans. by Alan C. M. Ross (Boston: Beacon Press, 1962), pp. 10–12.

25. Ibid., pp. 27–32.

26. Frantz Fanon, *A Dying Colonialism*, trans. by Haakon Chevalier (New York: Grove Press, 1967), particularly the chapter entitled "Algeria Unveiled."

27. Saadia-et-Lakhdar, *L'Aliénation colonialiste et la résistance de la famille algérienne* (Lausanne, Switzerland: La Cité-Editeur, 1961), passim.

28. Between 1919 and 1935 only 1,631 Algerians took advantage of fairly liberal naturalization laws. The total number of naturali-

zations between 1865 and 1934 was about 2500. The rate of naturalization did not change much between 1935 and 1954. See Julien, *L'Afrique du Nord en marche*, p. 31.

29. In 1911, some had simply left Algeria rather than to be subject to induction into the French army. See Julien, *L'Afrique du Nord en marche*, p. 104. Also interesting in this context is the popular verse reproduced in Y. Lacoste, A. Nouschi and A. Prenant, *L'Algérie: passé et présent* (Paris: Edition Sociales, 1960), p. 437: "The French have taken the eighteen year olds, I bid adieu to my parents; We take leave of each other before death. The French have taken the eighteen year olds, Next year they'll take the seventeen year olds . . ."

30. Faucher, *L'Algérie rebelle*, p. 81. Paradoxically, many Algerian families were to have men fighting on both sides. This was true especially after 1956 when the French finally seized the initiative. Fathers and sons or brothers can, of course, disagree on political issues, but it seems more likely that many Algerian families chose to hedge their bets by having representatives in both camps.

31. Kraft, *The Struggle for Algeria*, p. 70; Behr, *The Algerian Problem*, pp. 64–65.

32. For Lyautey's own definition of his strategy for pacification see Louis Hubert Lyautey, *Lettres du Tonkin et de Madagascar: 1894–1899* (Paris: Colin, 1946), pp. 629–653. Lyautey borrowed heavily from General Galliéni, to whom this book is dedicated and who also wrote a great deal about the subject of pacification. One of Galliéni's best and most easily accessible collections of essays and letters is Hubert Deschamps and Paul Chauvet, eds., *Galliéni pacificateur: Ecrits coloniaux de Galliéni* (Paris: Presses Universitaires de France, 1949).

33. David Galula, *Counter-Insurgency Warfare: Theory and Practice* (New York: Praeger, 1964), p. 74.

34. James Eliot Cross, *Conflict in the Shadows: The Nature and Policies of Guerilla War* (New York: Doubleday and Co., 1963), p. 15. Mr. Cross points out that in underdeveloped countries the groundwork for insurgency is already laid. Also, repressive regimes are especially vulnerable to guerrilla war. Algeria fulfilled both these conditions.

35. Galula, *Counter-Insurgency*, p. 75.

36. Brace and Brace, *Ordeal in Algeria*, p. 92.

37. Clark, *Algeria in Turmoil*, pp. 126–127.

38. Ibid., pp. 131–135.

39. Ibid. One could easily follow the spread of nationalism by

reading the *New York Times* or *Le Monde* for the last two months of 1954 and the first few months of 1955.

40. Benoit, "Chronologie de la guerre en Algérie," p. 6.

41. Favrod, *Le F.L.N. et l'Algérie*, pp. 169–172.

42. Clark, *Algeria in Turmoil*, p. 112; Duchemin, *Histoire du F.L.N.*, p. 60; Mandouze, *La Révolution algérienne par les textes*, p. 157; Le Tourneau, *Evolution Politique*, p. 386.

43. Duchemin, *Histoire du F.L.N.*, pp. 94–95.

44. Faucher, *L'Algérie rebelle*, p. 242.

45. Ibid.

46. Duchemin, *Histoire du F.L.N.*, p. 67.

47. Clark, *Algeria in Turmoil*, pp. 136–137.

48. Saadi Yacef, *Souvenirs de la bataille d'Alger* (Paris: Julliard, 1962), p. 12. Favrod claims that Bitat was arrested in February 1955. See Favrod, *Le F.L.N. et l'Algérie*, p. 155.

49. R. Eoche-Duval, "Aspects locaux et perspectives de la rénovation rurale en Algérie," CHEAM—3631 (1961), pp. 3–4.

50. Saadia-et-Lakhdar, *L'Aliénation colonialiste et la résistance de la famille algérienne*, passim.

51. Le Tourneau, *Evolution politique*, p. 386.

52. Clark, *Algeria in Turmoil*, p. 111.

53. See nn. 40–42 above and corresponding text. See also n. 35 of chapter 4.

6. Revolutionary Institutions and Organization

1. English terms for geographical units are used rather than the Arabic terms that the nationalists themselves used. Two exceptions are *douar* and *fraction*. The latter is self-descriptive and the former is typically Algerian and could hardly be translated. Other terms, such as *wilaya* (province), *nahia* (region) and *kism* (sector), however, are translated in order to avoid undue complications in the text.

2. The MTLD had six *wilaya* (provinces), although the Sahara wilaya was not used, thirty-three *daira* (districts) and one hundred or so *kasma* (sectors). (*Kasma* is plural of *kism*.) The FLN had six provinces. It had *mintaga* (zones) and *nahia* (regions) but apparently no *daira* between the province and the sector. On the organization of the MTLD see Clark, *Algeria in Turmoil*, p. 71.

3. Cdt. Bérard, "La Rebellion algérienne vue à travers ses chefs," CHEAM—3288 (1959), p. 5.

4. See for example Duchemin, *Histoire du F.L.N.*, pp. 97–98, passim; and Faucher, *L'Algérie rebelle*, pp. 129 ff.

5. Duchemin, *Histoire du F.L.N.*, p. 95.

6. Most of the information about the organization of the ALN and the FLN presented in this chapter comes from Lucien Poirier, "Un instrument de guerre subversive: Le F.L.N. (suite et fin)," *Revue Militaire d'Information*, CCXC (January 1958): 69–92. Material not specifically from this excellent source is cited as usual.

7. There is an interesting discussion of the Communist vocabulary borrowed by the FLN-ALN in Michel Déon, *L'Armée d'Algérie et la Pacification* (Paris: Plon, 1959), pp. 51–55.

8. Poirier, "Un instrument de guerre subversive: Le F.L.N. (suite et fin)," p. 79.

9. Ibid., pp. 79–80; Duchemin, *Histoire du F.L.N.*, p. 94.

10. Lavie, *Le Drame algérien*, p. 119. Lavie, however, refused to reproduce any part of the adapted French training manual which he claimed to have seen.

11. Faucher, *L'Algérie rebelle*, p. 119.

12. Ibid.

13. Duchemin, *Histoire du F.L.N.*, p. 98.

14. Faucher, *L'Algérie rebelle*, pp. 119–120.

15. Duchemin, *Histoire du F.L.N.*, pp. 102–103.

16. André Mandouze, *La révolution algérienne par les textes*, pp. 89–92. The nationalists, with the exception of the Reformist Ulama, were much too proletarian and not interested in independence for the sake of religious consideration; however, it might be well to define *moudjahidin, mousseblin* and *fida'iyin* in terms of their religious implications: *Moudjahidin* were regular soliders of the ALN, described by the nationalist journal *El Moudjahid* as the "mold in which the great moral forces of the past and the exalted hopes for the future blend, . . . bringing forth the extraordinary enthusiasm of a whole people that has decided to live in freedom." The reference to the past is a reference to Islam, to fighting of the jihad or holy war, hence to religious values and motives, but the propagandists seemed determined to avoid a specific religious definition.

The *mousseblin* (those who fight God's battle), again according to *El-Moudjahid*, made the whole system of the rebels work in a material sense—intelligence, logistic support, day to day political control on the local level. It was also the *mousseblin* who most often performed the duties of the *fida'iyin*, fanatic terrorists who, according to

nationalist propaganda, lived solitary lives of complete devotion to
assigned missions and were often ascetics. Here again there is a veiled
reference to the religious implications of the role played by the individual *fidaï*, but nationalist propagandists preferred, at least by 1956,
not to stress this characteristic. The term itself implies a sense of
religious sacrifice.

17. Favrod, *Le F.L.N. et l'Algérie*, p. 147.
18. Duchemin, *Histoire du F.L.N.*, p. 96.
19. Le Tourneau, *Evolution politique*, p. 390.
20. Ibid., p. 391.
21. Clark, *Algeria in Turmoil*, p. 136.
22. Ibid., p. 124.
23. With the building of an electrified barricade along the Al-
gerian-Tunisian border, the rebels' contraband was severely curtailed.
Also, the French army was much better organized to fight revolutionary warfare by the end of 1957 than it was earlier.
24. Le Tourneau, *Evolution politique*, p. 391.
25. And, of course, Ben Bella and his fellow travelers, Ait Ahmed,
Mohamed Khider, Mohamed Boudiaf, and Mustapha Lacheraf, were
caught when their airplane was forced to land in Algeria on October
22, 1956. See Martin, *Histoire de l'Algérie française*, p. 395.
26. Duchemin, *Histoire du F.L.N.*, pp. 97–98.
27. Ibid., p. 112.
28. See for example D. M. Condit, "Kenya," in D. M. Condit, Bert
H. Cooper, Jr., et al., *Challenge and Response in Internal Conflict,
The Experience in Africa and Latin America*, II (Washington: Center
for Research in Social Systems, 1968), pp. 280, 283, 288, 293. Also in-
formative are Elizabeth M. Thompson, "Madagascar," ibid., p. 327;
and William Zartman, "Portuguese Guinea," ibid., p. 359.
29. Poirier, "Un instrument de guerre subversive: Le F.L.N. (suite
et fin)," p. 79.
30. J. Bernhardt, "La Pacification dans un quartier d'Alger: 1957–
1959," CHEAM–3077 (1959), pp. 15–16; G. Philippe, "Que disait le
colonel d'Alger?" *Défense de l'Occident* X–XI (January–February
1961): 83; Benoit, "Chronologie de la guerre en Algérie," p. 6.
31. Poirier, "Un instrument de guerre subversive: Le F.L.N. (suite
et fin)," p. 74.
32. Ibid., p. 75.
33. Ibid. See also Favrod, *Le F.L.N. et l'Algérie*, p. 148. Favrod calls
the People's Assembly a consultative assembly and simply states that
it was elected by direct suffrage.

34. Poirier, "Un instrument de guerre subversive: Le F.L.N. (suite et fin)," p. 78.

35. Ibid., p. 75; Paul Thibaud, "Ce qu'est le F.L.N.," *Perspectives Socialistes* XXXIX–XL (August–September 1960): 15.

36. Poirier, "Un instrument de guerre subversive: Le F.L.N. (suite et fin)," p. 75.

37. Ibid., p. 78.

38. Ibid., p. 76.

39. Cross, *Conflict in the Shadows*, p. 44.

40. Bernhardt, CHEAM–3077, pp. 15–17.

41. Poirier, "Un instrument de guerre subversive: Le F.L.N. (suite et fin)," p. 78.

42. Bernhardt, CHEAM–3077, p. 19.

7. Some Motives for Support of the FLN-ALN

1. There are several accounts of OPA cells by officers who participated in the war. See for example Cdt. Berard, CHEAM–3072; and D. Bogros, CHEAM–3474. Other similar reports will be mentioned throughout this chapter. In addition, there are several published accounts of the war by officers who treat the subject of the OPA. See for example Philippe Heduy, *Au Lieutenant des Taglaïts* (Paris: Table Ronde, 1960); Jean-Jacques Servan-Schreiber, *Lieutenant en Algérie* (Paris: Julliard, 1957); François Denoyer, *Quatre ans de guerre en Algérie* (Paris: Flammarion, 1962).

2. See for example Mandouze, *La Révolution algérienne par les textes*; Kessel and Pirelli, *Le Peuple algérien et la guerre;* and Clark, *Algeria in Turmoil*.

3. For example, one *garde champêtre*, who was interviewed in 1963, had served the French before the revolution and continued in their pay until 1955 after having joined the FLN in 1954. Then he had gone to the *maquis* with the ALN. After independence he had resumed his police work for the new government. Asked why he had joined the ALN, he simply smiled; on other subjects, he was very talkative.

4. See Zohra Driff, *La Mort de mes frères* (Paris: Maspéro, 1961); Kessel and Pirelli, *Le Peuple algérien et la guerre,* p. 126.

5. Interviews with former ALN soldiers in the Fort National and Ouadiahs regions have led the author to this conclusion. Not to be able to own a gun was the most frequently mentioned grievance against the colonial administration.

6. The story was heard in Algeria by the author when he was a child and again in 1963.

7. See for example Charles Richard, *Du Gouverneur arabe et de l'institution qui doit l'exercer* (Algiers: Bastide, 1848), p. 91; and General Trézel, "Observations sur le projet d'ordonnance créant les troupes indigènes en Afrique, 12 juin 1839," H226 (Algérie, Mémoires Diverses), Archives du Ministère de la Guerre, Section Moderne, Chateau de Vincennes, Paris.

8. "Francs propos d'un africain," CHEAM—3491 (1955), p. 4. See also Saadia-et-Lakhdar, *L'Aliénation*, p. 46.

9. An Algerian barber of Fort National, who joined the rebels in 1955, told such a story about service in restaurants when he was interviewed in 1963. He was a thoughtful person, the chief of his village, well dressed in the Western style and faultless in his manners. The rest of the information in this paragraph is based on the author's personal experience.

10. The incident was related to the author by his father, W. N. Heggoy, who was a missionary in Algeria for thirty years.

11. This is the tone, for example, of Amar Ouzegane, *Le Meilleur combat* (Paris: Julliard, 1962). See also Paul Bert, *Lettres de Kabylie* (Paris: A. Lemerre, 1885), p. 10. Bert claims that there were sixteen marriages of Muslims and Europeans in 1883. The average number of mixed marriages must have been higher in the twentieth century, but the generalization remains true. See also Khaled Chaoui, "Pourqoi la rébellion?" CHEAM—3504 (1961), p. 11.

12. Saadia-et-Lakhdar, *L'Aliénation*, pp. 149–195.

13. Ageron, *Histoire de l'Algérie*, p. 86. In 1954 there were 354 native lawyers and 28 engineers. In addition there were 185 teachers and 165 doctors, pharmacists, and dentists. Ninety per cent of the total native population of nearly nine million, however, were illiterate. See also Julien, *L'Afrique du Nord en marche*, p. 68.

14. Saadia-et-Lakhdar, *L'Aliénation*, p. 44.

15. "Francs propos d'un Africain," CHEAM—3491, p. 15.

16. Condit, "Kenya," pp. 274–295.

17. Ageron, *Histoire de l'Algérie*, pp. 81–86. The birth rate in Egypt was 1.84 per cent. See also Tillion, *Algeria: The Realities*, p. 17.

18. Nouschi, *La naissance du nationalisme algérien*, p. 114.

19. Ageron, *Histoire de l'Algérie*, pp. 81–86.

20. Ibid.; M. Rager, "L'Emigration des Musulmans algériens en France," CHEAM—2691 (1965), passim.

21. Favrod, *Le F.L.N. et l'Algérie*, p. 147; Brace and Brace, *Ordeal in Algeria*, p. 110.

22. John Steward Ambler, *Soldiers Against the State: The French Army in Politics* (New York: Doubleday and Co., 1968), p. 167. Some of those who had more nearly achieved positions of equality in the colonial system were sometimes slow to join the FLN. Ferhat Abbas was, of course, an example of a successful man for whom the step from a political to a revolutionary attack on the French system was not easy.

23. Robert Barrat, "Un journalist français chez les 'hors-la-loi' algériens," *France-Observateur* CCLXXIX (15 September 1955): 16–18.

24. Faucher, *L'Algérie rebelle*, p. 97.

25. Merle, *Ahmed Ben Bella*, pp. 74, 77, passim.

26. Michel Boisard, *La Guerre d'Algérie à travers la litterature: 1954–1961*, thesis (Institut d'Etudes Politiques of the University of Paris, 1962), p. 75. Boisard refers to Servier's story of young Muslims who dared death by stretching themselves out across highways by night to see if cars would stop in time. This was the symptom of a need which the rebellion could fulfill. See Jean Servier, *Demain en Algérie* (Paris: Laffont, 1959), p. 54.

27. Jacques Vieillot, "Monographie de la S.A.S. d'Ain Boucif," CHEAM—2870 (1958), p. 28.

28. Barrat, "Un journaliste," *France-Observateur* CCLXXIX (1955): 17.

29. Ibid.

30. Le Tourneau, *Evolution politique*, pp. 397–398; and Brace and Brace, *Ordeal in Algeria*, pp. 101–102.

31. There were advantages and disadvantages in this system. After the French built the border barrier along the Tunisian and Moroccan borders, the ALN soldiers in foreign sanctuaries could rarely get into Algeria to fight.

32. Capt. P. Rohard, "L'Evolution sociale et politique dans le Guerrouma (arrondissement de Palestro)," CHEAM—3334 (1960), p. 51. See also Capt. Bogros, "Quelques aspects du contrôle des nomades en guerre subversive," CHEAM—3474 (1961), p. 24; and Vieillot, CHEAM—2870, p. 32. A native Francophile claimed the same thing. See Kebaili, *La Grande Kabylie*, p. 4. On the problem of secrecy in general, see Cross, *Conflict in the Shadows*, pp. 44–45.

33. John S. Putsay, *Counter-Insurgency Warfare* (New York: The Free Press, 1965), p. 66.

34. Bourdieu, *The Algerians*, p. 145.

35. Driff, *La mort de mes frères*, passim.

36. For various examples see Kessel and Pirelli, *Le Peuple algérien et la guerre*, pp. 126, 128, 131, passim. To the information given by Kessel and Pirelli might be added that available in books such as Abdelhamid Benzine, *Le camp* (Paris: Editions Sociales, 1962).

37. Favrod, *Le F.L.N. et l'Algérie*, pp. 100–104; Duchemin, *Histoire du F.L.N.*, pp. 29–31.

38. P. Haegeli, "L'Attentisme des classes bourgeoises musulmanes de l'Est Constantinois," CHEAM—3584 (1962); Vieillot, CHEAM—2870, p. 23 and p. 27; L. Lafage, "Un important chapitre de l'histoire politique de l'Algérie: Ferhat Abbas et l'Union Démocratique du Manifeste Algérien," CHEAM—3934 (1964), p. 18.

39. Bourdieu, *The Algerian*, p. 154.

40. Camus, *Actuelles III: Chronique algérienne: 1939–1958* (Paris: Gallimard, 1958), p. 113.

41. G. Guvan, "Etudes de quelques motivations et comportements du nationalisme musulman d'Algérie," mimeographed report, CHEAM—3614, September 1961, p. 28.

42. Barrat, "Un journaliste," p. 17.

8. France Takes the Initiative:
Institutional Reforms in Algeria (1956)

1. Pierre Fontaine, *Dossier secret de l'Afrique du Nord* (Paris: Les Sept Couleurs, 1956), p. 18.

2. Quoted in Ibid., p. 20.

3. The argument about whether Algeria was a colony or not is academic. As far as Algerians were concerned it was; they could not rule over their own affairs.

4. Michel Déon, *L'Armée d'Algérie et la pacification* (Paris: Plon, 1959), p. 5; Girardet, *La crise militaire française*, pp. 186 ff.

5. Paul Carpentier, "L'armée après six ans de guerre," *Perspectives Socialistes*, XXXIX–XL (August–September 1960): pp. 27 ff.

6. Faucher, *L'Algérie rebelle*, p. 75; Alfred Fabre-Luce, *Demain en Algérie* (Paris: Plon, 1958), p. 11.

7. Soustelle, *Aimée et souffrante Algérie*, p. 63; Andrews, *French Politics and Algeria*, p. 70.

8. Ageron, *Histoire de l'Algérie*, pp. 96–97.

9. Ibid., p. 97.

10. For a contemporary analysis, see "Ou en est l'Algérie?"

L'Afrique et l'Asie (1st trimester 1948), pp. 36–39. See also C. Faivre, "Une révolution administrative en Algérie: La réforme communale," CHEAM–3740 (1962), p. 9.

11. L. H. Gann and P. Duignan, *White Settlers in Tropical Africa* (Baltimore: Penguin Books, 1962), p. 142. Although this book does not include an analysis of Algeria, the problems discussed are similar.

12. As a schoolboy the author, who attended school in France but spent vacations in Algeria, asked the inevitable question: "If this is France, why do they look through my baggage?" Clearly Algeria was a colony in spite of legalistic arguments to the contrary.

13. The best English account of the French government in Algeria can be found in an official publication. See Algeria, Gouvernement Général, *Essential Notions about Algeria* (Paris: Imprimerie Georges Lang, 1949), p. 5. See also Roland Miette, "Le destin algérien," CHEAM–2515 (1956), p. 2. Another good account is Herbert Liebesny, *The Government of French North Africa* (Philadelphia: University of Pennsylvania Press, 1943).

14. Ageron, *Histoire de l'Algérie,* p. 93.

15. Ibid., p. 95.

16. The question of Muslim women's voting is well covered in Pierre Marmey, "Le droit de vote de la femme musulmane algérienne," CHEAM–2909 (1958); see also Boissenot, "Les conditions de l'émancipation de la femme musulmane," CHEAM—3061 (1959).

17. Pierre Marmey, "L'Electeur Musulman," CHEAM–2910 (1957).

18. Ancel, "L'Administration à l'échelon de l'arrondissement en Algérie," CHEAM–2973 (1959), pp. 1, 11.

19. Jean Laburthe, "L'Evolution de la djemaa kabyle dans la commune mixte de Fort-National," typed memoir, 1946, pp. 49–50. Although this memoir was prepared for the entrance competition of CHEAM in 1947, the copy read by this writer was owned by an inhabitant of Kabylia. The memoir has a long annex made up of pages from a personal journal kept by the same author.

20. Ministère de l'Algérie, *Guide de l'Officer des Affaires Algériennes* (Paris: Imprimerie Georges Lang, 1957).

21. General Cherrière, "Les Débuts de l'Insurrection Algérienne," *Revue de Défense Nationale,* CCLXXX (December 1946): 101.

22. Algeria, Ministère de l'Algérie, *Guide de l'Officier des Affaires Algériennes.*

23. Algeria, Cabinet du Ministre Résident, *L'Algérie 1956* (Algiers: Baconnier, 1956), section entitled "Mesures de Pacification."

24. Soustelle, *Aimée et souffrante Algérie,* p. 63.

25. Esquer, *Histoire de l'Algérie*, p. 101.

26. Algeria, Service de l'Information du Cabinet du Ministre Résident en Algérie, *Programme et action du gouvernement en Algérie: Mesures de pacification et réformes* (August 1956), pp. 63–65.

27. Ibid., pp. 125–126.

28. Ahmed Bennamour, "L'Accession des Musulmans à la fonction publique," CHEAM–3033, n.d. [1958?].

29. Anonymous, "Francs propos d'un Africain," CHEAM–3491 (1955).

30. Georges Zebert, "Etude d'un projet d'aménagement pouvant permettre dans un laps de temps relativement bref l'accession rapide des musulmans aux divers postes qu'ils soient d'execution ou de maitrise," CHEAM–3075 (1959).

31. Algeria, Service de l'Information, *Programme et action* (1956), 46. References are in old francs.

32. Ibid., pp. 52–55.

33. Ibid., pp. 117–119.

34. Merlet, "Evolution de l'organisation administrative de l'Algérie," CHEAM–2911 (1957), p. 8.

35. See for example Jean Meningaud, *La France à l'heure algérienne* (Paris: Paris Livres, 1956), p. 45.

36. Merlet, CHEAM–2911, passim but especially a chart at the end of this report.

37. Germaine Tillion, "Démocratie: II," p. 17.

38. Ibid.; Thibaud, "Ce qu'est le F.L.N.," p. 16.

9. COMPETITION FOR POWER AND INFLUENCE IN 1956

1. Ageron, *Histoire de l'Algérie*, pp. 101–102.

2. Kessel and Pirelli, *Le Peuple algérien*, p. 19, f.n. 9.

3. Ibid., p. 46.

4. Esquer, *Histoire de l'Algérie*, p. 101.

5. Favrod, *La Révolution algérienne*, p. 222.

6. The vote that counted was on a motion not to put the Algerian question on the agenda. The motion was defeated by a vote of 27 to 28 with 5 abstentions. See Mohamed Alwan, *Algeria Before the United Nations* (New York: Robert Speller and Sons, 1959), p. 31. See chapter 15 of this study for further information.

7. Le Tourneau, *Evolution Politique*, p. 407.

8. Ibid., p. 405.

9. Ibid., p. 407.

10. Favrod, *La Révolution algérienne,* p. 224.

11. Moroccan independence was recognized *de facto* on November 6, 1955, and *de jure* on March 2, 1956.

12. Tunisian independence was proclaimed on March 20, 1956.

13. Delmas, *La Guerre révolutionnaire,* pp. 63 ff. This was especially true of Tunisia, but Morocco also had armed guerrilla units. See also Behr, *The Algerian Problem,* pp. 99–100.

14. Pierre Boyer da Latour, *De l'Indochine à l'Algérie: Le Martyre de l'Armée française* (Paris: Les Presses du Mail, 1962), passim; and Suzanne Labin, *Vie ou mort du monde libre* (Paris: La Table Ronde, 1961), passim. A more specific reference can be found in François Kuntz, *L'officier français dans la nation* (Paris: Charles Lavauzelle et Cie., 1960), p. 165. On the attitudes of many military leaders, see George Armstrong Kelly, *Lost Soldiers: The French Army and Empire in Crisis* (Cambridge: M.I.T. Press, 1965), particularly part four, pp. 143 ff.

15. Esquer, *Histoire de l'Algérie,* p. 97.

16. Jean Raymond Tournoux, *Secret d'État* (Paris: Union Générale d'Editions, 1960), pp. 105 ff; Merle, *Ahmed Ben Bella,* pp. 114–130.

17. Behr, *The Algerian Problem,* p. 127. Tournoux, *Secret d'État,* p. 122 ff.

18. "Courbes théoriques et réelles de la puissance militaire et de l'action terroriste," *La Semaine en Algérie* XXXVI (April 6 to April 12, 1959). The rest of this paragraph is based on the same graphic description of the Algerian war from 1954 to 1959. Note that the figures used are official French figures; there may be a tendency to lower actual numbers of exactions.

19. Duquesne noted that there was triple pressure—Algerian, international, and national—from 1956 on. These pressures led to the *loi cadre* of 1958, a radically different approach to Algerian institutional realities; it was vaguely federalist. See Duquesne, "Septs ans de politique algérienne," *Revue d'Action Populaire,* CLVI (March 1962): 281.

10. THE SOUMMAM CONGRESS

1. Le Tourneau, *Evolution politique,* pp. 386–388 ff.

2. Ibid., p. 413.

3. Numerical strength was up to more than 400,000 men. See Benoit, "Chronologie de la guerre en Algérie," p. 8.

4. Duchemin, *Histoire du F.L.N.,* p. 179; Favrod, *Le F.L.N. et l'Algérie,* p. 148.

5. Ibid.

6. Delisle, "Les origines du F.L.N.," p. 31.

7. Thomas Oppermann, *Le problème algérien*, trans. from German by J. Lecerf (Paris: Maspéro, 1961), p. 116, f.n. 127.

8. Ben Bella was captured on October 22, 1956. See Mandouze, *La Révolution algérienne*, p. 22.

9. Oppermann, *Le problème algérien*, p. 116, f.n. 127.

10. Oppermann, *Le problème algérien*, p. 116 (text and f.n. 26, which mentions an article by W. Plum that deals specifically with this question). See chapters 1 and 2 of this study for a description of the 1949 event.

11. Favrod, *Le F.L.N. et l'Algérie*, p. 148.

12. One need simply note the number of times *El Moudjahid* referred to this platform to become convinced of this point. The texts collected by Mandouze in *La Révolution algérienne* are also instructive in this context. Even the post-independence pamphlet *Tous Algériens*, n.p., n.d. (1962?), published to induce Europeans to remain in Algeria, quotes the platform of the Soummam Congress and elaborates on it. See p. 28 ff.

13. Déon, *L'Armée d'Algérie*, pp. 30–31.

14. Ibid., p. 31.

15. Ibid., p. 32.

16. Duchemin, *Histoire du F.L.N.*, pp. 198–199. Here Duchemin presents an interpretation of the platform.

17. Ibid., pp. 207–212. These pages contain a reproduction of the Soummam platform's section on propaganda. The next several paragraphs are based on this source.

18. Ibid., pp. 211–212.

19. Ibid., p. 201.

20. The chapter on revolutionary organization, Chapter 6, was largely based on the platform of the Soummam Congress.

21. Oppermann, *Le problème algérien*, pp. 116–117, reproduces part of the platform, on which this author bases his analysis. Duchemin, *Histoire du F.L.N.*, pp. 191–212, reproduces an interpretation of the platform written by leaders of the autonomous zone of Algiers.

22. Le Tourneau, *Evolution politique*, pp. 412–416.

23. Oppermann, *Le problème algérien*, p. 122.

11. SOME INSTITUTIONS OF COUNTERINSURGENCY

1. Reference is made here to revolutionary warfare, the type with

which this study is concerned throughout. This kind of war is graphically described by Alexis Martin, who presents it in the following equation: "guerre de guerrillas + action psychologique = guerre revolutionnaire." See Alexis Martin, *Technique de la guerre occulte* (Paris: Flammarion, 1963), p. 101. Martin's book might be compared to Maurice Megret, *L'action psychologique* (Paris: Fayard, 1958), passim, and to Delmas, *La guerre révolutionnaire,* passim. An excellent article on psychological action was Capt. Souyris, "L'action psychologique dans les Forces Armées," *Revue Militaire et Information* CCXCVIII (October 1958): 34–45.

2. There may have been a connection between the resort to acts of individual terrorism in late 1956 and the truce worked out in the same year between the Parti Communiste Algérien and the FLN; see chapter 15.

3. On paper, this is what was achieved by the Soummam Conference. See the chapters on rebel organization and on the Soummam Conference.

4. The Algerian Communists continued to try to tell the FLN leaders that they must organize passage to superior forms of the struggle. See Bachir Hadj Ali, *Notre peuple vaincra* (Geneva: Du Fennac, 1960), p. 89 ff. Communist advice was not well received; see Ouzegane, *Le meilleur combat,* passim. For a typical example of the seizure, then evacuation, of a portion of the "national" territory, see Meziane Noureddine, *Un Algérien raconte* (Paris: Seuil, 1960), p. 101 ff.

5. See n. 2 above; Ageron, *Histoire de l'Algérie,* p. 104; and Behr, *The Algerian Problem,* pp. 99 ff. Behr retells the chronology of events surrounding Germaine Tillion's conversations with rebel leaders, particularly with Saadi Yacef.

6. See for example Jean Yves Alquier, *Nous avons pacifié Tazalt: Journal de marche d'un officier parachutiste* (Paris: Laffont, 1957), pp. 24, passim.

7. Ibid. See also Raoul Girardet, *Victoires et servitudes des capitaines* (Paris: Imprimerie de "Combat" et Presse de France, 1960), p. 3. Other accounts by officers who were active in Algeria between 1954 and 1962 also have pertinent information.

8. See Jacques Boutin, "De certains aspects de la guerre de pacification en Algérie," CHEAM–3089 (1959), p. 20; and Haegeli, CHEAM–3584, passim.

9. Delmas, *La guerre revolutionnaire,* passim.

10. The potential strength of the Forces of Order mounted to

400,000 men with the recall of reservists on April 13, 1956. A number of reservists had already been called up in May and August 1955. See Benoit, "Chronologie de la guerre en Algérie," pp. 6–8; and Jean-Jacques Servan-Schreiber, *Lieutenant in Algeria,* trans. by Ronald Mathews (New York: Alfred A. Knopf, 1957), p. 55.

11. Ambler, *Soldiers Against the State,* p. 164.

12. See for example Servan-Schreiber, *Lieutenant in Algeria,* p. 68; and Heduy, *Au Lieutenant des Taglaïts,* p. 41.

13. See nn. 20 and 21 below.

14. On psychological action see Megret, *L'action psychologique,* passim; and Souyris, "L'action psychologique dans les Forces Armées," passim.

15. Lieut.-Col. De Mareuil, "Le Centre d'Instruction de Pacification et de Contre-Guerilla d'Arzew," CHEAM—3383 (1961). Practically all the material on the Arzew school presented here was taken from De Mareuil's excellent report. Other notes given in this context are simply included to direct readers to additional information.

16. Ibid.

17. On the French Army's adaptation to the Algerian insurgency see Girardet, *La crise militaire française,* and Delmas, *La guerre révolutionnaire.* French military journals published excellent articles on the problem. Those articles that appeared in the *Revue Militaire d'Information* were particularly good.

18. *Le Semaine en Algérie,* started in 1958, gives a clear example of an exaggerated stress on statistics. This weekly was apparently aimed at representatives of the press and was quite different from the nationalist organ *El Moudjahid.*

19. De Mareuil, CHEAM—3383, p. 5.

20. Ibid., p. 14.

21. De Mareuil does not give the answer that was offered to students at Arzew, although he does mention that many officers were bothered by the question of torture. For the military justification see "En Algérie: de l'utopie au totalitarisme. Le reseignement contre la pacification," *Le Monde* (Feb. 2, 1937). The pertinent passage is quoted in Oppermann, *Le problème algérien,* p. 150. See also Delegation of the National Liberation Front, *Genocide in Algeria* (Cairo: 1957), and Pierre Vidal-Naquet, *Torture: Cancer of Democracy,* trans. by Barry Richard (Baltimore: Penguin Books, 1963), passim.

22. See Oppermann, *Le problème algérien,* pp. 146–147.

23. De Mareuil, CHEAM—3383, pp. 5 ff.

24. Servan-Schreiber, *Lieutenant in Algeria,* p. 97 and passim.

25. It is interesting to note that the word pacification was the same term as that used during the nineteenth century when it meant conquest and colonization. This fact was not lost on the nationalists, who accused the French of engaging in a colonial war of reconquest. See Hocine Ait Ahmed, *La guerre et l'après-guerre* (Paris: Editions de Minuit, 1964), p. 20, 26–27, and passim.

26. This coincides with what Lacoste said could be expected of the French Army. See "La Politique Française en Algérie," *Revue Militaire d'Information* CCLXXXIII (May 1957): 52–66.

27. Again, Ait Ahmed called the French moves exactly. See Ait Ahmed, *La guerre et l'après-guerre*, p. 21.

28. Kessel and Pirelli, *Le Peuple algérien et la guerre*, p. 25.

29. *Journal Officiel* (July 30, 1955), p. 4531. Part of Deputy Durroux's intervention was quoted by Kessel and Pirelli, *Le Peuple algérien et la guerre*, p. 25.

30. Kessel and Pirelli, ibid., pp. 25–27.

31. Numbers painted on houses could still be seen nearly everywhere in Algeria when the author traveled there in 1963 and 1964. See Claude Laurent, "La naissance d'une commune musulmane," CHEAM–3524 (1961), p. 21.

32. Group d'Etudes, "Les centres de regroupement en Algérie," CHEAM–3277 (1960), p. 5. Also enlightening is M. de Montalembert, "Action des S.A.S. en Algérie," CHEAM–3264 (1959), passim.

33. See for example *La Semaine en Algérie*, which from 1958 on broke down casualties into categories. The number of Muslims killed in any one month was easily four times as high as that of Europeans; the proportion was often higher. On free resettlements, see Vincent, CHEAM–3584.

34. Group d'Etudes, CHEAM–3277 (1960), p. 1; Maurice Dubarry, "Rôle de l'officier, chef de S.A.S. dans le reforme communale en Kabylie," CHEAM–3264 (1959), passim.

35. Servan-Schreiber, *Lieutenant in Algeria*, passim, relates several incidents that show that shooting on sight often occurred even in legitimately populated areas. On actual policy in closed zones see Paul Depis, "Notes sur le problème des refugiés algériens du Maroc oriental," CHEAM–3597 (1962), passim.

36. Mostefa Lacheraf, "Constantes politiques et militaires dans les guerres coloniales d'Algérie," *Les Tempes Modernes* CCLXXVII (January 1961): 786 ff. Also interesting is Jacques Charby, *L'Algérie en prison* (Paris: Editions de Minuit, 1961). On cataloguing see Laurent, CHEAM–3524, p. 20.

37. This point would be rather difficult to document. How the process might occur, however, should be clear from a reading of such reports as Claude Laurent, "Implantation d'une S.A.S. en zone d'insecurité," CHEAM–3655 (1962), pp. 15–16. The nationalists' propaganda made a point of claiming adherents within the regroupments. See *El Moudjahid,* passim. Some particular cases will be discussed elsewhere in this study.

38. See n. 40 below.

39. The Arab proverb that claims that "the stick comes from heaven" may illustrate the reason why people did so. See Vieillot, CHEAM–2870, p. 25. This might also result from simple obedience to rebel orders and lack of money. See Boutin, CHEAM–3089, passim. On payments made see Captain Borja, "Sidi Salem: cité nouvelle de l'Algérie nouvelle," CHEAM–2842 (1958), p. 31. Haegeli, CHEAM–3584 also has information.

40. This particular information comes from conversations with secretaries in town halls throughout Kabylia during the years 1963–1965. While the secretaries themselves could not give such authorizations, requests for permission had to be processed by them and they were the officials who kept records of previously cashed checks.

41. One million out of about eight million, according to Doctor George Martin, "Centres de regroupement et mille villages en Algérie," CHEAM–3526 (1959). See also n. 34 above.

42. There is no difficulty in documenting this point. One need simply to have traveled in Algeria during the revolutionary period, as did the author in December 1961. Conversations with Europeans and Algerians who lived through the events complement this information.

43. "Mesures reglementaires prises dans le Constantinois en vue de mettre obstacle au ravitaillement des rebelles," CHEAM–50660. This document was apparently designed to be read by French officers and was produced by the staff of the 10th military region, ZNC-BSND.

44. Ibid.

45. Boutin, CHEAM–3089, p. 38.

12. The Special Administrative Sections

1. Algeria, *Programme et action*, p. 26.

2. Dubarry, CHEAM–2888, passim; Christiane Fournier, *Nous avons encore des héros* (Paris: Plon, 1957), pp. 49–50.

3. The order establishing *quadrillage* was given on April 25, 1956. See Benoit, "Chronologie . . . ," *La Nef* 12–13 (October 1962–January 1963): 7.

4. Alexander Werth, *The Strange History of Pierre Mendès-France and the Great Conflict Over French North Africa* (London: Barrie Books Ltd., 1957), p. 328.

5. Algeria, *Programme et action*, p. 27.

6. As quoted in "La politique française en Algérie" (extracts of official speeches), *Revue Militaire d'Information* 283 (May 1957): 52–66. The rest of this paragraph is based on the same sources.

7. See for example Werth, *The Strange History*, p. 344. Soldiers themselves have complained about this. See François Denoyer, *Quatre ans de guerre en Algérie: Lettre d'un jeune officier* (Paris: Flammarion, 1962), pp. 57, 84, 169–170.

8. The opposite argument, that the *quadrillage* helped gather information and hence allowed the French to fight the rebels more efficiently is presented in Gabriel Bonnet, *Les guerres insurrectionnelles et révolutionnaires de l'antiquité à nos jours* (Paris: Payot, 1958), pp. 254–255. Soldiers who fought in Algeria seem to have resented duty in the *quadrillage* system. See Jean-Yves Alquier, et al., *Ceux d'Algérie: Lettres de rappelés precedées d'un débat* (Paris: Plon, 1957), pp. 35, 39, 43.

9. Denoyer, *Quatre ans*, pp. 97, 105, 113; Heduy, *Au lieutenant des Taglaïts*, p. 83; Bonnet, *Les guerres insurrectionnelles*, p. 256.

10. Soldiers who had served in Viet Nam and in Algeria were quick to criticize the U. S. for trying to arm helicopters against the Viet Cong. They believed the results would be inadequate and that other fire cover would provide better protection. But then the terrain and the nature of the enemies' armament in Viet Nam and Algeria were so different that comparison may be invalid.

11. De Montalembert, CHEAM—3264, p. 3.

12. Refers to the general directive by Lacoste, reproduced in Algeria, *Programme et action*, and in the Resident-General's speech extracts, some of which appeared in the *Revue Militaire d'Information* 283 (May 1957).

13. Boutin, CHEAM—3089, p. 33.

14. Ibid., p. 36. See map No. 5.

15. "Le rôle des Sections Administratives Specialisées," in *Perspectives*, II (March 1957). Dubarry, CHEAM—2888, p. 3.

16. C. Faivre, "Une révolution administrative en Algérie: La reforme communale," CHEAM—3740 (1962), p. 9. Most Algerians con-

sidered it dangerous to be seen shaking the hand of an official. On this, see Servier, *Dans l'Aurès sur les pas des rebelles*, p. 133.

17. Alquier, *Nous avons pacifié Tazalt*, pp. 22 and passim.

18. Alquier, *Nous avons pacifié Tazalt*, pp. 35 and passim. Dubarry, CHEAM—2888, p. 17. Many persons who were asked to serve as special delegates fled to Algiers or France.

19. R. Petitjean, "Les opérations de regroupement et la création de nouveaux villages dan l'arrondissement de Tablat," CHEAM—3613 (1962), pp. 1–3. On the creation of new villages in general, see Xavier de Planhol, *Nouveaux villages algérois* (Paris: Presses Universitaires de France, 1961).

20. Claude Laurent, "Implantation d'une S.A.S. en zone d'insecurité," CHEAM—3655 (1962), pp. 1–2.

21. R. Holstein, "La fin d'une commune-mixte algérienne," CHEAM—2909 (1957), p. 7.

22. Petitjean, CHEAM—3613, pp. 1–3.

23. Ibid.

24. Capt. Dubarry, "Rôle de l'officier, chef de S.A.S., dans la reforme communale en Kabylie," CHEAM—2888 (1957), pp. 1–3.

25. Ibid., p. 2. On problems in general see Vieillot, CHEAM—3025, p. 8.

26. Germaine Tillion, *France and Algeria: Complementary Enemies*, trans. by Richard Howard (New York: Alfred A. Knopf, 1961), pp. 9–10 ff.; and Laurent, CHEAM—3655, pp. 5–6.

27. De Montalembert, CHEAM—3264, p. 3.

28. Ibid.

29. Servan-Schrieber, *Lieutenant in Algeria*, pp. 52 ff.

30. See Heduy, *Au Lieutenant des Taglaïts*, pp. 41, 63. Servan-Schreiber, *Lieutenant in Algeria*, p. 68, describes how some serious questions were inevitably raised in the minds of French soldiers about the loyalty of Algerians. Only one Algerian, for example, survived a vicious ambush that cost several lives. Was this soldier loyal? The same author also writes of one Algerian who, during an attack, was crouched down next to the machine gun he should have manned.

31. See for example the novel by Thadée Chamski, *La Harka* (Paris: Robert Laffont, 1961). The same attitude is reflected in some of Claude Dufresnoy's interviews: *Des officiers parlent* (Paris: Julliard, 1961).

32. De Montalembert, CHEAM—3264, p. 3; Servan-Schreiber, *Lieutenant in Algeria*, p. 54; Laurent, CHEAM—3655, p. 18.

33. Alquier, *Nous avons pacifié Tazalt*, pp. 94, 126; and Fournier, *Nous avons encore des héros*, p. 147.

34. Fournier, *Nous avons encore des héros*, p. 79; Gerard Periot, *Deuxième classe en Algérie* (Paris: Flammarion, 1962), pp. 137–163.

35. See for example Merry and Serge Bromberger, *Les 13 complots du 13 mai* (Paris: Fayard, 1958); De Montalembert, CHEAM–3264, p. 5; and Alquier, *Nous avons pacifié Tazalt*, pp. 94, 100–101.

36. Holstein, CHEAM–2909, p. 7.

37. De Montalembert, CHEAM–3264, p. 5. Even as thoughtful a soldier as François Denoyer, *Quatre ans de guerre en Algérie* (Paris: Flammarion, 1962), preferred action to S.A.S. service. This attitude is expressed throughout the letters of this man, who became a war casualty.

38. De Montalembert, CHEAM–3264, p. 3.

39. Jean Servier, *Adieu Djebels* (Paris: France-Empire, 1958), p. 110.

40. Dubarry, CHEAM–2888, p. 9.

41. Ibid., p. 11.

42. Algeria, Cabinet du Ministre Résident, *Guide de l'officier des Affaires Algériennes* (Paris: Imprimerie Georges Lang, 1959).

43. Descriptions of the Gounod S.A.S. given in the next several paragraphs are taken from the excellent 18-page memoir by Claude Laurent, "Implantation d'une S.A.S. en zone d'insecurité," CHEAM–3655. There is also some pertinent information in Dubarry, CHEAM–2888, p. 11.

44. Laurent, CHEAM–3655, p. 8.

45. Ibid., p. 10.

46. Ibid., p. 18.

47. De Montalembert, CHEAM–3264, p. 4.

48. Gen. Sauvagnac in the preface to Alquier, *Nous avons pacifié Tazalt*. Gen. Sauvagnac was the commanding general of Alquier's unit, the 25th Parachute Division.

49. Ibid.

50. Ibid., pp. 201–203.

51. Ibid., p. 272.

52. Mouloud Ferraoun, *Journal: 1955–1962* (Paris: Seuil, 1962), pp. 193–198 and passim. Farraoun clearly expresses the reaction of Algerians, even pro-French Algerians, who had to live under pressure beyond their control.

53. Servier, *Adieu Djebels*, p. 174.

54. Laurent, CHEAM–3655, pp. 8–9. Barbed wire around villages could still be seen in scattered areas in Algeria in 1963.

55. Servier, *Adieu Djebels*, pp. 87 ff.

56. Ibid., p. 89.

57. Ibid., p. 90.

58. Ibid., pp. 91–93.

59. Ibid., pp. 103, 109 and 174.

60. This information is based on the author's personal observations but was corroborated by several Westerners who had lived in Algeria for 15 to 35 years.

61. Alquier, *Nous avons pacifié Tazalt*, pp. 32–33, 88–89.

62. Periot, *Deuxième classe en Algérie*, pp. 142–143; Servier, *Adieu Djebels*, p. 109.

63. Bourdieu, *The Algerians*, p. 63 (under fig. 7), argues that the war speeded up a movement already in progress. The argument is continued on pp. 164 ff.

64. Fournier, *Nous avons encore des héros*, p. 45; Bourdieu, *The Algerians*, p. 63. Bourdieu shows that emigration to the cities was widespread and affected all urban centers in Algeria. The same author claims that the population of Algiers increased by 203,000 between 1954 and 1960.

65. Bourdieu, *The Algerians*, pp. 65 and passim. See also the excellent study by Robert Descloitres, et al., *L'Algérie des bidonvilles: Le tier monde dans la cité* (Paris: Mouton and Company, 1961).

66. Fournier, *Nous avons encore des héros*, pp. 49–50.

67. Ibid., p. 51.

68. Ibid., p. 54.

69. Laurent, CHEAM–3665, p. 18.

70. Bourdieu, *The Algerians*, pp. 163–184.

71. Pierre Sas et Yves Romanetti, *Vie d'un peuple mort: clefs pour la Kabylie* (Paris: Editions du Scorpion, 1961), p. 211.

72. De Montalembert, CHEAM–3264, p. 4.

73. Dubarry in CHEAM–2888, p. 11, shows he was bitter about the character of "French" (occasionally naturalized Kabyles) mayors and their selfish habits even during the revolution.

74. Laurent, CHEAM–3655, p. 18; Fournier, *Nous avons encore des héros*, p. 54.

75. Algeria, *Programme et action*, pp. 125–126.

13. The Resettlement Policy and the Refugee Problem

1. Servier, Alquier, Bourdieu, and many other writers make reference to the refugee problem and to the motives that pushed many

Algerians to leave their homes. Kessel and Pirelli and Mandouze have presented interesting documents of importance in this respect. No specific references will be given here since each point will be more carefully presented in the development of this chapter.

2. The most accessible and perhaps the best study of this question that also described the feelings of the people involved is Bourdieu, *The Algerians,* trans. by Alan C. M. Ross. There is a specific chapter on the resettlement policy and its effects beginning on p. 163.

3. Groups d'Etudes, "Les Centres de regroupement en Algérie," CHEAM—3277 (1960), p. 1. There are several authors each of whom took responsibility for one portion of the report as a whole. Further references to this document will supply the particular author and the document number.

4. The reverse was true of the OAS in 1961. See Kelly, *Lost Soldiers,* p. 334. The idea itself is so well known that it needs not be documented.

5. Bourdieu, *The Algerians,* p. 163. Two interesting pamphlets that contain relevant information are *The Resettlement Camps,* ed. by the Algerian Red Crescent, probably in 1960, printed in Rabat and in Tunis; and *Genocide in Algeria: The Resettlement Camps,* prepared by the Ministry of Information of the Algerian Republic (GPRA), October 1960. The two pamphlets are, of course, very similar and quote the same sources.

6. The 25% figure given is from *The Resettlement Camps;* Group d'Etudes, CHEAM—3277, p. 1, gives the 15% figure.

7. This first resettlement was discussed in Ch. 3. See Duchemin, *Histoire du F.L.N.,* p. 59; Favrod, *Le F.L.N. et Algérie,* p. 128; and Brace and Brace, *Ordeal in Algeria,* p. 95.

8. Algerian Red Crescent, *The Resettlement Camps,* second page inside the cover.

9. Groupe d'Etudes, CHEAM—3277, p. 3.

10. Ibid., pp. 3–4.

11. Ibid., p. 4.

12. Bourdieu, *The Algerians,* pp. 63, 142–143 (figs. 7 and 14 and explanatory texts).

13. Bourdieu, *The Algerians,* pp. 163–184. The number of references to this one source should indicate its importance. There is indeed no better sociological study of Algerian society as a whole and of the effect of the war on Algerians.

14. Florentin in CHEAM—3277, p. 4.

15. Ibid., pp. 3–4.

16. Jules Roy, *La guerre d'Algérie* (Paris: Julliard, 1960), passim. The whole book expresses a feeling which is relevant to the point made in the text. For specific examples see pages 81, 92, 161, and others.

17. Florentin in CHEAM—3277, pp. 10–11.

18. P. Manière, "Un Essai de suppression des bidonvilles: Création Cité de Sidi-Salem à Bône," CHEAM—3005 bis (1959), p. 1.

19. Ibid., p. 3.

20. Manière, CHEAM—3005 bis, pp. 3–4.

21. Ibid., p. 5.

22. Ibid., p. 6.

23. Ibid., p. 7.

24. Ibid.

25. Laurent, "La naissance d'une commune musulmane," CHEAM—3524 (1962), pp. 20–21.

26. Petitjean, CHEAM—3613, p. 1. See also Manière, CHEAM—3005 bis, p. 5.

27. Capt. Espeisse, "Les regroupements de populations dans l'arrondissement de Tlemcen," CHEAM—3102 (1959); Petitjean, CHEAM—3613.

28. Algerian Red Crescent, *The Resettlement Camps*, passim.

29. The two pamphlets on the resettlement camps mentioned above have pertinent information and photos. See also the special number of *Témoignages et Documents* XII (May 1959). All the articles in this issue are pertinent.

30. "Les Regroupements sont mal connus," *Témoignages et Documents* XII (May 1959), 1–2.

31. Petitjean, CHEAM—3613, p. 1.

32. Ibid., p. 1.

33. Manière, CHEAM—3005 bis, p. 7.

34. This, of course, would be the meaning of accusing France of waging a war of extermination against the Algerian people. See "La France poursuit ses crimes en Algérie," *El Moudjahid* IX (August 20, 1957): 112–113; and "De la guerre d'extermination au triomphe de la révolution," ibid. XVIII (February 1, 1957): 300–304.

35. Pettitjean, CHEAM—3613, passim; Planhol, *Nouveau village Algérois*, passim.

36. Captain Bogros, "Quelques aspects du controle des nomades en guerre subversives," CHEAM—3473 (1961), p. 2.

37. "Excerpts from a memorandum addressed to the Secretary General of the United Nations by A. Chanderli, F.L.N. Delegate in

New York," as quoted in GPRA, *Genocide in Algeria: The Resettlement Camps,* p. 29.

38. Pierre Macaigne, *France-Soir* (July 22, 1959), as quoted in Algerian Red Crescent, *The Resettlement Camps.*

39. *France-Soir* (April 16, 1960), as quoted in Algerian Red Crescent, *The Resettlement Camps.*

40. Bogros, CHEAM—3484, passim.

41. Depis, CHEAM—3597, p. 3. See also the appropriate maps entitled "Interdicted Zones Along the Moroccan Border," which were adapted from a map prepared by M. Depis.

42. Ibid., p. 4.

43. See map entitled "Resettlements in Morocco," also based on work already done by M. Depis and presented in CHEAM—3597.

44. Depis, CHEAM—3597, p. 2. See also n. 48 below.

45. "Conséquences tragiques de la guerre: La situation des refugiés algériens," *El Moudjahid* (November 15, 1957), pp. 10, 180–181. This study was continued in later issues.

46. Heduy, *Au Lieutenant des Taglaïts,* p. 82. The establishment of interdicted zones had disadvantages for the French as well. See Déon, *L'Armée d'Algérie,* p. 153.

47. Depis, CHEAM—3597, p. 8.

48. Ibid., p. 9; Denoyer, *Quatre ans de guerre en Algérie,* p. 166.

49. Depis, CHEAM—3597, p. 10.

50. Ibid., pp. 18–21.

51. Kessel and Pirelli, *Le peuple Algérien,* pp. 36–45, 302–306.

52. Mohammed Bedjaoui, *Law and the Algerian Revolution* (Brussels: International Association of Democratic Lawyers, 1961), pp. 53 ff. A parallel problem was the desertion of young Algerians drafted into the French Army. See Kessel and Pirelli, *Le peuple Algérien,* pp. 483 ff.

53. This is not to imply that the rebels were no longer active within Algeria. In the last week of September 1958, the rebels killed 58 persons, wounded 48, and kidnapped more than 100. The French forces, meanwhile, claimed to have killed or wounded 500 rebels, to have captured another 92, and to have recovered some 238 weapons. See *La Semaine en Algérie,* IX (September 15–17, 1958).

14. THE BATTLE OF ALGIERS AND THE USE OF TORTURE

1. The fight against the MNA continued and led to atrocities as the Melouzza massacre in May 1957.

2. See chapter 9 of this study and Brace and Brace, *Ordeal in Algeria*, p. 92.

3. The capture of the *Athos* is indicative. See Bedjaoui, *Law and the Algerian Revolution*, p. 152.

4. Full utilization of the frontier barriers was announced in May 1957; the construction was essentially completed by the end of September 1957. See Le Tourneau, *L'Afrique du Nord Musulmane*, p. 420.

5. The first really effective search and destroy operation such as the Operation Arquebuse made things very difficult for the ALN from mid-1959 on. See Benoit, "Chronologie . . . ," *La Nef* XII–XIII (October 1962–January 1963): 8.

6. On concern about impressing the U.N. see: Jacques Le Prevost, *La Bataille d'Alger: Janvier-février 1957* (Algiers: Baconnier, 1957), 9.

7. Jean-Ph. Talbo, "Qu'est-ce que la résistance?" *Partisans* VI (September–October 1962): 97. Tillion, *France and Algeria*, p. 146. (Between 37 and 53 dead and 280 homeless according to Tillion.)

8. Behr, *Dramatique Algérie*, pp. 107–108.

9. Tillion, *France and Algeria*, pp. 150–151.

10. Le Tourneau, *L'Afrique du Nord Musulmane*, p. 419; Ageron, *Histoire de l'Algérie*, p. 104.

11. Behr, *Dramatique Algérie*, p. 113; Kessel and Pirelli, *Le Peuple algérien*, p. 94; Favrod, *Le F.L.N. et l'Algérie*, p. 217.

12. Tillion, *France and Algeria*, pp. 148 ff.

13. Ibid. Many writers have relied heavily upon Tillion's book for this information. Communists had their own reasons for interpreting events along similar lines. See for example Talbo, "Qu-est que la résistance?" p. 97.

14. To what Talbo has to say (see n. 13 above) one might add the interpretations presented by Ageron, *Histoire de l'Algérie*, p. 107; and by Le Tourneau, *L'Afrique du Nord Musulmane*, p. 420.

15. Yacef, *Souvenirs de la bataille d'Alger*, is still the best source for information about how active rebels reacted to Massu's methods and activity.

16. Tillion, *France and Algeria*, pp. 151–153. This is probably the best short description of the problem of "identification."

17. Le Prevost, *La Bataille d'Alger*, p. 83.

18. The island or ilôte thesis is taken from Ageron, *Histoire de l'Algérie*, p. 104.

19. Kessel and Pirelli, *Le Peuple algérien*, p. 91. Le Prevost, *La Bataille d'Alger*, passim, argues in defense of French activity dur-

ing the battle and blames "stupid extremists"—European counter-terrorists, not the army—for the excesses, which he condemned.

20. Tillion, *France and Algeria*, pp. 150–153.

21. Le Prevost, *La Bataille d'Alger*, pp. 75 ff. Here the author points to volunteers who gave service and blood for victims of bombings whether the wounded were Algerians or Europeans. Le Prevost almost anticipates the feeling of May 13, 1958, in this passage.

22. Kessel and Pirelli, *Le Peuple algérien*, p. 94.

23. Lacoste used the word "emmerder," which has been translated politely. See Behr, *Dramatique Algérie*, pp. 112–113.

24. Kessel and Pirelli, *Le Peuple algérien*, pp. 91–112, passim; G. Mustapha, *Barberousse* (Paris: Pierre Jean Oswald, 1960), passim.

25. Vidal-Naquet, *Torture*, pp. 169–179.

26. Ibid., p. 51.

27. Ibid.

28. Favrod, *Le F.I.N. et l'Algérie*, p. 217.

29. The many complaints reproduced in Kessel and Pirelli, *Le Peuple algérien*, and in other similar publications bring out this point very clearly.

30. Vidal-Naquet, *Torture*, pp. 52 ff.

31. Alleg, *The Question*, passim.

32. Alleg's books, as well as many articles on the Algerian question banned by the government, were in fact published by certain underground newspapers or presses. The Editions de Minuit is an example of a press that published studies critical of official policies in Algeria, usually by Communist authors. A newspaper that appeared irregularly but always presented articles that had been banned from legal newspapers was entitled *Témoignages et Documents sur La Guerre d'Algérie*. Number 14 (July 1959) included as a supplement the text of Alleg's book, which had been published by the Editions de Minuit and which had been promptly banned.

33. Le Prevost, *La Bataille d'Alger*, p. 7.

34. Soldiers were irritated by parliamentary commissions. It was outside interference of the same kind as that of journalists who forced Lacoste's irritated comment reported above. (See f.n. 21). Alquier in *Nous Avons pacifié Tazalt*, p. 186, openly asked when a parliamentary delegation would fall in ambush to men and weapons from Tunisia. The question reflected a defiant attitude.

35. Le Prevost, *La Bataille d'Alger*, p. 131. See also chart 10 in the present study.

36. Ibid., pp. 75–76 and 132.

37. Ibid., p. 131.

38. Ibid., p. 44.

39. A moving description of the Algerian Robin Hood appears in the book written by Ali's chief, Saadi Yacef, *Souvenirs,* pp. 73–87.

40. As a result, no. 7 (February 1957) never appeared. See preface to the June 1962 reedition of *El Moudjahid* I: 3. This was printed in Yugoslavia.

41. Le Tourneau, *L'Afrique du Nord Musulmane,* p. 420.

42. The paragraph that follows is based on the analysis given by M. Le Tourneau, *L'Afrique du Nord Musulmane,* p. 420.

43. Denoyer, *Quatre ans de guerre,* pp. 155–156. What Heduy says in *Au Lieutenant des Taglaïts,* pp. 154–155, passim, should lead readers to the same conclusion.

44. Benoit, "Chronologie . . . ," *La Nef* XII–XIII (October 1962–January 1963): 11.

45. The newspaper coverage of the Sidi-Sakiet incident was so thorough that there is really no need to footnote this further.

46. Vidal-Naquet, *Torture,* p. 52.

47. Mustapha G., *Barberousse,* p. 16.

48. On *fida'iyin* and ALN recruitment, see Le Prevost, *La Bataille d'Alger,* p. 42.

49. De Montalembert, CHEAM–3264, p. 5.

50. Vidal-Naquet, *Torture,* p. 55.

51. Ibid.

52. Ibid.

53. Ibid., pp. 53–54.

54. Kessel and Pirelli, *Le Peuple algérien,* pp. 102, 153, 162–166, 227, passim.

55. Alleg, *The Question,* passim.

56. Vidal-Naquet, *Torture,* p. 55.

57. Paul Henissart, *Wolves in the City: The Death of French Algeria* (New York: Simon and Schuster, 1970), p. 32.

58. Tillion, *France and Algeria,* pp. 31 ff.

15. COMMUNISM, THE UN, AND THE ALGERIAN REVOLUTION

1. Le Prevost, *La Bataille d'Alger,* p. 17.

2. This was clearly the meaning of a memoire written in 1951 or 1952. See Comité Central de Hautes Etudes Administrative sur l'Asie et l'Afrique Moderne, "Mémoire sur la machination par les gouverne-

ments des Etats Arabes pour déloger la France de ses positions en Afrique du Nord," CHEAM—50.018. Other sources on this point include George Sauge, *L'Armée face à la guerre psychologique* (Paris: Centre d'Etudes Politiques et Civiques, 1959), p. 11; Pierre Hofstetter, "Quel jeu joue la Suisse," *Défense de l'Occident* IX (November 1960): 38; Georges Albertini, "La guerre que nous devons faire," *Revue Militaire Générale* (March 1961), pp. 373–381; Soustelle, *Aimée et souffrante Algérie*, p. 140.

3. Le Tourneau, *L'Afrique du Nord Mulsulmane*, pp. 312 ff.

4. France, Ministère des Affaires Etrangères, *Discours prononcé par M. Christian Pineau, Ministre des Affairs Etrangères, le 4 février 1957 devant la Commission Politique de l'Assemblée Générale des Nations Unis* (Paris: La Documentation Française, 1957), p. 8.

5. Ibid.

6. Julien, *L'Afrique du Nord en marche*, p. 133. See also Glories, "Quelques observations," p. 16.

7. Déon, *L'Armée d'Algérie*, pp. 37–38; Joseph Folliet, *Guerre et paix en Algérie: Réflexions d'un homme libre* (Lyons: Imprimerie du Sud-Est, 1958), p. 38.

8. Soustelle, *Aimée et souffrante Algérie*, p. 140.

9. Nouschi, *La naissance du nationalisme algérien*, pp. 156–157.

10. Ibid., pp. 158–159.

11. France, Ministère des Affaires Etrangères, *Discours prononcé par M. Christian Pineau . . . le 4 février 1957 . . .* , p. 9.

12. Ibid., p. 10.

13. Thierry Maulnier, *Le Figaro* (March 4, 1958). This article is quoted in André Morice, *Les Fellagha dans la cité* (Nantes: Imprimerie générale, n.d. [1959?], pp. 31–32.

14. De la Bastide, CHEAM—3716, p. 1; Glories, "Quelques observations," p. 25.

15. Glories, "Quelques observations," p. 25, f.n. 23.

16. *El Moudjahid*, as quoted by Glories, ibid., p. 16.

17. Morice, *Les Fellagha*, p. 30.

18. Ibid., p. 27.

19. Ibid.

20. Glories, "Quelques observations," p. 25.

21. There exist several articles that analyze press reaction during the first week of revolution in Algeria. A good example is Duquesne, "Sept ans . . . ," pp. 275–288.

22. Soustelle, *Aimée et souffrante Algérie*, p. 140.

23. Jean Bruhat, "Nation algérienne et opinion française," *La Pensée: revue du rationalisme moderne*, New Series XCV (January–February 1961): 6.

24. Duquesne, "Sept ans . . . ," p. 278.

25. Bachir Hadj Ali, *Aspects actuels de la guerre de libération en Algérie*, ed. by *La Nouvelle Revue Internationale* (Paris: Richard, n.d. [1959?]), passim.

26. Jacques Couland, *L'Eveil du Monde Arabe* (Paris: Editions Sociales, 1963).

27. Pierre Lombard, *La Crise algérienne vue d'Alger* (Alger: Editions Fontana, 1958), p. 23.

28. Jules Monnerot, "La guerre subversive," *Défense de l'Occident* X–XI (January–February 1961): 37; G. J. Allard, "O.A.T.N. et A.L.N.," *Revue de Defense Nationale* (June 1958), p. 14.

29. Candelier, "Information et propagande radiophonic en pays arabes," CHEAM–3737 (1959).

30. Two excellent studies of the Algerian question and the UN are Mohamed Alwan, *Algeria Before the United Nations* and Mohammed Bedjaoui, *Law and the Algerian Revolution*. Bedjaoui's interest is international law, but he has much interesting information on the UN as well. Much of the interpretation on this question will be based on these two sources, although the books will not be cited specifically each time they are used.

31. Naudy, "L'Affaire algérienne à l'O.N.U.," CHEAM–3572 (1961), pp. 3–4.

32. Although three Communist nations—North Viet Nam, North Korea, and China—gave *de jure* recognition to the Algerian state and government in September 1958, that is, at the same time as did all the Arab and many African states, the USSR granted only *de facto* recognition and that only in 1961. See Bedjaoui, *Law and the Algerian Revolution*, p. 138.

33. For the most concise presentation of the French case see France, Cabinet du Ministère de l'Algérie, *Algérie: 1957*.

34. Alwan, *Algeria Before the United Nations*, pp. 21–30.

35. Ibid., pp. 33, 40; and Naudy, CHEAM–3572, p. 8.

36. Naudy, CHEAM–3572, p. 8.

37. Andrews, *French Politics and Algeria*, p. 29.

38. Alwan, *Algeria Before the United Nations*, p. 99.

39. Le Prevost, *La Bataille d'Alger*, p. 12.

40. Bernhardt, CHEAM–3077, p. 2.

41. Benoit, "Chronologie de la guerre en Algérie," pp. 9, 18.

42. Duquesne, "Sept ans . . . ," p. 280.

43. Claude Delmas, "Les Evenements d'Afrique du Nord," *Revue Militaire d'Information* CCXC (January 1958): 110.

44. Duquesne, "Sept ans . . . ," p. 280.

45. Delmas, "Les Evenements . . . ," p. 111.

46. Naudy, CHEAM—3572, p. 12.

47. Alwan, *Algeria Before the United Nations*, p. 98.

48. Le Tourneau, CHEAM—3768, p. 23.

49. Duquesne, "Sept ans . . . ," p. 280.

50. Delmas, "Les evenements . . . ," p. 101.

51. A. Morice, "Algérie ou les occasions perdues," *Revue politique Idées Inst.* XLVIII (March 1959): 137–140.

52. Otto Heilbrunn, *Warfare in the Enemy's Rear* (New York: Praeger, 1963), p. 199.

CONCLUSION

1. *La Semaine en Algérie,* No. 66 (December 28, 1959–January 3, 1960), p. 19.

2. Abdelkader Rahmani, *L'Affaire des officiers algériens* (Paris: Editions du Seuil, 1959), pp. 9 and passim.

3. Chamski, *La Harka,* passim.

4. Philippe, "Témoignages pour l'Algérie française," *Défense de l'Occident* X–XI: 40.

5. Andrews, *French Politics and Algeria,* chapters 2 and 3.

6. Frantz Fanon, *A Dying Colonialism,* trans. by Haakon Chevalier (New York: Grove Press Inc., 1967), pp. 29, 31, and passim.

Index

Abbane, Ramdane, 239

Abbas, Ferhat: as Elected Muslim, 13; describes Algerian problem, 14; in World War II, 25; leader of AML, 25; appeals to UN, 35; recommends nonviolence, 45; joins FLN, 157, 297*n22*; accusations against, 166; leads nationalist government, 239–240

Abd el Krim: and CRUA in Cairo, 60, 61

Abd el Qader, Hadj Ali: founder of ENA, 22

Agricultural workers: wage reform, 149

Ait Ahmed, Hocine: creates OS, 32, 54; CRUA member, 49, 55; military experience, 52; early life, 54–55

Algeria: conquered, 4; as French department, 5; French territorial organization of, 108–9

Algerians: poverty, 133; birth rate, 134; unemployment, 134

Algerian Assembly: opposes French administration, 82; *colon* control of, 145; delegates to, 145; support of nationalists, 155; dissolved, 156, 188

Algerian customs: in arming of a village, 205–6; importance of, 206–7

Algerian Front for the Defense and Respect of Liberty: nationalist coalition, 247, 248

Algerian Muslim Congress: formation of, 16; membership, 16; presents Charter of Muslim Demands, 17, 18; failure of, 20

Algerian women: traditional role of, 97

Algiers, battle of: causes of, 232; Muslim sectors sealed off, 234; as French tactical victory, 235; na-